BUSINESS CYCLES
AND FINANCIAL CRISES

BUSINESS CYCLES AND FINANCIAL CRISES

A. W. Mullineux

HARVESTER WHEATSHEAF
New York   London   Toronto   Sydney   Tokyo   Singapore

First published 1990 by
Harvester Wheatsheaf
66 Wood Lane End, Hemel Hempstead
Hertfordshire HP2 4RG
A division of
Simon & Schuster International Group

© A. W. Mullineux 1990

All rights reserved. No part of this publication may be reproduced, stored in a retrieval system, or transmitted, in any form or by any means, electronic, mechanical, photocopying, recording or otherwise, without prior permission, in writing, from the publisher.

Typeset in 10/12pt Times
by Witwell Ltd, Southport

Printed and bound in Great Britain by
BPCC Wheatons Ltd, Exeter

British Library Cataloguing in Publication Data

Mullineux, A. W. (Andrew William), *1952–*
  Business cycles and financial crises.
  1. Trade cycles
  I. Title
  338.5'42
  ISBN 0-7450-0545-4

1 2 3 4 5   94 93 92 91 90

To Ruth and Joe

CONTENTS

Preface ix

1 The nature of the business cycle 1
   1.1 Definitions 1
   1.2 The Monte Carlo hypothesis 6
   1.3 Are business cycles symmetric? 12
   1.4 The Frisch–Slutsky hypothesis 19
   1.5 Has the business cycle changed since the War? 29
        Notes 35

2 Business cycle theory in the 1980s 37
   2.1 Introduction 37
   2.2 Equilibrium business cycle (EBC) modelling 45
   2.3 Nonlinear cycle theory 54
        Notes 60

3 The financial instability hypothesis 62
   3.1 Introduction 62
   3.2 The role of money and credit in pre-Keynesian business cycle literature 63
   3.3 The financial instability hypothesis (FIH) 72
        3.3.1 Minsky on financial instability 72
        3.3.2 Financial instability and the banking sector 78
        3.3.3 Kindleberger's model and the international dimension 85
   3.4 Rational speculative bubbles 91
   3.5 Conclusion 99
        Notes 102

4 Towards a theory of dynamic economic development 105
   4.1 A brief overview of cycle modelling 105
   4.2 Schumpeter on economic evolution 108

	4.3	The long swing hypothesis and the growth trend	113
		4.3.1 The long swing hypothesis	113
		4.3.2 The growth trend	119
	4.4	Shackle on the business cycle	122
	4.5	Goodwin's macrodynamics	127
	4.6	Concluding remarks	131
		Notes	133
5	**The unfinished research agenda**		**135**
		Notes	140
References			141
Index			157

PREFACE

The purposes of this book are to update and extend the discussion in my previous book on business cycles, entitled *The Business Cycle After Keynes: A contemporary analysis*.[1] That book was based on a series of lectures given to final-year economics students at the University of Birmingham and was designed to supplement standard macroeconomics textbooks aimed at final-year specialist undergraduate and postgraduate students, which tended to confine their discussion of the business cycle to a section or chapter on multiplier–accelerator interaction. In order to keep the size of this book – which is aimed primarily at graduate students and academic economists – manageable, no attempt is made to incorporate the contents of the previous book or to cover the burgeoning literature on long swings.

Since writing *The Business Cycle After Keynes*, my lecturing and research activities have been in the money, banking and finance area as a result of my involvement in the establishment of a Money, Banking and Finance degree programme at the University of Birmingham. Last summer my interest in business cycles was rekindled by Professor Jim Ford, who introduced me to Shackle's much-neglected work on business cycles (discussed in Chapter 4). I then had the idea of merging my interests in business cycles and money and banking because I felt that the role of the latter in the propagation, as opposed to the impulse, mechanism had been largely neglected by mainstream business cycle theorists. This book is the result of further reflection on the business cycle in the light of my subsequent studies. No new theories are offered. There are numerous competing theories that have fundamentally different approaches already. Instead it is argued that the time has come for a major research programme designed to consider the empirical evidence in order to cast light on the numerous unanswered questions concerning business cycles.

[1] Published by Wheatsheaf in the United Kingdom and Barnes and Noble in the Unites States.

I would like to thank Judith, who was successfully completing the final year of the Social Administration degree programme at the University of Birmingham and our children, Ruth (8) and Joe (5), for participating in what amounted to a fantastic family team effort in the 1987/8 academic year. I must also thank Joyce Bradshaw for typing the manuscript accurately and quickly despite the demands of her young daughter and the child she was carrying. Finally, I would like to express my gratitude to an anonymous referee for his/her helpful comments and to Robert Bolick of Harvester Wheatsheaf for his editorial assistance.

Andy Mullineux
Department of Economics
University of Birmingham

1 · THE NATURE OF THE BUSINESS CYCLE

1.1 DEFINITIONS

Perhaps the most widely quoted and influential definition is that of Burns and Mitchell (1946, p.1)[1] who state that:

> Business cycles are a type of fluctuation found in the aggregate economic activity of nations that organise their work mainly in business enterprises: a cycle consists of expansions occurring at about the same time in many economic activities, followed by similarly general recessions, contractions, and revivals which merge into the expansion phase of the next cycle; the sequence of changes is recurrent but not periodic; in duration cycles vary from more than one year to ten or twelve years; they are not divisible into shorter cycles of similar character with amplitudes approximating their own.

A number of features of this definition should be highlighted. Firstly, it stresses only two phases of the cycle, the expansionary and contractionary phases. It will be seen in section 1.2 that the peak or upper turning point and the trough or lower turning point are not analysed as distinct phases but are merely used to identify business cycles in aggregate economic time series. Many economists, however, regard the turning points as particular phases requiring separate explanation. This is especially evident in the discussion of the financial instability hypothesis, which stresses the role of financial crises in terminating the boom phase, in Chapter 3.

The second main feature is the emphasis on the recurrent nature of the business cycle, rather than strict periodicity. Combined with the wide range of acceptable durations, encompassing both major and minor cycles (Hansen 1951), this means that cycles vary considerably in both duration and amplitude and that the phases are also likely to vary in length and intensity. Minor cycles are often assumed to be the result of inventory cycles (Metzler 1941), but Burns and Mitchell reject these as separable events as postulated by Schumpeter (1939), among others.[2] Finally, and perhaps most importantly, they emphasise comovements as

2 THE NATURE OF THE BUSINESS CYCLE

evidenced by the clustering of peaks and troughs in many economic series. This is a feature stressed in numerous subsequent business cycle definitions, a sample of which are discussed below.

The original National Bureau of Economic Research (NBER) work of Burns and Mitchell concentrated on the analysis of non-detrended data. In the post-war period such analysis has continued but the NBER has also analysed detrended data in order to identify growth cycles,[3] which tend to be more symmetric than the cycles identified in non-detrended data. The issue of asymmetry is an important one because it has implications for business cycle modelling procedures; it will be discussed further in section 1.3.

Concerning the existence of the business cycle, there remain bodies of atheists and agnostics. Fisher (1925, p. 191) is often quoted by doubters and disbelievers. He states:

> I see no reason to believe in the Business Cycle. It is simply a fluctuation about its own mean. And yet the cycle idea is supposed to have more content than mere variability. It implies a regular succession of similar fluctuations constituting some sort of recurrence, so that, as in the case of the phases of the moon, the tides of the sea, wave motion or pendulum swing we can forecast the future on the basis of a pattern worked out from past experience, and which we have reason to believe will be copied in the future.

The work done at the NBER has subsequently attempted to show that there is indeed more to the business cycle than mere variability. Doubters remain, however, and tests of Fisher's so-called Monte Carlo hypothesis will be discussed in section 1.2.

The NBER view that there is sufficient regularity, particularly in comovements, to make the business cycle concept useful is shared by two of the most distinguished students of cycle theory literature, Haberler (1958, pp. 454–9) and Hansen. Hansen (1951) notes that some would prefer to substitute 'fluctuations' for cycles but concludes that the usage of the term cycles in other sciences does not imply strict regularity. This point is also made by Zarnowitz and Moore (1986) in a recent review of the NBER methodology.

Lucas (1975) helped to rekindle interest in business cycle theory[4] by reviving the idea of an equilibrium business cycle. The cycle had tended to be regarded as a disequilibrium phenomenon in the predominantly Keynesian contributions to the post-war cycle literature. Lucas (1977) discussed the cycle in more general terms and stressed the international generality of the business cycle phenomenon in decentralised market economies. He concluded (p. 10) that:

> with respect to the qualitative behaviour of comovements among series, *business cycles are all alike*.

And that this:

> suggests the possibility of a unified explanation of business cycles, grounded in the *general* laws governing market economies, rather than in political or institutional characteristics specific to particular countries or periods.

The intention here is not to deny that political or institutional characteristics can influence actual cycle realisations and help account for their variation between countries and periods. It is rather to stress the existence of general laws that ensure that a market economy subjected to shocks will evolve cyclically. Research that aims to gauge the extent to which the US business cycle has changed since the Second World War is reviewed in section 1.5.

Sargent (1979, p. 254) attempts to formalise a definition of the business cycle using time series analysis. He first analyses individual aggregate economic time series and arrives at two definitions. Firstly:

> A variable possesses a cycle of a given frequency if its covariogram displays damped oscillations of that frequency, which is equivalent with the condition that the non-stochastic part of the difference equation has a pair of complex roots with argument . . . equal to the frequency in question. A single series is said to contain a *business cycle* if the cycle in question has periodicity of from about two to four years (NBER minor cycles) or about eight years (NBER major cycles).

Secondly, Sargent argues that a cycle in a single series is marked by the occurrence of a peak in the spectral density of that series. Although not equivalent to the first definition, Sargent (1979, Ch. XI) shows that it usually leads to a definition of the cycle close to the first one.

Sargent (1979, p. 254) concludes that neither of these definitions captures the concept of the business cycle properly. Most aggregate economic time series actually have spectral densities that display no pronounced peaks in the range of frequencies associated with the business cycle,[5] and the peaks that do occur tend not to be pronounced. The dominant or 'typical' spectral shape – as dubbed by Granger (1966) – of most economic time series is that of a spectrum which decreases rapidly as frequency increases, with most of the power in the low frequency, high periodicity bands. This is characteristic of series dominated by high, positive, low order serial correlation, and is probably symptomatic of seasonal influences on the quarterly data commonly used. Sargent warns, however, that the absence of spectral peaks in business cycle frequencies does not imply that the series experienced no fluctuations associated with business cycles. He provides an example of a series which displays no peaks and yet appears to move in sympathy with general business conditions. In the light of this observation Sargent

(1979, p. 256) offers the following, preferred, definition, which emphasises comovements:

> The business cycle is the phenomenon of a number of important economic aggregates (such as GNP, unemployment and lay offs) being characterised by high pairwise coherences[6] at the low business cycle frequencies, the same frequencies at which most aggregates have most of their spectral power if they have 'typical spectral shapes'.

This definition captures the main qualitative feature or 'stylised fact' to be explained by the cycle theories discussed in Chapter 2.

The dominant methodology of business cycle analysis is based on the Frisch–Slutsky hypothesis discussed in section 1.4. Low order linear deterministic difference or differential equation models cannot yield the irregular non-damped or non-explosive cycles typically identified by the NBER, but low order linear stochastic models can yield a better approximation,[7] as Frisch (1933) and Slutsky (1937) observed. Sargent (1979, pp. 218–19) observes that high order non-stochastic difference equations can, however, generate data that looks as irregular as typical aggregate economic time series. By increasing the order of the equation, any sample of data can be modelled arbitrarily well with a linear non-stochastic differential equation. This approach is generally not adopted, however, because the order usually has to be so high that the model is not parsimonious in its parameterisation (Box and Jenkins, 1970) and there will be insufficient degrees of freedom to allow efficient estimation. Further, it allocates no influence at all to shocks. An alternative to high order linear models that can also produce an essentially endogenous cycle, in the sense that the shocks merely add irregularity to a cycle that would exist in their absence, is to use nonlinear models which can have stable limit cycle solutions (see section 2.3). While it is generally accepted that stochastic models should be used, because economies are subjected to shocks, there is no general agreement over the relative importance of the shock-generating process and the economic propagation model in explaining the cycle, or on whether linear or nonlinear models should be used. The dominant view, however, appears to be that linear propagation models with heavy dampening are probably correct and that we should look to shocks as the driving force of the (essentially exogenous) cycle. Blatt (1978), however, showed that the choice of a linear model, when a nonlinear one is appropriate, will bias the empirical analysis in favour of the importance of shocks. It is in the light of this finding that the empirical results discussed in the following chapters, which are invariably based on econometric and statistical techniques that assume linearity, should be viewed.

A related issue is the tendency to regard the business cycle as a deviation from a linear trend.[8] Burns and Mitchell (1946) expressed concern about such a perspective and analysed non-detrended data as a consequence. In the post-war period, however, even the NBER has begun to analyse detrended data in order to identify growth cycles, although the trend used is not linear.[9] Nelson and Plosser (1982) warn of the danger of this approach, pointing out that much of the so-called cyclical variation in detrended data could be due to stochastic variation in the trend which has not in fact been removed. If the trend itself is nonlinear, linear detrending is likely to exaggerate the cyclical variation to be explained and introduce measurement errors. This and related issues will be discussed further in sections 1.2 and 4.3.2.

Despite the voluminous empirical work of the NBER and the work of other economists, a number of questions remain unresolved. Firstly, are there long cycles and/or nonlinear trends? This question will be considered further in section 4.3. It is of crucial importance because the analysis of the business cycle requires that it must somehow first be separated from trend and seasonal influences on the time series.[10] The appropriate method of decomposition will not be the subtraction of a (log) linear trend from the deseasonalised series if the trend is not (log) linear. Secondly, to what extent is the cycle endogenously and exogenously generated? Most business cycle research assumes that linear models can be used to describe an economic system which is subjected to shocks. The stochastic linear models employed can replicate observed macroeconomic time series reasonably well because the time series they produce possess the right degree of irregularity in period and amplitude to conform with actual realisations. Such models are based on the Frisch–Slutsky hypothesis, discussed in section 1.4. The hypothesis assumes that linear models are sufficient to model economic relationships. Because the estimated linear econometric models display heavy dampening, cycle analysts have increasingly turned their attention to trying to identify the sources of the shocks that offset this dampening and produce a cycle. Chapter 2 reviews some recent work on the sources of shocks which drive cycles in the US economy. The current trend is, therefore, towards viewing the cycle as being driven by exogenous shocks rather than as an endogenous feature of the economy. However, nonlinear mathematical business cycle modelling provides the possibility that stable limit cycles, which are truly endogenous, might exist; recent literature on such models is reviewed in section 2.3.[11]

Mullineux (1984) discusses the work of Lucas (1975, 1977), who stimulated renewed interest in the equilibrium theory of the business cycle. Lucas's cycle was driven by monetary shocks but subsequent work has emphasised real shocks; consequently, there has been a resurgence of the old debate over whether cycles are real or monetary in origin. Section

2.2 reviews the theoretical contributions to the debate, section 1.5 looks at work attempting to identify the main sources of shocks, and in Chapter 3 it is argued that monetary and financial factors are likely to play at least some role, alongside real factors, in cycle generation.

In the next section, the question of the business cycle's very existence will be considered, while in section 1.3 the question of whether or not cycles are symmetric, which has a bearing on the appropriateness of the linearity assumption, will be explored.

1.2 THE MONTE CARLO HYPOTHESIS

Fisher (1925) argued that business cycles could not be predicted because they resembled cycles observed by gamblers in an honest casino in that the periodicity, rhythm, or pattern of the past is of no help in predicting the future. Slutsky (1937) also believed that business cycles had the form of a chance function.

The Monte Carlo (MC) hypothesis, as formulated by McCulloch (1975), is that the probability of a reversal occurring in a given month is a constant which is independent of the length of time elapsed since the last turning point. The alternative (business cycle) hypothesis is that the probability of a reversal depends on the length of time since the last turning point.

The implication of the MC hypothesis is that random shocks are sufficiently powerful to provide the dominant source of energy to an econometric model which would probably display heavy dampening in their absence. The simulations with large scale econometric models in the early 1970s showed that random shocks are normally not sufficient to overcome the heavy dampening typical in these models and to produce a realistic cycle. Instead serially correlated shocks are required.[12] If shocks were in fact serially correlated the gambler (forecaster) could exploit knowledge of the error process in forming predictions and we would move away from the honest MC casino. The need to use autocorrelated shocks could alternatively indicate that the propagation model is dynamically misspecified.

McCulloch (1975) notes that if the MC hypothesis is true then the probability of a reversal in a given month is independent of the last turning point. Using as data NBER reference cycle turning points, McCulloch tests to see if the probability of termination is equal for 'young' and 'old' expansions (contractions). Burns and Mitchell (1946) did not record specific cycle[13] expansions and contractions not lasting at least fifteen months, measured from peak to peak or trough to trough. The probability of reversal is therefore less for very young expansions (contractions) than for median or old expansions (contractions), and McCulloch (1975) disregards months in which the probability of reversal has been reduced.

A contingency table test, based on the asymptotic Chi-squared distribution of the likelihood ratio, with 'young' and 'old' expansions (contractions) as the two classes, is performed. Since the sample is not large, the total number of expansions being twenty-five, McCulloch feels that it is more appropriate to use a small sample distribution than the asymptotic Chi-squared distribution. The small sample distribution is calculated subject to the number of old expansions equalling the number of young expansions. Results are reported for the United States, the United Kingdom, France and Germany. In order to facilitate a test of whether post-war government intervention had been successful in prolonging expansions and curtailing contractions, two periods are analysed for the United States.[14] In both periods the test statistic is insignificant, according to both the small sample and asymptotic Chi-squared distribution cases. Thus the implication is that the probability of termination of young and old expansions is the same for both expansions and contractions and that US government intervention had had no effect. For France the null hypothesis cannot be rejected for expansions or contractions, and a similar result is derived for Germany. In the United Kingdom, however, it is not rejected for contractions but it is rejected, at the 5 per cent significance level, for expansions in both the asymptotic and small sample distribution cases. The hypothesis would not have been rejected for the United Kingdom at 2.5 per cent significance level and McCulloch suggests that the significant statistic can be ignored anyway, since it is to be expected under the random hypothesis. He concludes that the MC hypothesis should be accepted.

McCulloch (1975) also notes that a lot of information is forfeited by working with NBER reference data rather than raw data, and that consequently tests performed using actual series are potentially more powerful. He assumes that economic time series follow a second order autoregressive process with a growth trend and fits such processes to logs of annual US real income, consumption and investment data for the period 1929–73, in order to see if parameter values which will give stable cycles result. The required parameter ranges are well known for such processes (see Box and Jenkins 1970, for example).

McCulloch points out that one cannot discount the possibility of first order autocorrelation in his results but the regressions do, in many cases, indicate that stable cycles exist. He concludes that, due to the potential bias from autocorrelation, no conclusions can be drawn from this approach with regard to cyclicality. The period is, however, calculated for each series that had point estimates indicating the presence of a stable cycle. These series were log real income, the change in log real income, log real investment and the change in log real investment, and log real consumption. The required parameter values were not achieved for the change in log real consumption and quarterly log real income and the change in log real income. Further, a measure of dampening used in physics, the Q statistic, is also calculated, and it indicates that the cycles that have been discovered are so damped that they are of little practical consequence.

Finally, McCulloch notes that spectral analytic results, especially those of Howrey (1968), are at variance with his results. His conclusion is that the spectral approach is probably inappropriate for the analysis of economic time series due to their non-stationarity, the absence of large samples, and their sensitivity to seasonal smoothing and data adjustment. (See section 4.3 for further discussion.)

Anderson (1977) also tested the MC hypothesis. The method employed is to subdivide the series into expansionary and contractionary phases; analyse the density functions for duration times between troughs and peaks, and peaks and troughs; and then compare the theoretical distribution, associated with the MC hypothesis, with the actual distributions generated by the time-spans observed. The MC hypothesis implies that the time durations of expansionary and contractionary phases will be distributed exponentially with constant parameters, α and β, respectively. A Chi-squared goodness of fit test is performed to see if the actual (observed) distribution of phase durations is according to the discrete analogue of the exponential distribution, the geometric distribution.

Unlike McCulloch, Anderson does not follow Burns and Mitchell in ignoring expansions and contractions of less than fifteen months since, by definition, this precludes the most prevalent fluctuations under the MC hypothesis, namely the short ones. The seasonally adjusted series used are total employment, total industrial production and the composite index of five leading indicators (NBER) for the period 1945-75 in the United States. The phase durations for each series are calculated by Anderson and are consistent with the MC hypothesis. They are short. The differences in length between expansions and contractions is attributed to trend.

The null hypothesis that expansionary and contractionary phases are geometrically distributed with parameters α' and β' was tested against the alternative that the phases are not geometrically distributed. The null hypothesis, and hence the MC hypothesis, could not be rejected. The hypothesis that the expansion and contraction phases were the same was also tested. The composite and unemployment indices showed no significant difference in the phase, but the hypothesis was rejected for the production series.

Savin (1977) argues that the McCulloch test based on NBER reference cycle data suffers from two defects. Firstly, because the variables constructed by McCulloch are not geometrically distributed, the test performed does not in fact test whether the parameters of two geometric distributions are equal and the likelihood ratio used is not a true likelihood ratio. Secondly, the criterion for categorising old and young cycles is random. The median may vary between samples and it is the median that forms the basis of the categorisation. An estimate of the population median is required in order to derive distinct populations of young and old expansions. Savin proposes to test the MC hypothesis by a method free from these criticisms. Like Anderson, he uses a Chi-squared goodness of fit test but he works with the NBER data used by McCulloch and concentrates on expansions. He too finds that the MC hypothesis cannot be rejected. McCulloch (1977) replied to Savin (1977), arguing that his constructed variables were indeed geometrically distributed and that the contingency table tests he had employed were more efficient than the goodness of fit test used by Savin.

Two methods have, therefore, been used to test the MC hypothesis: Chi-squared contingency table tests, as used by McCulloch, and Chi-squared goodness of fit tests, as used by Savin and Anderson. In both testing procedures there is some arbitrariness in choice of categories, and although Savin uses rules such as 'equal classes' or 'equal probabilities' to select his classes, he ends up with an unreliable test.[15]

In view of these findings on the MC hypothesis, one might wonder whether further cycle analysis would be futile. The tests are, however, confined to hypotheses relating to the duration of the cycle alone. Most economists would also take account of the comovements that are stressed by both Burns and Mitchell (1946) and more recent students of the cycle such as Lucas (1977) and Sargent (1979). There are, however, two sources of evidence that can stand against that of McCulloch, Savin and Anderson. Firstly, there are the findings from spectral analysis, the usefulness of which should be weighed in the light of the problems of applying spectral techniques to economic time series (see section 4.3). Secondly, there are the findings of the NBER, which will be considered in the next section.

As noted in the previous section, the NBER defines the business cycle as recurrent but not periodic. The variation of cycle duration is a feature accepted by Burns and Mitchell (1946), who classify a business cycle as lasting from one to ten or twelve years. It seems to be this range of acceptable period lengths that has allowed the test of the MC hypothesis to succeed. The approach pioneered by Burns and Mitchell was described by Koopmans (1947) as measurement without theory. It leaves us with a choice of accepting the MC hypothesis or accounting for the variability in duration. However, the sheer volume of statistical evidence on specific and reference cycles produced by the NBER and, perhaps most strikingly, the interrelationships between phases and amplitudes of the cycle in different series (comovements) should make us happier about accepting the existence of cycles and encourage us to concentrate on explaining their variation.

Koopmans (1947) categorises NBER business cycle measures into three groups.[16] The first group of measures is concerned with the location in time and the duration of cycles. For each series turning points are determined along with the time intervals between them (expansion, contraction, and trough to trough duration of 'specific cycles'). In addition turning points, and durations, are determined for 'reference cycles'. These turning points are points around which the corresponding specific cycle turning points of a number of variables cluster. Leads and lags are found as differences between corresponding specific and reference cycle turning points. All turning points are found after elimination of seasonal variation but without prior trend elimination – using, as much as possible, monthly data and otherwise quarterly data. The second group of measures relates to movements of a variable within a cycle specific to that variable or within a reference cycle.[17] The third group of measures expresses the conformity of the specific cycles of a variable to the business or reference cycle. These consist of ratios of the average reference cycle amplitudes to the average specific cycle amplitudes of the variable for expansions and contractions combined and indices of conformity.[17]

Burns and Mitchell (1946) are well aware of the limitations of their approach which result from its heavy reliance on averages. In Chapter 12 of their book they tackle the problem of disentangling the relative importance of stable and irregular features of cyclical behaviour, analysing the effects that long cycles may have had on their averages. In Chapter 11 they analyse the effects of secular changes. The point that comes out of these two investigations is that irregular changes in cyclical behaviour are far larger than secular or cyclical changes (see also section 4.3). They observe that this finding lends support to students who believe that it is futile to strive after a general theory of cycles. Such students, they argue, believe that each cycle is to be explained by a peculiar combination of conditions prevailing at the time, and that these combinations of conditions differ endlessly from each other at different times. If these episodic factors are of prime importance, averaging will merely cancel the special features. Burns and Mitchell try to analyse the extent to which the averages they derive are subject to such criticisms, which are akin to a statement of the MC hypothesis.

They accept that business activity is influenced by countless random factors and that these shocks may be very diverse in character and scope. Hence each specific and reference cycle is an individual, differing in countless ways from any other. But to measure and identify the peculiarities, they argue, a norm is required because even those who subscribe to the episodic theory cannot escape having notions of what is usual or unusual about a cycle. Averages, therefore, supply the norm to which individual cycles can be compared. In addition to providing a benchmark for judging individual cycles, the averages indicate the cyclical behaviour characteristic of different activities. Burns and Mitchell argue that the tendency for individual series to behave similarly in regard to one another in successive business cycles would not be found if the forces that produce business cycles had only slight regularity. As a test of whether the series move together, the seven series chosen for their analysis are ranked according to durations and amplitudes, and a test for ranked distributions is used.[18] Durations of expansions and contractions are also tested individually and correlation and variance analysis is applied. They find support for the concept of business cycles as roughly concurrent fluctuations in many activities. The tests demonstrate that although cyclical measures of individual series usually vary greatly from one cycle to another, there is a pronounced tendency towards repetition of relationships among movements of different activities in successive business cycles. Given these findings, Burns and Mitchell argue that the tendency for averages to conceal episodic factors is a virtue. The predictive power of NBER leading indicators provides a measure of whether information gained from cycles can help to predict future cyclical evolution and consequently allows an indirect test of the MC hypothesis.

Evans (1967) concluded that some valuable information could be gained from leading indicators since the economy had never turned down without ample warning from them and they had never predicted false upturns in the United States (between 1946 and 1966). For further discussion of the experience of forecasting with NBER indicators see Daly (1972).

Largely as a result of the work of the NBER a number of 'stylised' or qualitative facts about relationships between economic variables, particularly their pro-cyclicality or anti-(counter) cyclicality, have increasingly become accepted as the minimum that must be explained by any viable cycle theory prior to detailed econometric analysis. Lucas (1977), for example, reviews the main qualitative features of economic time series which are identified with the business cycle. He accepts that movements about trend in GNP, in any country, can be well described by a low order stochastic difference equation and that these movements do not exhibit uniformity of period or amplitude. The regularities that are observed are in the comovements among different aggregate time series. The principal comovements, according to Lucas, are as follows:

1. Output changes across broadly defined sectors move together in the sense that they exhibit high conformity or coherence.
2. Production of producer and consumer durables exhibits much more amplitude than does production of non-durables.
3. Production and prices of agricultural goods and natural resources have lower than average conformity.
4. Business profits show high conformity and much greater amplitude than other series.
5. Prices generally are pro-cyclical.
6. Short-term interest rates are pro-cyclical while long-term rates are only slightly so.
7. Monetary aggregates and velocities are pro-cyclical.

Lucas (1977) notes that these regularities appear to be common to all decentralised market economies, and concludes that business cycles are all alike and that a unified explanation of business cycles appears to be possible. Lucas also points out that the list of phenomena to be explained may need to be augmented in an open economy to take account of international trade effects on the cycle. Finally, he draws attention to the general reduction in amplitude of all series in the post-war period (see section 1.5 for further discussion). To this list of phenomena to be explained by a business cycle theory, Lucas and Sargent (1978) add the positive correlation between time series of prices (and/or wages) and measures of aggregate output or employment and between measures of aggregate demand, like the money stock, and aggregate output or employment, although these correlations are sensitive to the method of detrending. Sargent (1979) also observes that 'cycle' in economic variables seems to be neither damped nor explosive, and there is no constant period from one cycle to the next. His definition of the 'business cycle' (see section 1.1) also stresses the comovements of important aggregate economic variables. Sargent (1979, Ch. XI) undertakes a spectrum analysis of seven US time series and discovers another 'stylised fact' to be explained by cycle theory, that output per man-hour is markedly pro-cyclical. This cannot be explained by the application of the law of diminishing returns since the employment/capital ratio is itself pro-cyclical.

1.3 ARE BUSINESS CYCLES SYMMETRIC?

Blatt (1980) notes that the Frisch-type econometric modelling of business cycles (see section 1.4) is dominant. Such models involve a linear econometric model which is basically stable but is driven into recurrent, but not precisely periodic, oscillations by shocks that appear as random disturbance terms in the econometric equations. Blatt (1978) had demonstrated that the econometric evidence which appeared to lead to the acceptance of linear, as opposed to nonlinear, propagation models was invalid (section 1.4). Blatt (1980) aims to show that all Frisch-type models are inconsistent with the observed facts as presented by Burns and Mitchell (1946). The qualitative feature or fact on which Blatt (1980) concentrates is the pronounced lack of symmetry between the ascending and descending phases of the business cycle. Typically, and almost universally, Blatt observes, the ascending portion of the cycle is longer and has a lower average slope than the descending portion. Blatt claims that this is only partly due to the general, but not necessarily linear, long-term trend towards increasing production and consumption. Citing Burns and Mitchell's evidence concerning data with the long-term trend removed, he notes that a great deal of asymmetry remains after detrending and argues that no one questions the existence of the asymmetry. De Long and Summers (1986a) subsequently do, however, as will be seen below.

Blatt (1980) points out that if the cyclical phases are indeed asymmetric, then the cycle cannot be explained by stochastic, Frisch-type, linear models. Linear deterministic models can only produce repeated sinuousidal cycles, which have completely symmetric ascending and descending phases, or damped or explosive, but essentially symmetric, cycles. Cycles produced by linear stochastic models will be less regular but nevertheless will be essentially symmetric in the sense that there will be no systematic asymmetry (see also section 3.3). Frisch-type models consequently do not fit the data which demonstrates systematic asymmetry. To complement Burns and Mitchell's findings, Blatt (1980) assesses the statistical significance of asymmetry in a detrended US pig-iron production series using a test implied by symmetry theorems in the paper and finds that the symmetry hypothesis can be rejected with a high degree of confidence. He concludes that the asymmetry between the ascending and descending phases of the cycle is one of the most obvious and pervasive facts about the entire phenomenon, and that one would have to be a statistician or someone very prejudiced in favour of Frisch-type modelling to demand explicit proof of the statistical significance of the obvious.

Neftci (1984) also examines the asymmetry of economic time series over the business cycle. Using unemployment series, which have no marked trend, he adopts the statistical theory of finite-state Markov processes to investigate whether the correlation properties of the series differ across phases of the cycle. He notes that the proposition that econometric time series are asymmetric over different phases of the business cycle appears in a number of major works on business cycles.[19] Neftci presents a chart showing that the increases in US unemployment have been much sharper than the declines in the 1960s and 1970s and his statistical tests, which compare the sample evidence of consecutive declines and consecutive increases in the time series, offer evidence in favour of the asymmetric behaviour of the unemployment series analysed in the paper.

Neftci (1984) then discusses the implications of asymmetry in macroeconomic time series for econometric modelling. Firstly, in the presence of asymmetry the probabilistic structure of the series will be different during upswings and downswings and the models employed should reflect this by incorporating nonlinearities to allow 'switches' in optimising behaviour between phases. Secondly, although the implication is that nonlinear econometric or time series models should be employed, it may be possible to approximate these models, which are cumbersome to estimate, with linear models in which the innovations have asymmetric densities. Further work is required to verify this conclusion, he notes.

De Long and Summers (1986a) also investigate the proposition of business cycle asymmetry. They note that neither the econometric models built in the spirit of the Cowles Commission nor the modern time series vector autoregressive (VAR) models are entirely able to capture cyclical asymmetries. Consequently, they argue, if asymmetry is fundamentally important then standard linear stochastic techniques are deficient and the NBER-type traditional business cycle analysis may be a necessary component of empirical business cycle analysis. The question of asymmetry is therefore one of substantial methodological importance.

De Long and Summers undertake a more comprehensive study than Neftci (1984) using pre- and post-war US data and post-war data from five other OECD nations. They find no evidence of asymmetry in the GNP and industrial production series. For the United States only, like Neftci (1984) they find some asymmetry in the unemployment series. They conclude that asymmetry is probably not a phenomenon of first order importance in understanding business cycles.

De Long and Summers observe that the asymmetry proposition amounts to the assertion that downturns are brief and severe relative to trend and upturns are larger and more gradual. This implies that there should be significant skewness in a frequency distribution of periodic growth rates of output. They therefore calculate the coefficient of skewness,[20] which should be zero for symmetric series, for the various time series. Overall they find little evidence of skewness in the US data. In the pre-war period they find slight positive skewness, which implies a rapid upswing and a slow downswing, the opposite of what is normally proposed. In the post-war period there is some evidence of the proposed negative skewness and in the case of annual GNP the negative skewness approaches statistical significance. Turning to data from other OECD countries, they find that skewness is only notably negative in Canada and Japan. There is no significant evidence of asymmetry in the United Kingdom, France or Germany.

De Long and Summers argue that the picture of recessions as short violent interruptions of the process of economic growth is the result of the way in which economic data is frequently analysed. The fact that NBER reference cycles display contractions that are shorter than expansions is a statistical artifact, they assert, resulting from the superposition of the business cycle upon an economic growth trend. The result is that only the most severe portions of the declines relative to trend will appear as absolute declines and thus as reference cycle contractions.[21] Consequently, they argue, even a symmetric cycle superimposed upon a rising trend would generate reference cycles with recessions that were short and severe relative to trend – even though the growth cycles (the cycle in detrended series) would be symmetric. Comparing the differences in length of expansions and contractions for nine post-war US NBER growth cycles they find them not to be statistically significant, in contrast to a similar comparison of seven NBER reference cycles. They conclude that once one has taken proper account of trend, using either a skewness-based approach or the NBER growth cycle dating procedure, little evidence remains of cyclical asymmetry in the behaviour of output. This of course assumes that detrending does not distort the cycle so derived and that the trend and growth are separable phenomena.[22]

De Long and Summers finally turn to Neftci's (1984) findings for US unemployment series, which contradict their results. They argue that Neftci's statistical procedure is inadequate and proceed to estimate the skewness in US post-war unemployment data. They discover significant negative skewness and are unable to accept the null hypothesis of symmetry. None of the unemployment series from other OECD countries displayed significant negative skewness, however. They are therefore able to argue that it reflects special features of the US labour market and is not a strong general feature of business cycles.

De Long and Summers are, as a result, able to conclude that it is a reasonable first approximation to model business cycles as symmetrical oscillations around a rising trend and that the linear stochastic econometric and time series models are an appropriate tool for empirical analysis. They consequently call into question at least one possible justification for using NBER reference cycles to study macroeconomic fluctuations. They note that an alternative justification for the reference cycle approach stresses the commonality of the patterns of comovements (section 1.1) in variables across different cycles and that Blanchard and Watson (1986) challenge this proposition (see section 1.5).

Within the context of an assessment of NBER methodology, Neftci (1986) considers whether there is a well-defined average or reference cycle and whether or not it is asymmetric. His approach is to confront the main assertions of the NBER methodology, discussed in the previous section, with the tools of time series analysis; these imply that NBER methodology will have nothing to offer beyond the tools of conventional time series if covariance-stationarity is approximately valid and if (log) linear models are considered. If covariance-stationarity and/or linearity does not hold, the NBER methodology may have something to contribute if it indirectly captures any nonlinear behaviour in the economic time series.

From each time series under consideration Neftci derives for the local maxima and minima of each cycle, which measure implied amplitudes, and the length of the expansionary and contractionary phases. This data, he argues, should contain all the information required for a quantitative measure of NBER methodology. Neftci first examines correlations between the phase length and maxima and minima and then between these variables and major macroeconomic variables. If the length of a stage is important in explaining the length of subsequent stages then the phase processes should be autocorrelated and the NBER methodology would, by implication, potentially capture aspects of cyclical phenomena that conventional econometrics does not account for. To investigate such propositions Neftci uses an updated version of Burns and Mitchell's (1946) pig-iron series.

Neftci finds that the length of the upturn does affect the length of the subsequent downturn significantly but that the length of past downturns does not affect the length of subsequent upturns. Using the series for local maxima and minima, Neftci examines the relationship between the drop and the increase during upswings and finds a significant relationship between the two. Again the result is unidirectional because he finds that the size of the upswing has no effect on the subsequent drop. Introducing the paper, Brunner and Meltzer (1986) note that the latter result confirms the important finding described by Milton Friedman in the 44th Annual Report of the NBER and that the unidirectional correlations run in opposite directions for the lengths series and the drop and increase series (which might imply stationarity; see Rotemberg 1986).

Neftci regards the results as tentative, given the small numbers of observations employed, but nevertheless concludes that sufficient information apparently exists in the series derived to represent NBER methodology to warrant investigating the information more systematically. To do this Neftci defines a new variable that can express the state of the current business cycle without prior processing of the data. This is done to avoid the possibility that selecting the turning points after observing the realisation of a time series will bias any estimation procedures in favour of the hypothesis that the reference cycle contains useful additional information not reflected in the time series, or, as Neftci puts it, a cyclical time unit exists separately and independently of calendar time.

The variable introduced is a counting process whose value at any time indicates the number of periods lapsed since the last turning point if the time series exhibits strong cyclicality but no trend. When a positive trend is present, however, the variable will be a forty-five degree line and when the series is strongly asymmetric, with large jumps being followed by gradual declines, then the variable will have a negative trend with occasional upward movements. It can, therefore, capture some of the nonlinear characteristics of the series. Counting variables were derived from various macroeconomic time series and included in vector and univariate autoregressions. The major findings from the vector autoregressions were the following. The counting variable significantly affects the rate of unemployment in all cases. It shows little feedback into nominal variables such as prices and money supply. The fact that the counting variable helps explain the variation in unemployment, which has no trend, implies that information about the stage of the cycle – reflected in the variable in the absence of trend – carries useful additional information. Since the counting variable is a nonlinear transformation of the unemployment series, the implication is that the NBER methodology may capture some nonlinear stochastic properties of the economic time series which are unexploited in the standard linear stochastic framework. The univariate autoregressions for major macroeconomic time series included lagged values of the counting variable and a time trend. For most of the macroeconomic variables the counting variable was significant and in many cases strongly so.

Neftci then considers the reasons for the significance of his findings that cyclical time units carry useful additional information. The first possibility he identifies is that turning points may occur suddenly and it may be important for economic agents to discover these sudden occurrences (Neftci 1982). The second is that the derivative of the observed processes has different (absolute) magnitudes before and after turning points. In other words, there is asymmetry as discovered by Neftci (1984) but disputed by De Long and Summers (1986a) (see discussion above). Thirdly, the notion of trend may be more complex than usually assumed in econometric analysis. It may for example be non-deterministic (see section 4.3); consequently it may be useful to work with cyclical time units rather than standard calendar time. From a different perspective one could argue that the stage of the business cycle may explicitly enter into a firm's or even a consumer's decision-making process.[23] If cyclical time unit, or average or reference cycle, can be consistently defined and successfully detected, then macroeconomic time series can be transformed to eliminate business cycles and highlight any remaining periodicity, or long cycles, in the trend component (see section 4.3).

The phase-averaging of data employed by Friedman and Schwartz (1982) and criticised by Hendry and Ericsson (1983) is a procedure that uses a cyclical time unit. Phase-averaging entails splitting a time series into a number of consecutive business cycles after a visual inspection of a chart of the series. The time series are then averaged over the selected phases of the cycle and the behaviour of the process during a phase is replaced by the average. Usually only the expansionary and contractionary phases are selected; consequently the whole cycle will be replaced by two points of observation. (See Neftci 1986, p.40, for a formal discussion.) The procedure effectively converts calendar time data into cyclical time unit observations. Following Hendry and Ericsson (1983), Neftci concurs that if a traditional linear stochastic econometric model with a possibly nonlinear trend is the correct model, then the application of phase-averaging, which is like applying two complicated nonlinear filters that eliminate data points and entail a loss of information, would be inappropriate, even if there was a cyclical time unit. Consequently, phase-averaging can be justified only if a linear econometric model is missing aspects of the cyclical phenomena which, if included, would provide some justification of phase-averaging. Neftci (1986) notes that users of phase-averaging[24] would reject the insertion of deterministic, rather than stochastic, trends in linear econometric models. In fact, Neftci argues, phase-averaging can be seen as a method of using the cyclical time unit to isolate a stochastic trend in economic time series.[25]

Neftci concludes that the introduction of the counting variable, which effectively involves a nonlinear transformation of the data, improves explanatory power and indicates that this was the result of the presence of (stochastic) nonlinearities. It therefore appears that nonlinear time series analysis will contribute to future analysis of the business cycle. Commenting on Neftci (1986), Rotemberg (1986) expresses concern about the general applicability of Neftci's procedure for identifying the stochastic trend. In series with trends where a growth cycle is present it is difficult to date local maxima and minima without first detrending, as the NBER has discovered in the post-war period.[26] One possible way round the problem, he suggests, is to use series without trends, such as unemployment, to date the peaks and troughs and then use these dates to obtain phase-averages in other series. Since the timing of peaks and troughs in different series will vary stochastically, it would be important to analyse 'clusters' of peaks and troughs in detrended series to arrive at appropriate dates.

1.4 THE FRISCH–SLUTSKY HYPOTHESIS

Econometric analysis of business cycles has tended to concentrate on testing various versions of the hypothesis arising out of the work of Frisch (1933) and Slutsky (1937). Frisch (1933) postulated that the majority of oscillations were free oscillations – the structure of the system determining the length and dampening characteristics of the cycle and external (random) impulses determining the amplitude. As noted in section 1.2, such systems can produce regular fluctuations from an irregular (random) cause. If Frisch is correct then cycle analysis can proceed to tackle two separate problems: the propagation problem, which involves modelling the dynamics of the system; and the impulse problem, which involves the identification of the sources and effects of shocks and modelling the shock-generating process. Frisch believed that the solution of the propagation problem would be a system providing cyclical oscillations, in response to shocks, which converge on a new equilibrium.

As an approximation to the solution of the 'propagation problem', Frisch derives a macrodynamic system of mixed difference and differential equations based on the theory of Aftalion (1927). The model solutions have the properties sought by Frisch, namely a primary, a secondary and a tertiary cycle with a trend and, most importantly, the cycles are damped.

Frisch's approach is clearly a useful one but unfortunately many students of economic cycles have forgotten that he tried to solve the 'propagation problem' prior to tackling the 'impulse problem'. The testing of the Frisch hypothesis often involves deriving a shock-generating mechanism with sufficient energy to produce cycles from an econometric model and thus gives undue attention to the solution of the impulse problem and inadequate attention to the solution of the propagation problem, i.e. dynamic specification. Frisch regarded his model as a first approximation, pointing to the work of Fisher (1925) and Keynes (1936) as sources of ideas for improvement. A systematic testing of various solutions to the propagation problem is noticeably lacking in the literature. Frisch's hypothesis that the propagation model should have damped, rather than self-sustaining, cycles has not been adequately tested. Questions that remain unanswered include the following. What degree of dampening, if any, should be expected? What are the relative roles of endogenous cycles and external shocks? Or, alternatively, to what extent is the cycle free or forced?[27] It is to be noted that even if self-sustaining (endogenous) cycles are postulated, shocks will have a role to play in that they will add irregularity; so a solution to the impulse problem is still required. The role of the impulse model will of course differ in such cases from that attributed to it by Frisch, which was the excitement of free (damped) oscillations generated by the propagation model.

Frisch proposed two types of solution to the impulse problem. First, expose the system to a stream of erratic shocks to provide energy; second, following Schumpeter (1934), use innovations as a source of energy. The result of the former, Frisch finds, is a cycle that varies within acceptable limits in its period and amplitude. The dynamic system thus provides a weighting system that allows the effects of random shocks to persist. Frisch suggests that erratic shocks may not provide the complete solution to the impulse problem and assumes that inventions accumulate continuously but are put into practical use (as innovations) on a large scale only during certain phases of the cycle, thus providing the energy to maintain oscillations. The resulting cycle he calls an automaintained cycle. Frisch illustrates with a description of a pendulum and a water tank, with water representing inventions. A valve releases the water for practical use at certain points in the swing of the pendulum (economy), thus providing energy. Frisch notes that the model could lead to continuous swings or even increasing oscillations, in which case a dampening mechanism would be needed. He seemed to have in mind here something that reduces and slows movement, such as automatic stabilisers, rather than Hicksian ceilings and floors (Hicks 1950). Frisch regarded these two types of solution as possibly representing equally important aspects of the cycle.

Frisch (1933), therefore, provides two possible solutions to the impulse problem: the Frisch I hypothesis that exogenous, purely random, shocks provide energy to a system (propagation model), with a damped cyclical solution, to produce the cycles observed in the economy; and the Frisch II hypothesis that the shocks are provided by the movement of the economic system and these shocks supply the necessary energy to keep the otherwise damped oscillations from dying out. These shocks are released systematically, but whether they are regarded as exogenous or endogenous depends on whether or not a theory of innovations is included in the model. It should be noted that the Frisch I hypothesis is a bit loose in the sense that the random shocks could apply to equation error terms, exogenous variables or parameters; and shocks to each have different rationalisations and, therefore, imply subhypotheses. Further, these various types of shock are not mutually exclusive.

Slutsky's (1937) work (see also Yule 1927) largely overlaps with that of Frisch (1933) and tends to confirm some of its major propositions, but there are some useful additional points made. Slutsky considers the possibility that a definite structure of connection of random fluctuations could form them into a system of more or less regular waves. Frisch (1933) demonstrated that this was possible. Slutsky distinguishes two types of chance series: those where probabilities are conditional on previous or subsequent values, i.e. autocorrelation within the series but not cross-correlation between series, which he calls coherent series; and those with independence of values in the sequence (i.e. no auto-correlation), which he calls incoherent series.

Slutsky derives a number of random series which are transformed by moving summation. We shall call the resulting series type I series. Slutsky then forms type II series by taking moving sums of type I series. Analysis of type I series shows that cyclical processes can be derived from the (moving) summation of random causes. Type II series display waves of a different order to those in type I series and, Slutsky notes, a similar degree of regularity to economic series. The type II series are subjected to Fourier analysis which reveals a regular long cycle. Slutsky also finds evidence of dampening and suggests the system consists of two parts: vibrations determined by initial conditions; and vibrations generated by disturbances. The disturbances, he suggests, accumulate enough energy to counter the dampening, and the vibrations ultimately have the character of a chance function, the process being described solely by the summation of random causes. Tests of whether the business cycle is adequately described as a summation of random causes, rather than by a complicated weighting of such random shocks through a 'propagation model' derived from economic theoretic considerations, were discussed in section 1.2.

It is common in stochastic simulations of econometric models to feed in autocorrelated shocks. Since this is essentially what has been done by Slutsky to yield type II series, which provide his best results, we may regard these as tests of the Slutsky hypothesis. In terms of Frisch's analysis, Slutsky hardly considered the propagation problem, using instead purely mechanical moving sums. His work is best regarded as a contribution to the solution of the impulse problem. One further point arises from the work of Slutsky, and related work by Yule (1927). This has become known as the 'Slutsky-Yule' effect (Sargent 1979, pp.248–51), which is that using moving averages to smooth data automatically generates an irregular periodic function. It is likely that a number of series, smoothed by the same moving average process, will show similar cycles. The Slutsky–Yule effect does not mean that cycles do not exist in economic series, but it does imply the need to be careful in dealing with series that have been smoothed or filtered, perhaps to eliminate trend or seasonal effects, since spurious cycles may be introduced. This problem is particularly relevant when tests of the 'long swing hypothesis' are considered, since it should be borne in mind that smoothing the series to eliminate shorter cycles could well have created longer cycles in the smoothed data. (See section 4.3 for further discussion.) This likelihood is demonstrated by Slutsky's finding that type II series had clearly identifiable long cycles whereas type I series did not.

It should be noted that the Frisch I hypothesis implies that economic oscillations are free (although damped), whereas Slutsky's hypothesis, that the cycle is formed by the summation of autocorrelated shocks, implies that oscillations are more likely to be forced. It is also possible that the method of summation or weighting implicit in the propagation model could, in the Slutsky case, impart significant cyclical features in addition to those 'forced' by the autocorrelated shocks.

The greater the dampening factor, the larger the shocks needed to produce a regular cycle. The problem is that it is always possible to produce random shocks that produce cycles if they are of the right size and occur with the required frequency. What is needed is an indication of a reasonable magnitude of shocks and the frequency with which they occur. If this 'reasonable' random shock series cannot produce acceptably realistic cycles then something is wrong.

Kalecki (1952) illustrates the point that, with heavier dampening, a cycle that was regular becomes irregular and of the same order and magnitude as that of the shock series. The erratic shocks used by Kalecki in his demonstration were from an even frequency distribution, i.e. shocks with large or small deviations from the mean occurring with equal frequency. Frisch (1933) and Slutsky (1937) also worked with shocks of even frequency. Random errors are, however, usually assumed to be subject to the normal frequency distribution, in accordance with the hypothesis that they themselves are sums of numerous elementary errors and such sums conform to the normal frequency distribution.

Kalecki observes that, whether or not random shocks in economic phenomena can be considered as sums of numerous elemental errors (random shocks), it seems reasonable to assume that large shocks have a smaller frequency than small shocks. Hence a normal frequency distribution of shocks will be more realistic than an even frequency distribution. Kalecki finds that the cycle generated by normally distributed shocks shows considerable stability with respect to changes in the basic equation which involve a substantial increase in dampening and, even with fairly heavy dampening, normally distributed shocks can generate fairly regular cycles from a linear equation.

The Frisch–Slutsky hypothesis, that the business cycle is the result of a series of shocks to a linear economic model, which imparts dampening effects, has formed the basis of post-war business cycle modelling. It is implicit in the Keynesian approach, as demonstrated by the simulation analysis of the large scale econometric models in the 1970s,[28] as well as the New Classical approach. Lucas and Sargent (1978) have explicitly observed that their equilibrium theory of the cycle (Mullineux 1984, Ch. 3) is also based on the Frisch–Slutsky hypothesis. In the New Classical models, the 'impulse problem' is solved by the real and monetary shocks that result in unanticipated price changes. The shocks are assumed to be random and non-autocorrelated with constant mean and variance. In order to explain the persistence of the effects of the shocks and to provide a model of the cycle, the impulse model must be supplemented with a propagation model. The 'Lucas supply hypothesis' (Lucas 1972, 1973) introduces a positive (negative) supply response to unanticipated price increases (decreases), so that a random, non-autocorrelated series for output would be expected to result from random shocks feeding through to prices (Mullineux 1984, Ch. 4). Lucas (1975, 1977) explains why these output effects might persist and thereby provides a solution to the propagation problem for these models, allowing them to explain the observed autocorrelation in output series. In Lucas's (1975) model, persistence is introduced by employing a modified accelerator hypothesis. The positive supply response leads to an increase in capital stock which cannot instantly be reversed if the supply response was incorrect, in the sense that it was a response to a monetary rather than a real shock. It must be reduced over time, at the rate of depreciation.[29]

When simulated, most econometric models, which are essentially linear or log linear, display stable growth rather than damped oscillations.[28] Thus these models cannot explain cycles, in the Frischian manner, when bombarded with random shocks and certainly cannot explain the cycle endogenously. Serially correlated shocks are usually required to simulate the economy to any degree of accuracy. Blatt (1978) calls this the modified Frisch–Slutsky theory. One interpretation of serial correlation in the shocks is that it indicates dynamic misspecification and, in particular, insufficient lags. The success of autoregressive integrated moving average (ARIMA) models, whose strength is lag specification, in forecasting economic time series also points towards the conclusion that the weakness of large scale econometric models was in their lag structure.[30]

Attempts to improve models by refining their lag structures could, however, lead to further misspecification if it is to nonlinearities that we should be looking to solve the propagation problem. Further, if the nonlinear approach is correct, then it may be necessary to replace the traditional trend (growth) and deviation from trend (cycle) analysis with an integrated theory of the dynamic development of the economy.[31]

One of the first problems to be resolved is whether a linear system can provide a reasonable approximation to the economy. (See also section 1.3 and Chapter 4.) If it can, then efforts should be made to improve dynamic specification, and the Frischian approach of seeking the solution to the propagation and impulse problems should be pursued. In the case of explosive rather than the damped cycles usually associated with the Frischian approach, it would also be necessary to consider 'billiard table' or type I nonlinearities,[32] such as ceilings and floors.

In specifying a model for testing a theory of the business cycle, it is necessary to consider the shock-generation mechanism or to solve the impulse problem because the dynamic path of the stochastic form of the model will differ from that of the deterministic form. The importance of the shock-generating mechanism will depend on the type of model being considered. It will be less important for a nonlinear model with a stable limit cycle solution (see section 2.3) than for a monotonically stable system.

To construct a cycle model one must first decide whether the principal active forces are endogenous or exogenous to the model. Haavalmo (1940) called the exogenous case an open model and the endogenous case a closed model. The choice between an open or closed model should ideally be made after a priori theory has allowed full dynamic specification of the model, which involves specification of nonlinearities and lags. The model would then be analysed using simulation and/or analytical techniques in order to determine whether maintained, damped or explosive oscillations were present. In the case of damped cycles, or monotonic dampening, it is necessary to assume an open model in order to simulate observed cycles, whereas for the maintained or explosive cycle cases shocks would accentuate the explosiveness and add irregularity. Type I nonlinearities would be required to contain the cycle, and the model would be essentially closed. A nonlinear model with a stable limit cycle, in which shocks simply add irregularity, is clearly a closed model.

In the open model case it is also necessary to consider whether the driving force is itself cyclical, resulting in 'forced oscillations', or whether the cycle is the result of the way the system responds to non-oscillatory stimulating forces, i.e. 'free oscillations'. In the cases of damped cycles or monotonic convergence, it is clear from the previous discussion of the Slutsky–Yule effect that an open model can generate business cycles. For many of the large scale macroeconometric models, random shock simulations proved inferior to autocorrelated shock simulations.[28] The resulting cycles were consequently forced oscillations, the driving force coming from the imposed error structure. In view of the fact that the presence of autocorrelation can be viewed as indicative of dynamic misspecification, it is not clear whether these oscillations should really be viewed as 'forced', on an otherwise monotonically stable system, or whether the system, with correct dynamic specification, would produce its own, perhaps damped, cycles that would be stimulated by random shocks to produce 'free' oscillations.

It is also to be noted that forced oscillations could arise from the exogenous variable generating process, a possibility largely ignored in the model simulation exercises of the early 1970s. With multiplicative errors, the exogenous variable generating process might even produce free oscillations, another virtually untested hypothesis.

Thus, especially where it is believed that the oscillations are forced, but also in the Frischian case, where random shocks solve the impulse problem and the model the propagation problem, it is essential to have a model of shock generation and also a model of exogenous variable generation. Further, to achieve a degree of realism, closed cycle models need to be analysed in stochastic form so that in this case too shock generation should be considered.

In order to formulate a theory in the forced oscillation case, it is essential to decide where the source of energy originates. Once the probable source of energy is located, and if we believe the dynamic specification of the model to be correct, it is not safe to assume that we can simply choose a (possibly ARIMA) process to generate the energy (impulses) to our propagation model that best simulates observed cycles. We ought to have a rationalisation for the forcing elements. In other words an impulse model is required. This is difficult to derive because the errors could represent omitted variables – which are omitted because they are unobservable, not believed to be relevant, or due to considerations of model size. If a propagation model cannot generate an acceptable cycle when hit by random shocks we should look at it critically, unless we have good a priori reasons to expect ARIMA generated shocks of a particular degree, given the risk that the autocorrelated error shocks could represent misspecification.

It is necessary to decide whether the shocks are to be applied via the error term or the exogenous variables. If they are then more attention must be paid to the prediction of exogenous variables. It seems desirable that, instead of trend predictions for exogenous variables in simulation experiments, ARIMA processes should be used to derive optimal linear forecasts based on past observations of the exogenous variables. The only relevant information in forecasting a truly exogenous variable should be its own past history. Sims (1980) opened up the whole question of the exogeneity and endogeneity of variables. He challenged the a priori approach to this choice and suggested that the division of variables, between exogenous and endogenous, should be based on causality tests and, at minimum, the a priori choice should be checked in this way. There seems to be some ambiguity in the choice of endogenous and exogenous variables which results from the size of model to be considered. For example, government policy variables have often been treated as exogenous because no government objective function is included in standard econometric models. If a government objective function is included, however, policy variables become endogenous.[33] Further, in concentrating on economic factors, it is common to treat non-economic factors such as weather and demographic trends as exogenous. There are, however, scientists who regard these variables as endogenous to their models. Thus in some cases it may be possible to utilise satellite models, for weather or population prediction for example, into which information can be fed to generate exogenous (to the economic model) variable processes.

Once these 'forecasts' for exogenous variables have been made they can be fed into the model, in place of linear trend predictions, in order to see how much energy is provided. The expected amount of energy can be gauged by comparing *ex post* simulations using true exogenous variables with those using trend generated exogenous variables instead. Further, the use of ARIMA forecasted exogenous variables for *ex ante* forecasting will introduce systematic or random shocks to the exogenous variables which are not provided by the trend extrapolation of exogenous variables. The size and nature of the random errors can be gauged by comparing *ex post* simulations, using true exogenous variables, with ARIMA generated exogenous variables. Once the propagation model, with its ARIMA forecasts of exogenous variables, has been simulated it may be possible to decide how much additional energy is required to solve the impulse problem. It is then necessary to identify realistic sources of energy rather than impose on the equation errors the form that produces representative time paths.

Haitovsky and Wallace (1972) suggested adding error terms to exogenous variables and to parameters in simulation experiments. The latter introduces multiplicative errors if we assume the errors on the stochastic coefficients follow the same process, or have a common factor. The aim is to prevent overstating the error in the equation residuals. One rationale for parameter shocks is the introduction of errors to account for irrationality or erratic behaviour in decision-making by economic agents.[34] Multiplicative, as well as additive, errors and therefore stochastic parameters should also be considered as part of the impulse model. The additive residual errors on the equations of a model are usually assumed to represent one of the following: measurement errors, aggregation errors, omitted variables or specification errors.

It is clear from the previous discussion that, if errors are applied to the exogenous variable generating process and parameter values (multiplicative errors), a clearer picture emerges of what energy is required from the equation errors to solve the impulse problem. It has been noted above that an estimate of the error process on exogenous variables can be generated using simulations. It is not clear how the error process on parameters is to be determined. The simplest solution is to assume errors are random. If the propagation model, with its exogenous variable generating process and stochastic parameters, still requires autocorrelated shocks to the equations in order to generate realistic simulations, then misspecification is a strong possibility and, in the absence of strong a priori reasons to expect autocorrelated shocks, an attempt should be made to identify it. It is not too difficult, using simulations experiments, to get a good idea of the ARIMA error process required to solve the impulse problem. This could be used if misspecification is not identifiable; if the error process is believed to represent common factors of lag polynomials so that the model is specified in its most efficient estimation form; or if it is believed to be due to the omission of unmeasurable variables.

Zarnowitz (1972) suggests that we might expect some autoregression (AR) in the errors as a result of structural change and that the cyclical aspects of the simulations would probably be strengthened by application of autocorrelated shocks not only to the equations with endogenous variables, but also to exogenous variables. He notes that wars, policy actions and technical change (innovations), *inter alia*, would frequently result in autocorrelated 'autonomous' shocks to the economy.[35] The simulations in Hickman (ed.) (1972), for example, reveal a neglect of exogenous variable generation and shocks. Exceptions are the work of the Adelmans (1959) and of the OBE group.[36] The OBE group found that cycles were increased in amplitude and showed absolute declines in GNP lasting three to five quarters when shocks were applied to the exogenous variables. This result suggests that movements commonly considered exogenous in large scale models may play a crucial role in the determination of business cycles. The review in section 2.2 will also show that AR shocks to equations have been used with some success and analysis of the forecasting performance of a number of models suggests that the errors may be AR due to dynamic misspecification of the lag structure.

Hickman (1972) points out that in broadening the class of shocks to include perturbations to exogenous variables and autocorrelated errors in the equations, the role of the model as a cycle maker is diminished. If the real roots dominate the cyclical ones and the lag structure does not propagate cycles from serially independent impulses, the model becomes simply a multiplier mechanism for amplifying the various shocks. There is still an impulse response mechanism but the cycles are inherent in the impulses rather than the responses. This could be the correct position, in which case we should model, as accurately as possible, the shock-generating process by analysing carefully the effects of innovations and other sources of shocks in order to solve the impulse problem.[37] Alternatively, if the autocorrelation in the errors does in fact represent misspecification of the structural model, more attention should be paid to the solution of the propagation problem, but a model of shock generation will still be required.

If the propagation model is believed to be 'correct' in that it forecasts well when subjected to AR errors, then omitted variables are likely to be the source of the AR errors. By definition large scale econometric models will be misspecified representations of the real world economy because the aim of a model is to explain the main features of the real world without being unmanageably large. To prevent the model becoming too large certain variables must be omitted by choice; yet other potential influences on the chosen endogenous variables are probably omitted as a result of our view of the world through the narrow blinkers of economic analysis, which prevent consideration of political, sociological, demographic and other factors. As a first approximation an ARIMA process can be used to generate the errors but identification of the likely sources of the errors is essential. For example, the period after a major war could be treated as a special period, and the time series could be divided into policy periods, technological periods and so on. De Leeuw (1972) suggested a systematic historical investigation of the role of identifiable exogenous influences. Further, to the extent that some external events (e.g. wars and oil crises) have a general impact on the economy, allowance should be made, in simulation experiments, for covariation between disturbance terms on exogenous variables and stochastic equations.

In order to test competing cycle theories each one has to be put into a testable form. This involves careful specification of the deterministic part of the model to solve the propagation problem. If the model is linear then careful attention must be paid to lag specification at this stage, and a priori theoretical considerations based on microeconomic foundations should be utilised, as far as possible, in order to avoid *ad hoc* dynamic specification. A fully specified cycle model should also have a well specified exogenous variable and shock-generating functions, representing a solution to the impulse problem. For nonlinear models with stable limit cycles, the role of the shock-generating mechanism will be different because the shocks merely introduce the required irregularity to simulated cycles. In this case the role of the deterministic model is not really one of propagating exogenous shocks. It is one of producing endogenous cycles.

In order to test competing cycle hypotheses it will be necessary to consider various alternative cycle-generating or propagation models, exogenous variable generating models and shock-generating models; all of which would be linked by an overall model.

1.5 HAS THE BUSINESS CYCLE CHANGED SINCE THE WAR?

The sustained growth of the United States and most other industrialised economies in the 1950s and 1960s raised the question: 'Is the business cycle obsolete?' A Social Science Research Council (SSRC) conference addressed this question in 1967 and the resulting papers are published in Bronfenbrenner (1969). Further light on the problem was shed by the NBER colloquium conference in 1970, the papers from which are published in Zarnowitz (ed.) (1972). Following the experiences of the 1970s, with its two oil price shocks, and the deep recession of the 1980s, a new perspective emerged from an NBER conference on the US business cycle in 1984, the papers from which were published in Gordon (ed.) (1986).

The 1967 conference was designed to be a successor to the 1952 conference on the business cycle in the post-war world (papers published in Lundberg (ed.) (1955)). It considered a number of papers outlining the post-Korean War economic experience of a number of countries, including the United States, United Kingdom and various European countries. The general conclusion was that the business cycle still existed, albeit without strict periodicity, but that its character had changed. The period and amplitude seemed to be decreasing, although neither was clearly smaller than in the fifteen to twenty year period prior to the First World War. The cycle seemed to be taking the form of a growth cycle, with alternating rates of growth rather than the expansions and contractions, involving negative growth, of the classical cycle. In addition some interest was shown in the possibility of a political business cycle (Mullineux 1984, Ch. 3) because of the observed alternation between government policies designed to reduce inflation and unemployment. R.C.O. Matthews expressed concern about the lags in policy and the possibility that the government might act out of phase with the cycle it was trying to cure, thus exacerbating it, and also about the severity of policy reactions in the United Kingdom to economic events.

An interesting by-product of the conference was the comparison of cycles in socialist and capitalist economies. The conference agreed that socialist planning in the USSR had reduced economic fluctuations to those due to random shocks emanating largely from political circumstances (e.g. Stalin's death) and natural phenomena, such as bad weather. Some doubts about the reliability of the Russian data were expressed and the conference conclusion was not unanimously supported. It was, however, felt that maintenance of a high degree of stability was compatible with capitalist organisation and that the catastrophe of 1929–33 was very unlikely to be repeated.

The comparison of socialist and capitalist economic experience could prove a fruitful avenue for further cycle research. If it could be shown that cycles in the Soviet economy result largely from exogenous shocks, then some measure of the size of the cycle expected from exogenous shocks could be imputed to other economies – the differences between these cycles attributable to shocks, and the observed cycles attributed to factors endogenous to the capitalist system. More generally, one could analyse the major differences between socialist and capitalist economies in the hope of isolating probable areas of cycle generation.

The 1970 NBER colloquium concluded that the business cycle, while not obsolete, had undergone important changes and that the evaluation of the economic system and its institutions required new tools of analysis. The papers by Mintz, Fabricant and Moore (all in Zarnowitz (ed.) 1972) considered various methods of analysing 'growth cycles'. It was argued that cumulative changes in the organisation of the economy can affect the nature of economic motion over time and that government attempts to reduce instability might alter the structure of the economy and change the character of economic fluctuations as a consequence. Although cycles were believed to have attenuated since the War, it was felt that they were still potentially dangerous and, as a further motivation for the continued study of the business cycle, Zarnowitz noted that good forecasting requires knowledge of business cycles.

In support of the hypothesis that cycles had become milder and shorter, Zarnowitz drew on results from NBER studies. The four recessions in the United States between 1948 and 1961 had an average duration of ten months, whereas the twenty-two recessions between 1854 and 1948 averaged twenty-two months and were more than ten months in all but three cases. Expansions had also become longer. Between 1949 and 1961 the average duration was thirty-six months and between 1961 and 1969 it was forty-nine months, whereas for the period 1854–1945 the twenty-two expansions had an average duration of twenty-nine months. This shortening of contractions and lengthening of expansions is clearly consistent with the growth cycle hypothesis. Romer (1986), however, finds that the methods used to construct the conventional US industrial production figures have exaggerated the fluctuations in the series, especially pre-First World War. This was consistent with Romer's previous findings that historical US unemployment and GNP series are excessively volatile, and suggests that the apparent stabilisation of the post-war economy might be a statistical artificat not warranting the status of a 'stylised fact'.

Zarnowitz postulates that the observed changes could originate from a number of sources. Firstly, the intensity of external shocks could have been reduced since the strongest shocks are probably caused by major wars. Zarnowitz looks at years excluding wars and still finds that the more recent cycles had more moderate contractions and longer expansions, though the expansions are perhaps a little less vigorous. As if to verify this view the 1970s brought larger shocks, particularly the oil price shocks of 1973 and 1979; these seem to have caused another structural change in the cycle, growth trends becoming less pronounced and zero and negative growth again being recorded in recessions. In addition, in the 1950s and 1960s the economies could still have been feeling the benefits of the major shock provided by the Second World War. In this connection the long swing hypothesis would suggest that the 1950s and 1960s represented an upswing of the long wave, with typically strong growth trends, and the 1970s brought a downswing of the wave, with weaker, and possibly zero or negative, growth trends. Advocates of this view include Mandel (1978a, 1978b, 1980) and Van Duijn (1983).

Secondly, the system could perhaps have become less vulnerable to shocks in the 1950s and 1960s as a result of the stabilising influences of structural, institutional and policy changes. The wider application of built-in stabilisers through the tax system and in transfer payments probably had such an effect. The role of government policy intervention also needed to be examined. In 1970 the belief seemed to be that although government policy reactions could sometimes get out of phase with the cycle – and had sometimes entailed overreaction and, therefore, had destabilising effects – government policy intervention, in the form of demand management, had contributed to the reduction in the amplitude of the cycle and to its conversion to a growth cycle in the post-war period. Alternative views of the role of the government in the business cycle are examined in Mullineux (1984, Ch. 3). In the 1970s, scepticism about the potential for the government to stabilise the economy using demand management grew. The disenchantment with demand management policies and the preoccupation with supply side policies in the late 1970s and early 1980s was prompted, in part, by the seemingly markedly different experience of the 1970s, in which inflation and unemployment were significantly higher and growth was lower than in the 1960s.

The general findings of the colloquium as outlined by Zarnowitz (1972), were as follows. First, economic fluctuations had become milder in the post-Second World War period in the United States and other developed countries, slowdowns in growth largely replacing declines in economic activity. Many features of these growth cycles are similar, though perhaps in modified form, to the classical business cycle. The Mintz paper shows that leading indicators are still useful for predicting declines and accelerations in growth. The Moore paper shows that rates of change of prices have a close correspondence with the US cycle. Fabricant finds that the 1969–80 diffusion indices resemble the patterns of past recessions. Second, structural changes were given much of the credit for the greater stability. The whole question of interactions between endogenous and exogenous forces, however, was judged to require further study, especially with reference to major historical changes. Research needed to be extended in three directions:

1. To examine the effects of fluctuations in and disturbances to exogenous variables.
2. To learn about the specification errors of existing models, in order to decide how much of the serial correlation is due to misspecification.
3. To include a greater variety of model, since most of the models analysed were Keynesian-dominated.

Further, whatever their causes, the moderation and modification of the business cycle in the 1950s and 1960s required a more complete reference chronology, ideally integrating classical and growth cycles. Finally, the 1969–70 US recession disclosed both important differences and similarities when compared with earlier recessions – the major difference being the persistence of inflation in the face of declining production and rising unemployment.

As noted above, this last point posed major problems for Keynesians, and the continuing experience of stagflation in the 1970s provoked speculation that there had been a further alteration in the structure of the business cycle. One of the major questions raised was the extent to which the essentially Keynesian, large-scale econometric models were misspecified, especially with regard to the monetary sector and inflation forecasting.

The purpose of the 1984 conference was to consider whether the US business cycle had changed since the War. Gordon (ed.) (1986) drew attention to the revival of interest in the business cycle, following the severe recessions of 1974–5 and 1981–2 and the intellectual ferment caused by the Lucas (1975) and subsequent equilibrium business cycle contributions.[38] He suggested that the stage had been reached where the terms macroeconomic theory and business cycle theory were virtually interchangeable and that another peak in the cycle of interest in business cycles had been reached following the trough in the 1960s. Seven of the twelve papers published in Gordon (ed.) (1986) consider specific components of economic activity, while the remaining five focus on aggregate economic activity. Of the latter, the papers by Eckstein and Sinai (1986) and Blanchard and Watson (1986) attempt to identify the shocks or impulses that generate business cycles, and the papers by De Long and Summers (1986) and Zarnowitz and Moore (1986) concentrate on changes in cyclical behaviour.

Gordon notes that, following the debates between Keynesians and the Friedmanite monetarists in the late 1960s and early 1970s, the oil shocks of 1973–4 and 1979–80 restimulated interest in the Frischian view that external impulses or real shocks, rather than the money supply or its rate of change, were a major source of business cycle fluctuation (Friedman and Schwartz 1963a, b). Because the oil price shocks were of a supply side nature, it has now become common to distinguish between three types of shock: monetary, real demand and real supply shocks. The recognition of the importance of supply side shocks, Gordon notes, meant the government could not be regarded as the sole source of mainly monetary shocks.

The overall picture to be gleaned from the 1984 conference is that the propagation model may change over time due to structural and institutional changes and changes in government policy perspectives. Such changes are likely to be slow and may take years to detect; nevertheless, it may not be appropriate to treat the post-war period as a whole any more. The 1970s and 1980s appear to be different from the 1950s and 1960s. In the 1970s it became evident that supply shocks could have a major impact, along with aggregate demand shocks. Thus the combinations of shocks hitting an economy may change over time. Although cycles may be all alike in the sense of being generated by the same, but possibly slowly changing, propagation model, they will still lend themselves to historical analysis since each cycle is caused by a unique combination of shocks, given the Frisch-inspired view of cycle generation. Historical analysis is also necessary to assess the impact of structural, institutional and policy changes. Further, the institutional and related differences between countries can be used to explain differences in cyclical behaviour between them. In the conference it was, however, noted that the business cycle might be in the process of becoming a fluctuation in world economic output due to the increased synchronisation of cycles in the OECD countries and growing international interdependence. But the evolution of the Third World debt problem[39] has demonstrated that the interdependence is increasingly North–South as well as intra-OECD. It may therefore make little sense to confine analysis to business cycles in one country, even as large and important as the United States, in future. The conference included remarkably little discussion, beyond the oil shocks, of open economy influences on the US business cycle and its post-war changes in behaviour.

Following the declaration that the cycle was alive and well in the early 1980s, one of the longest sustained recoveries in the post-war period has been witnessed, particularly in the United States and the United Kingdom, since the recession of the early 1980s, which hit economies on both sides of the Atlantic very badly. Although sustained, the average rate of growth has been considerably below that of the 1960s. In the summer of 1988, signs of a buildup of inflationary pressure were beginning to emerge. These are commonly associated with boom conditions and in the past all booms have eventually bust. Nevertheless, this experience of sustained growth, in countries that have experienced 'Reaganomics' and 'Thatcherism' respectively, has again raised the question of the cycle's obsolescence. Others point to the possibility that the changes wrought by the Reagan and Thatcher governments have increased the risk of a future depression, probably on a worldwide scale, and financial crises – the 1982 Mexican debt crisis and the October 1987 worldwide stock market price collapse merely being a presage of worse to come. These changes, which included the weakening of automatic stabilisers and deregulation, run counter to the positive influences on increased post-war stability identified in the 1984 conference.

US, UK and other OECD governments are adapting their tax systems to achieve 'fiscal neutrality' and increasing the proportion of expenditure-related tax revenue relative to income-related tax revenue. These changes are reducing the degree of progressiveness in the tax structure. At the same time, particularly in the United Kingdom, unemployment benefit is declining in relation to average wages and being made harder to qualify for. The automatic stabilisers are, therefore, likely to be less effective. Further, a number of OECD governments have succeeded in reducing the rate of growth of their expenditure. In the United Kingdom, the government's share of total GNP has been declining and the government was able to announce a fiscal surplus in 1988. Working in the opposite direction, the financial liberalisation and innovation since the mid-1970s in the United States and in the 1980s worldwide have increased the access of consumers to credit and therefore their ability to smooth consumption flows in the face of income fluctuations. (See Mullineux 1987b, c for further discussion.) The result may, however, be that financial crises will have a greater impact in the future unless central banks can avert them. Central banks were apparently successful in curtailing the economic impact of the October 1987 stock market crashes by adding liquidity to the financial, and especially the banking, system and/or reducing interest rates. In hindsight, they may even have overdone it since by the summer of 1988, world growth projections were being increased and talk of recession had been replaced by that of inflation. A co-ordinated interest rate increase was engineered by the central banks of the major OECD countries in August 1988 to dampen inflationary expectations.

The financial liberalisation has also included the removal of capital controls.[40] This has allowed international capital flows to react to interest rate differentials and other factors very rapidly and has further increased international economic interdependence. The implications of this are discussed further by Eichengreen and Portes (1987), who note various parallels between the 1970s and 1980s and the 1920s, when financial liberalisation was also a prominent feature (see Chapter 3 for further discussion). The other major change in the 1980s was the decline in the inflation rate, following the post-war peaks of the 1970s, and the rise in the real interest rate to post-war high positive levels. This has been attributed, *inter alia*, to the high, by historical standards, US budget deficit at a time when the savings ratio was low in the United States, perhaps due to falling inflation. Whatever their cause, the high positive real interest rates may account for the lower investment and slower average growth in many of the OECD countries in the 1980s compared with the 1960s. But their effect on the nature and shape of the business cycle warrants further investigation if, rather than the real wage, they are indeed the most important price in the whole economy, as De Long and Summers (1986) assert.

NOTES

1. See Gordon (1986, p.736) for a recent quotation and discussion of the definition.
2. See section 1.5 for further discussion.
3. See Zarnowitz and Moore (1986) for further discussion.
4. See Mullineux (1984, Ch. 3).
5. See also section 4.3.1, which briefly reviews spectral analyses of the long swing hypothesis.
6. See Sargent (1979, Ch. XI) for further discussion and evidence of high pairwise coherence.
7. See section 2.3 and Mullineux (1984, Appendix) for further discussion.
8. See Nelson and Plosser (1982) for references to studies adopting this approach.
9. See Zarnowitz and Moore (1986) on the NBER detrending method.
10. Unless it is inseparable from the trend and should be seen as part of the process of dynamic economic evolution, as argued by Schumpeter (1939), Goodwin (1955) and Kaldor (1954), for example. See Chapter 4 for further discussion.
11. See also Mullineux (1984, Ch. 2).
12. See papers in Hickman (ed.) (1972), for example.

13. See below on NBER specific and reference cycles.
14. See section 1.5 for further discussion of the impact of government intervention in the post-war period.
15. This is because the rule of thumb that each class in the test should have at least five observations is violated in both cases.
16. See Zarnowitz and Moore (1986) for a recent discussion of NBER methods.
17. See Koopmans (1947) and Burns and Mitchell (1946) for further discussion.
18. Designed by Milton Friedman.
19. E.g. Keynes (1936), Hicks (1950) and Mitchell (1927).
20. In symmetric distributions the mean, median and mode coincide. When distributions are asymmetric they do not and their deviations can be used to measure skewness; see Kendall and Stuart (1969) for details.
21. In the post-war period, at least until the early 1970s, the cycle appeared to have become a growth cycle with growth alternating between above and below trend rates – the latter phase being termed a growth recession to distinguish it from the negative growth associated with pre-war depressions. The growth recessions are emphasised in detrended data and consequently a different cycle dating, from the reference cycle approach, is likely to result.
22. See note 10 and section 4.3.
23. Via a Duesenberry (1949) ratchet effect, for example.
24. See Burns and Mitchell (1946) and Friedman and Schwartz (1963a, b).
25. Neftci (1986) provides an example; see also Long and Plosser (1983) and section 4.3.
26. As noted above, but unless the nature of the trend is known then detrending risks introducing measurement errors or noise. It seems safest to work with the rawest, least filtered data available, as Burns and Mitchell (1946) concluded.
27. See section 1.5 for further discussion of sources and contributions of shocks.
28. See papers in Hickman (ed.) (1972), for example.
29. See Mullineux (1984, Ch. 3) and Barro (1981) on alternative sources of persistence, and Chapter 2 below on real equilibrium theories of the business cycle.
30. See Cooper (1972), Howrey, Klein and McCarthy (1974), Nelson (1972), Naylor et al. (1972), and Granger and Newbold (1975, 1977) for further discussion.
31. As advocated by Schumpeter (1934), Kaldor (1954) and Goodwin (1955). See Chapter 4 for further discussion.
32. See Samuelson (1947) and Mullineux (1984, Ch. 2) for further discussion.
33. See Mullineux (1984, Chs. 3 and 5) for further discussion.
34. Tinsley et al. (1980) and Driscoll and Ford (1980) discuss alternative rationalisations for stochastic parameters.
35. Note that Kondratieff (1935) regards wars as endogenous and Schumpeter (1935) regards waves of innovations as endogenous to the capitalist system.
36. The OBE simulations are reported in Hickman (ed.) (1972).
37. The papers in Gordon (ed.) (1986) show evidence of this approach.
38. On the rediscovery of the business cycle, see also Volcker (1978). On the equilibrium business cycle, see Mullineux (1984, Ch. 3) and section 2.2 below.
39. See Mullineux (1987a, Ch. 5) and UNCTAD (1987) for further discussion.
40. In 1979 in the United Kingdom and 1980 in Japan, for example; see also Mullineux (1987c).

2 · BUSINESS CYCLE THEORY IN THE 1980s

2.1 INTRODUCTION

It has frequently been observed that interest in business or trade cycle theory is itself cyclical (e.g. Zarnowitz 1985, p.524). In periods of sustained prosperity interest wanes, as it did in the 1960s and early 1970s when research into macroeconomic dynamics concentrated on growth theory. At the end of the 1960s the continued existence of business cycles was questioned (see section 1.5). The experiences of the 1970s and early 1980s, especially following the 1973 and 1979 oil price shocks, brought a resurgence of interest in business cycles. In this introductory section, the main themes in business cycle research in the 1980s will be reviewed. In section 2.2, the equilibrium approach to business cycle modelling, which has been dominant in the 1980s, will be discussed in more detail. In section 2.3, recent contributions by economists who do not accept that the business cycle can be adequately modelled using the linear Frisch-Slutsky approach, and that nonlinearities must be introduced, will be surveyed in order to update the survey of nonlinear business cycle models in Mullineux (1984, section 2.5). This chapter does not seek to provide a comprehensive survey of the vast literature on business cycles. Zarnowitz (1985) has recently made a Herculean attempt at this.

Mullineux (1984, Ch. 3) traces the renewed interest in business cycle theory to the contributions of Nordhaus and Lucas in the mid-1970s. Nordhaus (1975) revived interest in the idea of a political business cycle (PBC) and Lucas (1975) utilised rational expectations to revitalise interest in the equilibrium business cycle (EBC). Nordhaus's contribution differed from previous PBC literature[1] in stressing the influence of the electoral period on the cycle in economic activity and drew on the ideas being developed by 'modern political economists' (e.g. Tullock 1976 and Frey 1978), who argue that governments manipulate the economy to maximise votes.[2] Lucas viewed Hayek (1933) as an antecedent of his work. Lucas's EBC model marked a major change from the Keynesian approach to business cycle modelling, which regarded the cycle as an essentially disequilibrium phenomenon. 'Rigidities' or 'frictions' in the economy, such as sticky nominal wages and prices, were the proximate cause of disequilibrium.

Lucas, and other members of the 'New Classical School',[3] aimed to derive the dynamic behaviour of the macroeconomy from the basic microeconomic principles of rational, maximising firms and individuals and in so doing made use of advances in microeconomic theory relating to intertemporal labour supply. In the latter connection, Lucas (1972) had developed the 'Lucas Supply Hypothesis' (LSH) which showed that, under rational expectations with restricted information, deriving from the 'islands market hypothesis' (Phelps 1972), a 'signal extraction problem' arises and labour and firms will tend to respond to a rise in price by increasing supply, even if they are uncertain if the price rise is a relative or an absolute one, in order not to miss out on profit maximising opportunities. (See Lucas 1977 for an informal discussion.) The LSH formed the basis of the Lucas (1975) EBC model.

One might have expected the 'New Classical School' to view the economy as essentially stable but to display erratic movements by virtue of being hit by a series of random shocks, as postulated by the Monte Carlo hypothesis (see section 1.2). Instead Lucas (1975) utilised a modified version of the acceleration principle, much favoured in Keynesian cycle models, to explain the persistence of the effects of the shocks and the findings of the NBER – which he then distilled into a number of 'stylised facts' discussed in Lucas (1977).

Although an equilibrium theory of the cycle, in the sense that all markets were assumed to 'clear' continuously, the Lucas (1975) model remained in the Frisch–Slutsky tradition that had dominated Keynesian econometric model building. The cycle was not endogenous. It was instead driven by external random shocks. In the Lucasian EBC and related models,[4] these were a combination of real shocks, entering via random error terms, and nominal shocks, caused by unanticipated changes in the growth of money supply. (For further discussion, see Mullineux 1984, section 3.2.) These shocks were transformed or 'propagated' by the Lucasian EBC models to generate a cyclical output, the cycle being assumed to occur around a log linear trend. In the absence of the modified accelerator, the Lucas (1975) model would have generated a Monte Carlo cycle. Barro (1981, Ch. 2) considers alternative sources of the persistent effects of shocks which introduce the rigidity necessary to lock economic agents into incorrect decisions.

As a result of the major recession, or depression, experienced in many Western economies in the early 1980s, interest in business cycles was sustained and the EBC approach remained dominant. The practical applicability of the modern PBC and Lucasian EBC models was, however, increasingly questioned. Despite the fact that journalistic economic commentary continues to imply that government economic policy-making is heavily influenced by the stage of the electoral period, mainstream academic interest in the PBC has not been sustained in the 1980s. This is perhaps surprising in light of the widespread belief that the large US budget deficit was a major cause of the worldwide stock market crashes in October 1987 and that no significant action on the deficit was likely prior to the November 1988 US Presidential election. There were also suggestions that the US Federal Open Market Committee (FOMC) had been unwilling to raise interest rates in the run-up to the election, despite a buildup of inflationary pressures. In the United Kingdom, there has been widespread acknowledgement of the contribution of Chancellor Nigel Lawson's tax cutting budget to the 1987 Conservative Party election victory. Not only has the modern PBC approach been largely dismissed, but so too has the Lucasian EBC model. It received little attention at the NBER conference reported in Gordon (1986) and was rejected in Gordon's overview of the conference (Gordon (ed.) 1986, p.9).

Mullineux (1984, Ch. 5) concluded that, although apparently contradictory, the modern PBC and Lucasian EBC models could be usefully developed and merged using game theory. The major weakness of the PBC theory was the incredible naivety of the electorate, who were assumed to allow themselves to be repeatedly conned by the government in a way that seemed to be inconsistent with rationality. A weakness of the EBC was the assumption that the government was completely benign and would never be tempted to manipulate the economy in its own interests. Backus and Driffill (1985a, b) have shown that, under rational expectations, the PBC can indeed be rationalised using game theory. Building on the work of Barro and Gordon (1983a, b), they show that a government can exploit the time inconsistency identified by Kydland and Prescott (1977). By building up credibility for its anti-inflationary policies, or an anti-inflationary reputation, the government can create an opportunity to manipulate the economy to improve its chances of winning the next election. The electorate, which Backus and Driffill assume to be atomistic, has effectively only one strategic choice in this game. That is to form expectations of inflation on the basis of the rational expectations hypothesis (REH). It turns out that they can indeed be duped as long as the government's anti-inflationary reputation or credibility is not dissipated.

This point is apparently illustrated by recent UK experience. Prior to the 1983 election, UK Chancellor Geoffrey Howe can be regarded as being in the process of building an anti-inflationary reputation. He declined to engineer a pre-election boom in 1983, paving the way for the subsequent Chancellor, Nigel Lawson, to boost the economy by relaxing monetary policy and cutting taxes. This is widely acknowledged to have contributed to the electoral success of the Thatcher government in the summer of 1987. By the summer of 1988, however, it appeared that anti-inflationary credibility was evaporating rapidly. Broad money targets had been abandoned in the 1987 tax cutting budget and it appeared that a policy of shadowing the EMS had been adopted instead. Uncertainty over the status of the exchange rate policy was increased significantly by a public disagreement between the Chancellor and the Prime Minister prior to the 1988 tax cutting budget. As a result the Chancellor was forced to encourage a rise in bank base rates from 7 per cent in March to 12 per cent in August.

Further progress along the lines of Backus and Driffill could perhaps be made if the assumption of an atomistic electorate were to be dropped, the existence of trade unions recognised and wage demands regarded as a strategic variable.[5] The economic game would then become richer and the two-player framework would need to be extended to allow for additional players.

In the 1980s there has been renewed interest in the analysis of economic decision-making under uncertainty, especially by 'New Keynesians'. Zarnowitz's survey article on business cycles (1985, section 5), draws attention to the fact that in models utilising the REH, economic behaviour is guided by subjective probabilities which agree, on average, with the true frequencies of the events in question. The REH therefore deals with risk, rather than uncertainty, in the sense of Knight (1921) and Keynes (1936). In particular there is no uncertainty as to what the objective probabilities are. Lucas (1977, p.15) goes so far as to argue that in cases of uncertainty, economic reasoning will be of no value. Shackle (1938) argued long ago that the view that we cannot theorise rationally about conduct that is not completely rational has inhibited the development of economic thought and caused a preference for the Walrasian equilibrium framework. It may also have generated widespread acceptance of the REH but as a result of this renewed interest in the implications of uncertainty, the applicability of the REH is being increasingly questioned.

Meltzer (1982) distinguishes formally between uncertainty, which is associated with variations in nonstationary means resulting from permanent changes in economic variables, and risk, which is associated with transitory, random deviations from stable trends. He argues that uncertainty should form an essential part of an explanation of the persistence of business cycle contractions by allowing permanent changes to occur without being identified immediately. Stochastic shocks, he argues, have permanent and transitory components which cannot be reliably separated and new information cannot completely remove the confusion. The rational response to such shocks may well be adaptive, taking the form of gradual adjustments of prior beliefs about the permanent values of endogenous variables.

If uncertainty prevails, then economic agents cannot behave atomistically[6] – as they are implicitly, in models employing the REH, and explicitly, by Backus and Driffill (1985a, b), assumed to do. Under uncertainty, instead of forming expectations independently, agents must take account of the weight of opinion guiding the activities of other agents in the manner of the Keynes (1936, p.156) 'beauty contest' example. Such complications are ignored under the REH and by the New Classical models that employ it.

Gordon (ed.) (1986, p.9) identifies two further problems with the New Classical EBC models. The first is their inability to explain how an information barrier of a month or two could generate the output persistence observed in the typical four-year US business cycle and in the twelve-year Great Depression. This is perhaps a bit harsh considering that Lucas (1975) generated persistence using a modified accelerator and the information lag merely gave time for decisions about investment to be made based on misperceptions. Further, the incompleteness of information upon which the investment decisions are made can be alternatively rationalised as being the result of costs of processing information rather than a lag in its availability – a view that Lucas (1987) seems to hold. The second problem is the internal inconsistency of stale information itself. If it is solely responsible for the phenomenon of business cycles, Gordon argues, then one would have expected an 'information market' to develop to diffuse the 'signal extraction problem'. This would also go some way towards removing the alternative rationalisation of the information deficiency, based on the cost of processing information, if the market could provide processed information at a sufficiently low price. Lucas would presumably counter, in line with the arguments in Lucas (1987), that because of the excessive volume of information to be processed this would not be the case. Alternatively, it can be argued that the information market cannot provide full information if the world is one in which uncertainty plays an important role, but it can, and probably already does, provide a picture of how other agents view the economy.

As well as attempting to model economic decision-making under uncertainty, the New Keynesian School, rather than accept the New Classical approach of deriving macroeconomic theory from traditional microeconomic foundations, is attempting to derive rationalisations for the key Keynesian rigidities from alternative micro foundations. Greenwald and Stiglitz (1987) review some of the contributions to the

New Keynesian literature, such as efficiency wage models, which attempt to explain wage rigidities, and analyses of equity and credit rationing and the implications of the latter for the role of monetary policy. The analysis relies heavily on imperfect information and asymmetries of information and, as such, is related to the work of Lucas, referred to above, and Friedman (1968), who used information asymmetries between workers and firms to explain how a rise in the money supply could have real effects in the short term.

Greenwald and Stiglitz (1987) claim that New Keynesian economics provides a general theory of the economy, derived from microeconomic principles, that can explain the existence of an equilibrium level of unemployment, based on efficiency wage theories, and business cycles. The latter result from the effect of shocks on the stock of working capital held by firms. They note that even in the absence of credit rationing, firms' willingness to borrow would be limited by their willingness to bear risk. Given risk aversion, the fixed commitments associated with loan contracts implies that as the working capital which is available declines, the risk of bankruptcy probability, associated with borrowing, increases. Thus a reduction in working capital will lead to a reduction in firms' desired production levels and it takes time to restore working capital to normal levels. The effects of aggregate shocks will, therefore, persist. They also argue that sectoral shocks (e.g. oil price shocks) will have redistributional effects via their influences on the stocks of working capital of firms in various sectors and, because it takes time to restore working capital to desired levels, there will be aggregate effects.

It is clear that the New Keynesian school also tends to adopt the linear Frisch–Slutsky approach and there are certain similarities with Lucasian EBC models in that incomplete information is stressed and shocks have persistent effects because of their influence on capital investment decisions. The New Keynesians do, however, stress that markets are not perfect and that markets do not clear continuously, as assumed by New Classical economists. They accept that the decisions of economic agents are based on future expectations and influenced by past decisions but reject the view that individuals have perfect foresight or rational expectations concerning the future. Instead, they postulate that events which economic agents confront appear to be unique and that there is no way that they can form a statistical model predicting the probability distribution of outcomes, as assumed in Lucasian EBC models. Decisions are made under uncertainty rather than risk.

Despite these criticisms, the EBC approach itself has not been abandoned. In its place real EBC (RBC) models have proliferated. These usually retain the REH but reject the information deficiencies inherent in the Lucasian EBC models. The RBC models retain the Frisch–Slutsky approach but postulate that real, as opposed to unanticipated monetary, shocks are the major source of impulses. The contributions of Kydland and Prescott (1982) and Long and Plosser (1983) have proved very influential. Kydland and Prescott relied on 'time to build' to form the basis of a propagation model which converts technology shocks into a cyclical output. These models will be discussed further in section 2.2. The coexistence of Lucasian EBC and RBC models in the early 1980s revived an old debate about whether the cycle is primarily real or monetary in origin. At present the theoretical literature appears to be dominated by the view that it is real. Some of the empirical studies reported in Gordon (ed.) (1986) attempted to identify the major sources of shocks and more work clearly needs to be done in this area. The issue runs deeper, however, because it is also important to decide on the roles real and monetary factors play in the models that propagate these shocks. Acknowledgement of this is evident in the synthetic EBC models suggested by Lucas (1987) and Eichenbaum and Singleton (1986), who attempt to introduce money into RBC models; this issue will be discussed further in section 2.2.

While conforming to the linear Frisch–Slutsky modelling strategy, the RBC approach does attempt to integrate growth and cycle theory by analysing stochastic versions of the neoclassical growth model. It does not attempt to derive a truly endogenous theory of the cycle. The majority of RBC models stress technological shocks and are therefore related to the work of Schumpeter (1935, 1939), which is discussed in section 4.2 and Shackle (1938), which is discussed in section 4.4. Schumpeter and Shackle, however, argued that innovations occurred in 'swarms' when favourable economic conditions prevailed, rather than as a random series of exogenous shocks.

The role of innovations and their dissemination has not, however, been completely neglected in the cycle literature of the 1980s. The experiences of the 1970s and 1980s have stimulated a revival of interest in long cycles or waves,[7] with the deceleration of growth following the 1950s and 1960s being interpreted as a downswing in the long wave (e.g. Mandel 1980). An alternative, and perhaps dominant, view is that the deceleration marked a response to major historical episodes in the form of oil price shocks.[8] The long cycle literature includes contributions which emphasise the impact of major innovations and the dissemination of technological innovations (e.g. Metcalfe 1984). No attempt will be made to review the literature in this chapter, which will concentrate on business cycle theory in the 1980s. If, however, innovations contribute to the business cycle, as well as the long cycle, then it will be important to pay attention to their dissemination. To do this, sectoral models that allow for input–output interactions, such as those developed by Goodwin and Punzo (1987) (see section 4.5), will be required and the tendency towards reduced form vector autoregressive (VAR) modelling will have to be reversed in favour of a more structural approach.

The relative roles of induced and autonomous investment remain unresolved but explanation of the dynamic economic development process will require a judicious mix of these elements with various 'multipliers'. Hicks (1950) used a trend in autonomous investment to bring about a gradual rise in the floor, while Kaldor (1954) and Goodwin (1955) groped for a richer mix to explain both the business cycle and growth. The division between growth and cycle theory had followed the decision by Harrod (1936) to concentrate on growth, leaving the cycle to be explained by multiplier–accelerator interaction. Goodwin and Kaldor, however, felt that the role of innovations in stimulating cyclical growth, as stressed by Schumpeter, had been overlooked and that undue stress had been placed on induced investment via the acceleration process and autonomous investment – which was regarded as a separable trend resulting from replacement investment and a steady stream of innovations. In particular, the Schumpeterian bunching of innovations had been ignored. They expressed the view that an integrated theory of dynamic economic development was required. As a consequence, it is incorrect to decompose economic time series into a linear trend and business cycles components because they are part of the same process and the statistical trend has no economic meaning. Nevertheless, Goodwin (1955) combined a nonlinear accelerator with a trend in autonomous investment, while Hansen (1951) made autonomous investment depend on a steady stream of innovations. Attempts to develop a theory of dynamic economic development will be discussed further in Chapter 4. In the next section the equilibrium approach, which adopts the linear Frisch–Slutsky approach and which was dominant in the 1980s, will be discussed and in the final section of this chapter recent developments in nonlinear business cycle modelling will be reviewed.

Before discussing the equilibrium theories of the business cycle, another influential contribution to the literature should be mentioned. Azariadis (1981) considers the possibility that, under uncertainty, business cycles are set in motion by factors, however subjective, that agents happen to believe to be relevant to economic activity. Such factors could include Keynes's 'animal spirits', consumer sentiment, pronouncements of Wall Street gurus, the growth of certain monetary aggregates, or even sunspots – if a sufficient number of people naively believe they influence economic activity, as Jevons (1884, Ch. 7) asserted they did. 'Sunspot theories' demonstrate that extraneous or extrinsic uncertainty is consistent and commonly associated with rational expectations equilibria in an aggregate overlapping generations model with no price rigidities and continuous market clearing. Azariadis finds that even well-behaved economies typically allow rational expectations equilibria in which expectations themselves spark cyclical fluctuations. This is because if individuals naively believe in indicators of future prices, such as sunspots or perhaps certain monetary aggregates, they take actions that tend to confirm their beliefs. These self-fulfilling prophecies are a source of indeterminacy which augment the multiplicity of equilibria that typically emerge in generalised monetary models with perfect foresight. A significant proportion of the equilibria may result from self-fulfilling prophecies and resemble perpetual cycles. It is also possible that equilibria resembling permanent 'recessions' or permanent 'booms' will result. Azariadis shows that such 'perpetual' and 'permanent' states may unravel if the uncertainty is reduced by introducing contracts, or as a result of the development of financial markets for claims contingent on predictions, which permit hedging.

2.2 EQUILIBRIUM BUSINESS CYCLE (EBC) MODELLING

EBC models differ from the traditional Keynesian business cycle models, which incorporate multiplier–accelerator interaction and wage–price rigidities, in assuming that markets clear continuously throughout the cycle. In this respect they also clearly differ from the alternative Keynesian models which stress constrained demand,[9] the New Keynesian models and models of financial instability, such as that of Minsky, which will be discussed in section 3.3. In the disequilibrium models stressing constrained demand, the importance of the interdependence of markets and sectors is highlighted. This feature is assumed away by the 'market islands' paradigm (originated in Phelps 1972) employed in Lucasian EBC models[10] and consequently the linkages underlying the Keynesian multiplier are decoupled. The cycle generated by Minsky's disequilibrium model is much more nearly endogenous than in traditional Keynesian multiplier–accelerator formulations, which rely heavily on external shocks. The potential for financial crises is generated endogenously by the interplay of real and financial factors and crises can be sparked by exogenous shocks or endogenous shocks, such as shifts in Keynesian 'animal spirits' leading to reduced optimism. The cycle is normally originated by real factors but money and credit play a significant role in the propagation of the cycle and are primarily responsible for speculative booms and crises. This contrasts with the Lucasian EBC model which utilises monetary shocks to derive a cycle from a real propagation mechanism.

Dissatisfaction with the Lucasian EBC model, which relies on monetary shocks and price misperceptions, which in turn result from limited information and give rise to a 'signal extraction problem' despite the assumption of RE, prompted experimentation with alternative models. Boschen and Grossman's (1982) paper was particularly influential in persuading New Classical economists to abandon the Lucasian approach and to focus on real factors instead. They found contemporaneous monetary data to be significantly (partially) correlated with real activity, as measured by output. This is inconsistent with the Lucasian approach, which stresses incomplete information and the role of unanticipated and unobserved, rather than anticipated or observed, monetary shocks, in particular, as a determinant of macroeconomic fluctuations. Tests of the rational expectations and structural neutrality hypotheses, which underlie the Lucasian approach, are discussed further in Mullineux (1984, section 4.2).

Zarnowitz (1985) distinguishes three main alternative approaches. The first was to reimpose Keynesian wage and price rigidities by introducing explicit (Taylor 1979, 1980a) and implicit (Okun 1980) multi-period contracts into RE models. These contracts were then given a microeconomic rationalisation in the New Keynesian literature (Greenwald and Stiglitz 1987). The second approach was to emphasise the role of the interest rate and harked back to the work of Wicksell, Myrdal, Keynes and Shackle, who had attempted a synthesis of Keynes's 'General Theory' with the work of Myrdal (see Shackle 1938 and section 4.4). This approach emphasises the importance of deviations from the natural rate of interest.[11] Additionally McCulloch (1981), in the Lucasian incomplete information mould, argued that business cycles are associated with unanticipated changes in the rate of interest that misdirect investment and lead to an incorrect mix of capital goods and distort the intertemporal production process in a Hayekian manner. McCulloch's models stress the role of the financial sector in adding to instability through 'misintermediation' or 'mismatching', which results when banks raise short-term finance to lend for longer periods. This adds to the uncertainty surrounding the rate of interest by creating imbalances in the term structure of interest rates, McCulloch argues. In another equilibrium model, Grossman and Weiss (1982) utilise a mix of random real shocks which affect production and the real interest rate, leading to investment and output fluctuations, and monetary shocks which affect inflation and the nominal interest rate, leading to amplification of the cycle. As in Lucasian EBC models, a 'signal extraction problem' arises from trying to infer *ex ante* real interest rates and inflation from observed nominal interest rates when agents cannot observe relative rates of return.

The third approach focuses on real factors and has led to the development of a class of EBC models called real business cycle (RBC) models. Zarnowitz observes that it entails the most extreme reaction to Friedmanite monetarist and Lucasian monetary shock theories by strong believers in general equilibrium models and the neutrality of money. While retaining the REH, these models assume that information is publicly and costlessly available. The 'signal extraction problem' that is such an important ingredient of Lucasian EBC models is thus diffused and consequently unanticipated monetary shocks play no role. The Lucasian approach is highly aggregated and effectively assumes a single product is produced on each market island. Black (1982) rejects the single goods approach to modelling. He argues that because specialisation increases efficiency, multi-product models must be considered. In his model unemployment can be explained by the fact that the effects of a large number of partly independent shocks hitting different sectors of the economy will persist for a considerable time because rapid transfers of resources are costly and will be more so the greater the specialisation.

The most influential contributions to the RBC literature have probably been those of Kydland and Prescott (1982) and Long and Plosser (1983). Long and Plosser adopt a highly restrictive formulation, which assumes the following:

1. Rational expectations.
2. Complete current information.
3. No long-lived commodities.
4. No frictions or adjustment costs.
5. No government.
6. No money.
7. No serial correlation in shock elements.

While not disputing the explanatory power of hypotheses inconsistent with these stringent assumptions, their aim was to focus on the explanatory power of fundamental hypotheses about consumer preferences and the production process. The preference hypothesis employed implies that consumers will want to spread unanticipated increases in wealth over both time and consumer goods, including leisure. There is, therefore, persistence in the effects of changes in wealth since they will alter the demand for all goods. The production possibility hypothesis allows for a wide range of intra- and intertemporal substitution opportunities. In emphasising the latter, their approach is consistent with the Lucasian EBC approach (see Lucas 1977 in particular), but it does not incorporate a Lucasian 'signal extraction problem' because it assumes complete information. The model allows for the interplay of the preference and production hypotheses and is used to analyse their cyclical implications. As in Black (1982), the business cycle equilibrium is preferred to non-business cycle alternatives because agents are willing to take risks to achieve higher expected returns. Random shocks are added to the outputs of numerous commodities, which are used for consumption or as inputs. Input–output relationships propagate the effects of output shocks both forward in time and across sectors but, unlike Black's model, there are no adjustment costs and so unemployment is difficult to explain. Despite the problems with the model, identified by Zarnowitz (1985, p.567), it usefully stresses the role of input–output relationships and in so doing is richer than the Kydland and Prescott (1982) single product model and moves away from the 'islands' hypothesis, inherent in Lucasian EBC models, which effectively denies the multiplier process.

Long and Plosser use stochastic simulations with random shocks to test whether their propagation model can produce a realistic cyclical output. The propagation mechanism is found to display damped cyclical responses following a shock and can, therefore, generate cycles in the Frisch-Slutsky tradition if hit by a series of shocks of suitable frequency and size. Further, comovements in industrial outputs can be identified as a result of input–output relationships.

Kydland and Prescott (1982) modify the neoclassical equilibrium growth model (e.g. Solow 1970) by introducing stochastic elements and an alternative 'time to build' technology in place of the constant returns to scale neoclassical production function and, in so doing, also reject the adjustment cost technology often emphasised in empirical studies of aggregate investment behaviour. Their approach is, therefore, to integrate neoclassical growth theory with cycle theory. They aim to explain the cyclical variation of short-term economic time series and especially the autocorrelation of output and the covariation of real output and other series. The main modification of the standard neoclassical growth model is the assumption that multiple periods are required to build new capital goods and only finished capital goods are part of the productive capital stock. The assumed preference function admits a great deal of intertemporal substitution of leisure, in line with Lucasian EBC models. This feature does not increase persistence in their model. The persistence of the effects of shocks is instead the result of the 'time to build' assumption.

The technology parameter is subject to a stochastic process with two components which differ in their persistence. Productivity itself cannot be observed but an indicator or 'noisy' measure of it can be observed at the beginning of the period. Consequently a 'signal extraction problem' is present, but it is different from the Lucasian one. The technology shock is the sum of a permanent and a transitory component, in the manner of permanent income models (Friedman 1957). The permanent component is highly persistent, and shocks are therefore autocorrelated.[12] When the technology parameter grows smoothly, steady state growth prevails but when it is stochastic, cyclical growth results. When estimated and empirically plausible parameters are introduced to the essentially linear model, investment varies three times as much as output and consumption only half as much. Kydland and Prescott found that most of the variation in technology had to come from the permanent component in order for the serial correlation properties of the model to be consistent with post-war US data. Their results proved to be sensitive to the specification of the investment technology and the 'time to build' lag is important, but the cycle is not particularly sensitive to the length of the lag.[13] Experiments with adjustment costs as an alternative source of persistence and lags proved unfruitful. This contrasts with the Black (1982) analysis but may reflect the lack of specialisation. Kydland and Prescott themselves felt that the introduction of more than a single type of productive capital with different 'time to build' and patterns of resource requirements would improve the performance of the model. As in Lucas (1975) there is a 'signal extraction problem', and capital is used to create persistence but the approach is different. Lucas uses a modified accelerator and relies on random monetary shocks while Kydland and Prescott use 'time to build' and autocorrelated real technology shocks. Zarnowitz (1985) notes that consequently the Kydland and Prescott model lacks the random shock property which EBC theorists had previously looked for in an essential propagator of the business cycle (see also Taylor 1980b).

The models of Long and Plosser and Kydland and Prescott are representative agent models with complete markets so that credit does not enter into the determination of real quantities. King and Plosser (1984) consider an extended version of an RBC model in which certain, perhaps information, 'frictions' in private markets lead to the creation of institutions specialising in the issuance of credit. They conclude that while credit may have a role to play in the propagation mechanism, the actions of the Federal Open Market Committee (FOMC) may not be an important independent source of fluctuations in real quantities and relative prices.

As a class,[14] RBC models analyse the role of basic neoclassical factors in shaping the characteristics of economic fluctuations. In particular, they concentrate on the specification of preferences, technology and endowments in order to derive a stochastic propagation model. RBCs are driven by shocks entering the economic system via a number of channels, including those to technology and preferences.[15] Within the basic neoclassical model it has proved necessary to incorporate substantial serial correlation in the productivity shocks, which are most commonly utilised in RBC models, to allow the generation of fluctuations resembling the post-war US experience. This was evident in Kydland and Prescott (1982) and Prescott (1986) and may imply that stochastic growth is at the heart of observed economic fluctuations, as postulated by Nelson and Plosser (1982). (See section 4.3.1 for further discussion.) RBC models can be regarded as stochastic versions of the neoclassical growth model and as permitting a unified analysis of growth and the cycle. They imply that the business cycle is exactly what should be expected to emerge from industrial market economies in which consumers and firms solve intertemporal optimisation problems in a stochastic environment. RBC models commonly assume the following:

1. The existence of a complete set of contingent claims to future goods and services based on the nonseparability of time preferences.
2. That agents have common information sets.
3. That the only frictions are due to technological factors modelled variously as 'time to build' or costs of adjustment.

They normally abstract entirely from monetary considerations and the fact that exchange in modern economies uses the medium of real money. They implicitly assume that monetary shocks have played an insignificant role in determining the behaviour of real variables.

In order to assess the importance of the RBC explanation of cycles, which assigns little or no role to monetary shocks, in the post-war period Eichenbaum and Singleton (1986) present and interpret evidence on the importance of monetary shocks as determinants of real economic activity. They note that in empirical investigations of RBC models it is common to assure their good fit by choosing the stochastic process appropriately. Little consideration had been given to the extent to which RBC models emerge as special cases of monetary models of the business cycle. Acknowledging that the work of King and Plosser (1984) had come closest to such an exercise, they derive an RBC model with money introduced using a cash-in-advance constraint of the type considered in Lucas and Stokey (1984). Eichenbaum and Singleton then use the model to investigate Granger-causal relationships between nominal and real aggregates and find little empirical support for the proposition that monetary growth or inflation Granger-cause output growth. They interpret this to mean that exogenous shocks to monetary growth are not an important independent source of variation in output and growth in the United States in the post-war period and consequently that real shocks are the predominant source of variation in real quantities over the cycle. In itself this does not imply that the RBC propagation model accurately characterises the economic environment, however, and in any case Granger-causality is difficult to interpret when expectations are taken account of. Like Lucas (1987), they conclude that acceptance or rejection of RBC models must be based in part on the plausibility of the variances and autocorrelations of technology shocks employed to generate realistic cycles. Kydland and Prescott (1982), for example, simply chose variances and levels of persistence of shocks that were consistent with those of observed variables and concentrated on the adequacy of the model for propagating them to give output comparable to US data.

There is, therefore, a need to quantify the various shocks that hit the economy in order to gain an insight into the magnitude and nature of real shocks in the real world, to assess the relative importance of different types of real shocks, and to compare the magnitude and persistence of real and monetary shocks. This can only be done within the context of a model complex enough to accommodate various types of shock.

Eichenbaum and Singleton derive an EBC model for a monetary economy in which monetary growth can have real effects. The cash-in-advance constraint is the only source of non-neutrality in the model. It is an extended version of the Garber and King (1983) model and is closely related to the Long and Plosser (1983) model. They examine the conditions under which the RBC special case, in which the cash-in-advance constraint is not binding, provides an accurate approximation to the monetary economy. They find a constant monetary growth rate to be both necessary and sufficient for the real allocations to be identical in the monetary EBC and RBC versions.

There is clear evidence, however, that monetary growth has not been constant. This alone is not sufficient to dismiss the RBC explanation of aggregate fluctuations, since the cash-in-advance constraint may be incorrectly imposed. They also show that when real shocks to tastes and technology predominate, the RBC will be a good approximation to the monetary EBC model with constant monetary growth, and money may not be seen to Granger-cause output.

Commenting on Eichenbaum and Singleton's paper, Barro (1986) emphasises their warning that the lack of significance of monetary shocks as a determinant of output does not imply that RBC models are correct. Keynes's model, as outlined in the 'General Theory', is clearly not an RBC model and yet would attribute a major role to endogenous shocks in the form of shifts in the optimism and pessimism, or animal spirits, of investors and the propagation mechanism would rely on wage–price rigidities. Barro's main concern with RBC models is the lack of important 'multipliers', which leads them to rely heavily on the frequency and size of shocks, and he argues that many economists are sceptical about whether shocks to preferences and technology are large and frequent enough. He notes that the oil price shocks of the 1970s clearly were large enough but this does not convince him that real shocks alone can explain the cycle throughout the post-war period in the United States.

Mankiw (1986), in another commentary, finds Eichenbaum and Singleton's conclusions surprising in the light of the work of Sims (1972, 1980) and argues that their failure to establish that money Granger-causes output might not have implications as far-reaching as they suggest. Mankiw uses examples, based on the Fischer (1980) contract model, to demonstrate that money need not Granger-cause output for it to be a determinant of output. He further notes that Granger-causality is unlikely to be detected for most of the post-war period because the Federal Reserve Board's goal was to allow money supply fluctuations to stabilise interest rates. Finally, Mankiw finds it suggestive that Eichenbaum and Singleton's results show some evidence of Granger-causality in the post-1979 period, when money supply targets replaced interest rate targeting. In the concluding discussion of Eichenbaum and Singleton's paper, Rotemberg questions the use of first differencing, which he believes led to the conflicting results on Granger-causality derived by Sims and Eichenbaum and Singleton.

Like Eichenbaum and Singleton, Lucas (1987) suggests a synthesis of RBC with EBC models, in which monetary shocks play an important role. He regards the Kydland and Prescott (1982) model as a useful definition of the frontier of business cycle research but feels that it incorrectly focuses on real, as opposed to monetary, considerations. Nevertheless he is impressed by its coherence and the fact that it is developed to the point where it can be empirically tested. Lucas demonstrates that money can be grafted on to the Kydland and Prescott model in a way that has no significant effect on its conclusions. He does not, however, believe money to be neutral and argues that the fluctuations observed in the real world are too large to be induced by a combination of real impulses and Kydland and Prescott's propagation mechanism. He draws attention to the work of Friedman and Schwartz (1963a, 1982), which clearly implies an influence of money on economic activity. If he is correct, he deduces, then either larger shocks, including monetary shocks, are required or the propagation model must be modified to include larger multipliers. Lucas points out that the problem is not to account for Friedman and Schwartz's evidence with a model in which the money supply responds passively to real events but plays no causal role. This is easy to do, he argues, and he demonstrates using a variant of the Lucas–Stokey (1984) model, as utilised by Eichenbaum and Singleton. This leads to a restatement of the 'Quantity Theory' in which money is neutral in the long run but monetary shocks can affect real variables. He argues that the problem is rather to account for real fluctuations without candidates for shocks that are of the right order by magnitude. Kydland and Prescott (1982), he observes, simply chose the variance of the technology shocks to assure consistency with the observed GNP variability. They did not attempt to provide independent evidence that technological shocks will have the required variance. Lucas doubts this to be the case and advocates that empirical work be done to settle the issue.

Lucas argues that the integration of the Lucas–Stokey (1984) insights with the real dynamics of Kydland and Prescott is slightly beyond the frontier of what is possible. Eichenbaum and Singleton (1984) do, however, make a stab at the impossible by introducing a cash-in-advance constraint into a model related to Long and Plosser (1983). Lucas does speculate about how a hybrid model with preferences and technology for producing goods akin to those postulated by Kydland and Prescott (1982), but trading not centralised, would behave. Instead of the centralised trading assumed by Kydland and Prescott he uses the Lucas–Stokey motivation for using money. Agents are assumed to trade in securities at the beginning of the period and use the cash acquired in the course of this trading to buy consumer goods later in the period. Lucas then postulates that the money supply is erratic, following a stochastic process with parameters fixed and known by agents, and considers the conditions under which monetary expansion will be associated with real expansions. One possibility would be to retain the full public information assumption, utilised by Kydland and Prescott and Lucas and Stokey, but to introduce price rigidity, perhaps using wage contracts in the manner of Taylor (1979). He adds that because of inflation tax considerations, non-neutrality must be recognised.

Lucas's preferred way of introducing monetary effects is to integrate Lucasian EBC models with RBC models. He notes that in a multi-product version of the Kydland and Prescott (1982) model, the volume of information would explode even if the full public information assumption is retained. If there is any sort of cost of processing information, then economic agents will economise and process only the information which materially sharpens their ability to make production or investment decisions. As a result, the 'signal extraction problem' will remain and a positive supply response to monetary shocks can be expected. Lucas believes that in a modified version of the Kydland and Prescott (1982) model, elaborated to admit limited information due to costs of processing it, shocks of a monetary origin would be 'misperceived' by agents as signalling a change in technology or preferences. Monetary shocks would then trigger similar dynamic responses to the technology shocks considered by Kydland and Prescott. He notes that Lucas (1975) had relied on 'misperceptions' over whether the shocks were real or nominal in origin but had not specified the source of the real shocks. They had been simply introduced through random error terms. Lucas cites Grossman and Weiss (1982), Grossman *et al.* (1983) and other models, surveyed in Scheinkman (1984), as examples of models employing limited information and allowing for an interplay of real and monetary shocks. Lucas finally draws attention to the Sargent (1976) paper, which demonstrated the 'observational equivalence' of models in which monetary non-neutrality is the result of limited information and those in which money affects real variables in some other way. He concludes his analysis by advocating the use of structural models that lay down specific economic hypotheses for testing, rather than the use of reduced form testing, and of dynamic game theoretic analysis, in the light of the 'Lucas critique' (see Lucas 1976). This accords with the conclusions of Mullineux (1984) and Chapter 5 of this book.

The proposed synthetic EBC model, in which real and monetary shocks hit a propagation model describing an economy which is always in equilibrium to produce a cycle, accords little importance to the financial sector as a propagator of cycles. Considered in the next section is recent work by economists who refuse to accept the Frisch–Slutsky approach and argue that nonlinearities must be employed to generate realistic cycles. In the next chapter, work on the financial instability hypothesis, which assigns much more importance to the financial sector in business cycle generation, will be reviewed.

2.3 NONLINEAR CYCLE THEORY

Zarnowitz (1985, pp. 540 and 544) argues that nonlinearities are likely to be very common in economic relationships. Business cycle models incorporating nonlinearities can generate limit cycles, which can be regarded as the equilibrium motion of the economy, whereas linear models cannot. Limit cycles occur when the energy dissipated over a period is compensated for endogenously so that there is neither a gain nor a loss of energy and a steady oscillatory state results. There may be equilibrium points or growth paths in nonlinear models that have limit cycle solutions, but these are unstable and the representative point will tend to follow the cycle instead. Limit cycle solutions need not be unique and may be stable or unstable. The limit cycle followed will, however, be independent of initial conditions. In the stable limit cycle case, the effect of adding shocks will be to increase irregularity by causing temporary deviations from the equilibrium orbit, which itself need not be symmetric (see also section 1.3). The sine wave produced by linear models is a conservative oscillator in the sense that no energy is dissipated. The cycle followed by the representative point in the conservative oscillator case will depend on the initial conditions. When hit by shocks, however, the conservative property leads to an explosive motion and consequently the practical usefulness of conservative models, which are also symmetric in linear formulations, is doubtful – unless a Hicksian approach is to be adopted and ceilings and floors imposed. But this entails dropping the original linearity assumption.

This accounts for the adoption of the linear Frisch–Slutsky approach, in which damped motions occur because energy is dissipated over time but new compensatory energy is supplied by exogenous shocks, as an alternative. The existence of a stable limit cycle implies that the economy will always be gravitating towards an endogenously determined cyclical motion. Nonlinear models with such solutions can be regarded as modern attempts to derive an endogenous theory of the cycle. They are therefore related to previous attempts to develop endogenous theories of the business cycle, which are reviewed briefly by Zarnowitz (1985, section III), and they contrast with the mainstream linear Frisch–Slutsky models, which rely on external shocks to supply energy and have dominated the post-war business cycle literature.

Some of the recent contributions to the literature on nonlinear business cycles will be reviewed in this section, which aims to update the survey in Mullineux (1984, section 2.5). It should be noted that economists working in this area often try to develop models of dynamic economic development, in which cycles and growth are part of the same macrodynamic process. Some of the ideas introduced in this section will be considered further in Chapter 4.

Chiarella (1986) analyses a model with a nonlinear demand for money function which is dependent on the expected rate of inflation. Initially the money market is allowed to adjust sluggishly with inflation expectations being formed adaptively. Chiarella shows that the model has a stable limit cycle if the expectations time lag is sufficiently small. By allowing the time lag to go to zero, perfect foresight is considered as a limiting case. It is found that the stable limit cycle persists. Apart from providing an additional demonstration[16] that plausible nonlinear functions can result in a stable limit cycle, Chiarella is able to cast light on the dynamic instability problem that arises because perfect foresight, in the sense that rate of change variables such as inflation can be correctly perceived, leads to saddle point instability. The introduction of a nonlinearity removed the instability commonly associated with linear perfect foresight models by replacing the unstable local saddle point equilibrium with a global stable limit cycle equilibrium.

Papers presented at an international symposium on nonlinear models of fluctuating growth[17] were published in Goodwin et al. (1984) and included a number of further extensions[18] to the Goodwin (1967) growth cycle model as well as other contributions to the theory of fluctuating growth. The symposium rejected, as analytically unsatisfactory, the simple superposition of fluctuations on growth trends because, it was argued, fluctuations and growth interact in a crucial way. Instead it advocated that a general theory of fluctuating growth be pursued. Such issues will be discussed further in Chapter 4. A central view of the symposium was that economic fluctuations are a natural, endogenously determined, consequence of the internal dynamic structures and conflicts inherent in capitalist economies and that advanced capitalist economies undergo fluctuations whether or not there is state intervention. Linear models were rejected as inadequate and judged incapable of representing the complex relationships inherent in capitalist economies.

The symposium judged the two keystones to an understanding of why capitalist economies evolve cyclically as having been provided by Marx, who stressed class conflict, and Schumpeter, who emphasised the role of technical progress. Goodwin's (1967) growth cycle model brought these two elements together using a model, drawn from biology, of the symbiotic relationship between predator and prey populations, with capitalists as predators and workers as prey, and spawned a series of studies on Marx/Goodwin cycles. These are listed in Goodwin *et al.* (1984). In Goodwin's seminal paper, technical progress was introduced as a trend and steady growth of the labour supply was also assumed. Growth was introduced via two log linear trends and was not fully integrated with the cyclical motion around it.

Desai (1973) extended the model by introducing inflation and expected inflation and by allowing the capital-labour ratio, assumed constant by Goodwin, to vary over the cycle as utilisation rates, proxied by employment, changed. The effect of introducing inflation is to complicate the wage bargaining process and has a stabilising influence unless workers are able to incorporate actual wage inflation into their wage demands. Desai and Shah (1981) further extend the model by reformulating the technical change relationship. They incorporate the Kennedy–Weizäcker technical change function (discussed in Samuelson 1965) and find that the introduction of induced technical progress changes the stability properties of the model. The conservative oscillations in Goodwin's original model are the result of the implicit assumption that each side in the class struggle has only one weapon. Workers can bargain for wages, their bargaining power being dependent on the level of employment, and the capitalists can determine the growth of employment by their investment decisions. Desai and Shah's model gives the capitalists an additional weapon: the choice of the induced rate of technical progress. As a consequence, an equilibrium point, rather than a conservative cyclical motion, results.

Van der Ploeg's (1984) contribution to the symposium was to consider the effect of introducing endogenous technical progress, based on Kaldor's (1957) technical progress function, and allowing workers to save and to receive dividends from share ownership. Goodwin (1967) had assumed that workers consumed all their income. The implication of the analysis is that the class conflict, and with it the cycle, is likely to die away as workers obtain an interest in capitalism.

Di Matteo (1984) considers the implications of introducing money into the Goodwin model and this enables him to examine the interplay between real and monetary factors. Two cases are examined. In the first, the money supply is assumed to be exogenously determined and it is found that the share of profits is inversely related to the rate of growth of the money supply. If it can control the money supply, the central bank can have a profound effect on the cycle and can in fact adopt a rule to eliminate it if certain initial conditions are satisfied. In the second case, it is assumed that the central bank sets the interest rate rather than the money supply and again, if certain initial conditions are satisfied, the central bank can adopt a rule to eliminate the cycle. Di Matteo stresses, however, that the analysis is highly abstract since it incorporates no theory of the behaviour of the banking sector. Such a theory is necessary to facilitate an analysis of the interplay between financial and industrial capitalists in the Schumpeterian tradition (see section 4.2).

The symposium includes other interesting extensions of Goodwin's model. Glombowski and Krüger (1984) examine the effects of introducing unemployment benefits while Balducci *et al.* (1984) use the theory of non-co-operative differential games to explain the effects of introducing the REH into the model. Balducci *et al.* find that the cycle remains under the REH. This indicates that the cycle is due not to myopia but to the fundamental conflicts inherent in economic development under capitalism which the model tries to capture. In an attempt to move away from the high level of aggregation which he now finds unsatisfactory, Goodwin's contribution was to analyse economic interactions within the framework of multi-sectoral models. The multi-sectoral approach has subsequently been developed by Goodwin and will be discussed further in section 4.5.[19]

Another significant contribution to the nonlinear cycle theory literature is that of Grandmont (1985), who used nonlinearities to generate an endogenous EBC. Unlike the Lucasian EBC and RBC models, it required no shocks to keep it alive and, in contrast to New Classical models, money turned out to be non-neutral. This was despite the fact that as in other EBC models, markets clear, in the Walrasian sense, at every date and in addition traders have perfect foresight. The latter can be regarded as rational expectations with full information, in contrast with the imperfect information imposed by the 'market islands' hypothesis employed in Lucasian EBC models. The equilibrium output is shown to be negatively related to the equilibrium level of the real rate of interest, and the employment of the nominal rate of interest as an instrument of monetary policy is shown to be extremely effective. A simple deterministic counter-cyclical policy can enable the monetary authorities to stabilise business cycles and force the economy back to a unique stationary state.

The source of Grandmont's endogenous deterministic cycles is the potential conflict between the wealth and intertemporal substitution effects, which are associated with real interest rate movements. Business cycles emerge when the degree of concavity of the traders' utility functions is sufficiently higher for older than younger agents. This follows from the assumption that older agents have a higher marginal propensity to consume leisure within the simple structure of an overlapping generations model. Grandmont's analysis implies that cycles of different periods will typically coexist. He feels his results suggest that economic theorists should look more closely at the sort of mechanisms that might be responsible for significant nonlinearities in the economic system if they wish to have a proper foundation on which to build a sound business cycle theory. He postulates that relaxation of the *ad hoc* Walrasian continuous market clearing assumption and the introduction of imperfect competition may lead to the sort of nonlinearities that give rise to endogenous economic fluctuations. It would also reduce reliance on variations in real interest rates through variations in relative prices by allowing quantity adjustment and thus mechanisms akin to multiplier–accelerator effects to play a role. A sound Keynesian, or non-Walrasian, business cycle theory could then be developed. This, he argues, might form the basis of the 'New Keynesian' business cycle research programme, referred to in the introductory section of this chapter, although most contributions[20] have so far tended to conform to the linear Frisch–Slutsky approach.

To conclude this section, the contributions of Day (1982) and Varian (1979) will be discussed. Varian (1979) employs catastrophe theory to examine a variant of the nonlinear Kaldor (1940) model.[21] Kaldor's model includes sigmoid savings and investment functions that intersect in a manner that generates a stable limit cycle solution (see Chang and Smyth 1970). Catastrophe theory was developed by Thom (1975) (see also Zeeman 1977) to describe biological processes and has since been widely applied. Catastrophe theoretic models entail a system of differential equations in which the parameters are not constant but change at a much slower rate than the state variables. There are, therefore, essentially two sets of variables. The 'fast', or state, variables can be regarded as adjusting towards a short-run equilibrium and the 'slow' variables, or parameters, as adjusting in accordance with some long-term process. Catastrophe theory, therefore, studies the movement of short-term equilibria as long-run variables evolve and would appear to be a particularly useful tool for business cycle analysis and the study of dynamic economic development. When a short-run equilibrium jumps from one region of the state space to another, a catastrophe is said to occur. Catastrophes have been classified into a small number of qualitative types, the simplest of which is the 'fold catastrophe'. This occurs when the system contains one 'slow' variable and one 'fast' variable. For a given value of the slow variable, the fast variable adjusts to a stable equilibrium. If the state space contains 'bifurcation points' at which there are abrupt changes in stability characteristics, as in the Kaldor model, then adjustment to a locally stable equilibrium can involve jumps or catastrophes. Things naturally get more complicated as more fast and slow variables are added. With one fast variable and two slow variables, for example, 'cusp catastrophes', which allow jumps and then either fast or slow returns to short-term equilibria, can occur.

Using a cusp catastrophe, Varian shows that if there is a small shock to one of the stock variables in the Kaldor model, a similar story to that analysed using the simpler fold catastrophe unfolds and an inventory recession of minor magnitude results. If the shock is relatively large, however, wealth may decline sufficiently to affect the propensity to save and a depression can result because the recovery can take a long time. This is related to the idea, discussed by Leijonhufved (1973),[22] that economies operate as if there is a 'corridor of stability', within which small shocks are damped out but large shocks are amplified. Large deflationary shocks may, for example, produce financial crises (see Chapter 3) and waves of bankruptcies which throw a normally stable system into a deep depression. Varian suggests that catastrophe theory might usefully form the basis for some further business cycle research.

Day (1982) applies the mathematical theory of chaos which, like catastrophe theory, is related to bifurcation theory,[23] to show that in the presence of nonlinearities and a production lag, the interaction of the propensity to save and the productivity of capital can generate growth cycles that exhibit a wandering, saw-toothed, pattern, not unlike observed aggregate economic time series. These 'chaotic' fluctuations need not converge to a cycle of regular periodicity and are not driven by random shocks. Periods of erratic cycling can be interspersed with periods of more or less stable growth. Under such circumstances, the future of the model solution cannot be anticipated from past realisations. A deterministic single equation model is found to be consistent with structural change and unpredictability. Such models allow periods of sustained growth, such as that experienced since the early 1980s, but suggest that recent claims that a combination of supply side initiatives and fine tuning have eliminated the cycle are likely to prove to be incorrect. Day's work indicates that even if there is substance to the Monte Carlo hypothesis (discussed in section 1.2) that there are no regular business cycles, economic fluctuations may still be a phenomenon to be reckoned with, and that random shocks may not be as important for driving cycles as the Frisch–Slutsky approach (discussed in section 1.4) indicates.

Goodwin[24] has employed catastrophe theory and related ideas drawn from bifurcation theory for the analysis of dynamic economic development. He adopts a multi-sectoral approach which makes nonlinear analysis intractable and finds it necessary to make linear approximations, which hold in the short run, and to view the long run as a series of short runs. The linear approximations are chosen carefully, however, to generate regions of stability and instability between which economic variables can bifurcate back and forth; Goodwin also makes use of fast and slow variables.

NOTES

1. See for example Kalecki (1943), who argued that the government or state represented the interests of the dominant capitalist class. See Mullineux (1984, section 3.3) for further discussion.
2. See Mullineux (1984, section 3.3) and Alt and Chrystal (1983) for further discussion.
3. Such as Barro (1976) and Sargent and Wallace (1975, 1976).
4. See Barro (1981, Ch. 2) for a survey.
5. See Cuckierman (1986) and Rogoff (1987) for surveys of the burgeoning literature in this area, and Tabellini (1987) for comments on work that has begun to tackle these issues.
6. See Frydman and Phelps (1983) and Zarnowitz (1985) for further discussion.
7. See Freeman (1984), Goldstein (1988) and Van Duijn (1983), for example.
8. And other structural changes such as the breakdown of the fixed exchange rate mechanism in the early 1970s and the increasing internationalisation of banking and capital markets.
9. See Clower (1965), Hines (1971), Barro and Grossman (1976) and Muellbauer and Portes (1978, 1979). These models have not had their dynamics developed sufficiently to be able to generate cycles.
10. Discussed further in Mullineux (1984, section 3.2).
11. See Leijonhufved (1981, Ch. 7) and Frydman and Phelps (1983).
12. That is, there is first order autocorrelation with the autocorrelation parameter close to one.
13. It mattered little whether three, four or five time unit construction periods were assumed.

14. Surveys are provided by Eichenbaum and Singleton (1986, section 2), Zarnowitz (1985, section 7.6) and Prescott (1986), among others.
15. See King and Plosser (1984) for a comprehensive definition of RBCs.
16. See Mullineux (1984, section 2.5) for a brief review of other examples.
17. Held in Sienna, Italy, in March 1983.
18. Supplementing those of Desai (1973) and Desai and Shah (1981), discussed below, among others.
19. The symposium also included analyses of long waves and endogenous technical progress along Kaleckian lines.
20. See Greenwald and Stiglitz (1987) for a review.
21. See Mullineux (1984, section 2.5) for a discussion of the Kaldor model.
22. See also Howitt (1978), Leijonhufved (1981) and Chapter 5 of this book.
23. See Goodwin and Punzo (1987, pp. 377-80) on the relationship between catastrophe and bifurcation theory.
24. In his contribution to Goodwin and Punzo (1987), which is discussed in section 4.5.

3 · THE FINANCIAL INSTABILITY HYPOTHESIS

3.1 INTRODUCTION

The possibility that the financial system might be a source of instability leading to crises was frequently discussed in pre-Keynesian business cycle literature, which will be reviewed briefly in the next section. The main focus of the chapter is the revival of interest in the financial instability hypothesis (FIH) in the 1970s and 1980s. The FIH does not attempt to provide a complete theory of business cycles but concentrates instead on explaining speculative booms and subsequent crises. In most versions the speculative boom and the financial crisis that terminates it are both triggered by shocks; consequently it is implied that we should not look for too much regularity in the periodicity and amplitude of cycles in which such crises occur and that crises may not occur in all cycles. They are essentially individual events with certain common features but the economy's reaction to them may be cyclical and basically similar in the sense that the comovements of various macroeconomic time series will be similar.

As noted in the previous chapter, the role of the banking and the wider financial system has been largely neglected in mainstream post-war business cycle literature except to the extent that a role is attributed to the money supply[1] or monetary shocks (e.g. Lucas 1975) in cycle generation. This is not the case in the historical literature.[2] The main issue to be resolved is whether the banking system itself is a major source of instability, as postulated by the FIH, or whether its importance lies in its tendency to spread the effects of shocks hitting some sectors of the economy to others. The following review of the theoretical literature does not resolve this issue. Empirical investigations need to be undertaken that are more rigorous than the existing historical analyses (such as that of Kindleberger 1978).

Although the post-war business cycle literature, particularly that inspired by Keynes's 'General Theory' (GT) (Keynes 1936), largely ignored the role of the banking system in the business cycle, the FIH can in fact be regarded as being a descendant of the GT. Minsky, its main proponent, certainly sees it as such (e.g. Minsky 1982a, b and 1986). Keynes did not progress to a full theory of the cycle. Instead he attempted to identify and explain the behaviour of variables which he regarded as essential components of cyclical movements. It was never absolutely clear which sectors and which variables were the prime movers and how they interrelated in cycles. Consequently various interpretations are possible. Nevertheless, Keynes did emphasise the role of uncertainty, as opposed to risk, in the sense of Knight.[3] Areas in which Keynes stressed decision-making under uncertainty, such as financial and investment decisions, should therefore feature strongly in a truly Keynesian theory of the cycle. Uncertainty is, however, more difficult to model than risk and leads naturally to instability if shocks or extraneous events cause rapid and fundamental reappraisals of the expectations concerning future events held by economic agents. It is perhaps because of the difficulty of analysing economic decisions under uncertainty[4] that it was essentially ignored in the multiplier–accelerator modelling of the cycle. As noted in the previous chapter, more recent cycle literature concentrates mainly on risk rather than uncertainty, again probably because analysis of stochastic models is more tractable in this case and normally assumes that the distributions of real and monetary stocks are known to the economic agents.

Following the brief review of the pre-Keynesian cycle literature in which financial instability played a part, the FIH will be discussed. The FIH does not fit well with modern analysis incorporating rational expectations (RE) but the latter has also been developed to provide models in which speculative bubbles can occur. Some of this work will be reviewed in section 3.4. The final section of the chapter will draw some conclusions concerning the implications of financial instability for economic policy designed to attenuate the business cycle, which may well need to encompass the regulation of the banking and perhaps the wider financial system.

3.2 THE ROLE OF MONEY AND CREDIT IN PRE-KEYNESIAN BUSINESS CYCLE LITERATURE

Hansen (1951) and Haberler (1958) provide excellent reviews of pre-Keynesian business cycle literature. Hansen takes a critical stance and largely dismisses pre-Keynesian theories[5] in favour of a multiplier–accelerator approach, stressing in particular the role of investment. In so doing he plays down the roles of innovation, uncertainty and the financial system in cycle generation and propagation. He is particularly critical of Hayek's work (Hayek 1931), which is regarded by many as perhaps the major pre-Keynesian theory and which attaches weight to both monetary and real factors. In the previous chapter it was noted that proponents of equilibrium theories of the business cycle regard Hayek's work as a seminal contribution. Haberler is more cautious about the post-Keynesian multiplier–accelerator approach and, having reviewed the Keynesian and pre-Keynesian literature, provides his own synthetic exposition of the nature and causes of business cycles in which innovations, uncertainty and the monetary and financial systems feature more prominently. Haberler makes the following observation, for example:

> Money and credit occupy such a central position in our economic system that it is almost certain that they play an important role in bringing about the business cycle, either as an impelling force or as a conditioning factor. (1958, p. 14)

Hansen (1951) traces concern over financial instability back to the early nineteenth century when 'overtrading' became a common explanation of commercial and financial crises. The original source of the 'overtrading' idea appears to be Adam Smith (1776), who described it as a general error committed by large and small traders when the profits from trade happen to be greater than normal. Carey (1816) observed that banks contributed to and significantly amplified commercial and financial crises because, rather than checking the spirit of overtrading, they fostered and extended it by discounting freely on demand. Then at the first sign of crisis they abruptly changed their practice and adopted a dramatically opposite stance and diminished their loans violently and rapidly. Mill (1848) devoted three chapters to the causes and effects of commercial crises. He perceived of a crisis as a commercial phenomenon caused by speculation in commodities – often, but not always, backed by an irrational extension of bank credit. Later Mills (1867)[6] stated categorically that every ten years or so a vast and sudden increase of demand in the loan market occurs, followed by a revulsion and a temporary destruction of credit or discredit, as it was sometimes called. He argued that the credit cycle breeds optimism which in turn breeds recklessness and leads to a crisis and stagnation. It was, therefore, governed by moral or psychological causes. Marshall and Marshall (1879) also regarded crises as being related to reckless inflation of credit, with the subsequent depressions attributed to a want of confidence which induced a state of commercial disorganisation. Hansen then turns to a critical review of the work of Hawtrey and Hayek, which he regards as monetary disequilibrium theories.

Haberler's review of the literature draws a useful distinction between purely monetary theories of the cycle, monetary over-investment theories and psychological theories, all of which attach importance to money and credit. In his view, Hawtrey's work[7] is the leading example of a purely monetary theory. Hawtrey argues that changes in the flow of money are the sole and sufficient cause of changes in economic activity, including the alternation of prosperity and depression and good and bad trade. In his theory aggregate demand, or consumer outlay as he calls it, is related to the money supply via the Cambridge version of equation of exchange, in which income velocity replaces transactions velocity. Consequently changes in consumers' outlay are principally due to changes in the quantity of money and the business cycle is a replica, on a small scale, of an outright money inflation and deflation. Depression results from a fall in consumers' outlay in response to a reduction in the circulating medium of exchange[8] and is intensified by a fall in the velocity of circulation. In prosperity the reverse holds. It follows that if the flow of money can be stabilised, cycles will disappear but, Hawtrey argues, stabilisation will not be easy because the modern money and credit system is inherently unstable. Hawtrey assumes that bank credit is the main means of payment and the money supply consists of bank credit and circulating legal tender. The banking system creates credit and regulates its quantity. The upswing of the trade cycle is caused by an expansion of credit brought about by banks through the easing of conditions attached to loans, including reductions in the discount rate.

Merchants are particularly sensitive to interest rate charges and play a strategic role in Hawtrey's theory. In the upswing prices will tend to rise, improving profitability, and so too will the velocity, thus reinforcing the expansionary tendencies. Prosperity is terminated when credit expansion is discontinued. In the expansionary phase the demand for transactions balances will increase, causing a drainage of cash from the banks and making them reliant on the central bank to alleviate the shortages. If the central bank declines to do so because of its exchange rate objective or out of concern over growing inflationary pressure, then the process of credit expansion will be terminated. The downswing that follows is also cumulative and is caused largely by a reversal of the processes prevailing in the upswing. During the depression, loans are liquidated, bank reserves accumulate, excess reserves build up, and interest rates fall to very low levels. Hawtrey argues that the abundance of cheap money, reinforced by central bank policy, will eventually spark a revival but acknowledges the possibility of a credit deadlock in which pessimism prevails. This he regards as a rare occurrence but one which can explain the drawn-out depression of the 1930s. Normally, however, banking policy can be relied upon to generate another upswing fairly soon after bank reserves have become excessive, and another over-expansion of credit will occur.

Haberler draws attention to the fact that Hawtrey's theory contends that changes in the rate of interest influence primarily the demand for working capital and particularly stocks of goods, hence the importance attached to merchants rather than investment in fixed capital. It is, therefore, distinguishable from monetary over-investment or neo-Wicksellian theories. In this category he places the work of Hayek (particularly 1931, 1933), among others.[9] Like Hawtrey's, such theories assume that the banking system regulates the quantity of money and recognise a complicated relationship between the interest rate, changes in the quantity of money and the price level. Wicksell (1907, 1934, 1936) provides the basis for their analysis by drawing a distinction between the money, nominal or market rate of interest, which is influenced by monetary factors including the policy of banks, and the natural rate of interest. The latter is defined as the rate which equates the demand for loan capital with the supply of savings. If banks lower the market rate below the natural rate, the demand for credit will rise to exceed the supply of savings, leaving banks to expand credit to meet the excess demand, and inflation will result. If the market rate is raised above the natural rate, the demand for credit will fall and savings will not be used for productive purposes.

In monetary over-investment theories the boom is brought about by the market rate of interest falling below the natural rate, which leads to a credit expansion and rising prices. This encourages further borrowing and credit expansion, possibly by causing a reduction in the real interest rate.[10] Monetary expansion through the increase of bank credit does not lead to a parallel increase in savings, and the natural or equilibrium rate of interest will tend to rise. If banks try to maintain the prevailing interest rate then the gap between it and the natural rate will rise, requiring even greater credit expansion to meet the growing excess demand for credit. Prices rise still higher, profits are raised further, and the inflationary spiral continues. So far the theory runs parallel with the purely monetary theory, Haberler observes.

Complementary to the monetary expansion-induced upswing, however, there will be distortions in the real sector because the rate of interest also influences the allocation of factors of production. As capitalism develops, with the ultimate goal of expanding the output of consumer goods, the process of production lengthens – in the sense of involving a greater number of intermediate stages in the production of intermediate goods such as machinery, components, raw materials and half-finished products. The percentage of capital stock in particular will tend to increase relative to the output of consumable goods, and entrepreneurs will tend to elongate the process of production in response to the availability of new capital and lower interest rates. If the rate of interest falls as a result of increased savings, then investment will increase, and the product in process will tend to lengthen.

The entrepreneur seeking to increase capital stock need not be concerned about whether the interest rate fall is due to an increase in voluntary saving or an expansion in bank credit. The fall in the interest rate will encourage investment, and means of production will be drawn away from consumption goods industries. This requires that the credit creation does not lead to an equivalent rise in the demand for consumer goods through rising aggregate income. Income may indeed rise but is assumed to do so after a lag so that prices will rise faster than disposable income and consumption will be curtailed. The rising prices and lower interest rates induce people to save more and result in 'forced saving' which, like voluntary saving, restricts consumption and releases productive resources for the production of additional capital goods.

According to the monetary over-investment theories, the process of monetary expansion and heavy investment cannot go on indefinitely because the artificial lowering of the interest rate encourages a lengthening of production which cannot continue unchecked. The structure of production becomes top-heavy as a result of over-investment, and it is increasingly evident that further investment should be curtailed; the investment boom then collapses. The proximate cause for the breakdown of the boom, Haberler observes, is normally attributed to the inability or unwillingness of the banking system to continue to expand credit. The mere stoppage of expansion can cause a collapse because of the long gestation of newly started investment projects which rely on the availability of credit over a long period. If the flow of credit is not forthcoming, the completion of new schemes becomes impossible, and this means that various sectors may not be able to work at full capacity because of inadequate demand as a result of input–output relationships.

Members of the over-investment school argue that the problem is not a purely monetary one; consequently, monetary measures cannot avert the crisis but can only postpone it, Haberler observes. The sustained monetary expansion would instead lead to inflation and then hyperinflation and the complete collapse of the monetary system. According to Haberler, Hayek provides the most elaborate analysis of the monetary over-investment process. At the end of the boom, near-full employment is likely to prevail, and it is postulated that there will be an increase in the demand for consumer goods relative to that for producer goods. It is not totally clear why this should occur. Hayek attaches importance to historic cost accounting which inflates the paper profits of entrepreneurs, tempting them to increase consumption, but the lagged effect of the over-investment boom on incomes might also stimulate consumer goods demands. The relative increase in demand for consumer goods will ensure that consumer goods industries' profitability will increase relative to that of producer goods industries, and factors of production will be bid away from 'higher' stages of production to 'lower' stages. This change causes a rise in interest rates because the prosperity of the consumer goods industries is expected to encourage them to invest and therefore increase their demand for the products of the producer goods industries. Producers in the 'higher' stages of production will therefore seek to lengthen the productive structures further and will try to raise the funds by borrowing from banks. Demand for credit rises but is not matched by an increase in supply and the interest rate rises.

This rise, Hayek argues, increases the production costs of the higher stages of production more than it does those of the lower stages, and a breakdown in the investment-led expansion process can be expected. It can be averted only if people can be induced to save more and consume less, and the rise in interest rates is judged by adherents to the monetary over-investment school to be insufficient to achieve this. They therefore conclude that every credit expansion will lead to over-investment and to a breakdown, and that it is impossible to achieve a continuous increase in the capital stock by means of 'forced' saving accomplished with the help of inflationary credit expansion. No collapse need occur if credit expansion and forced saving could continue indefinitely; but forced saving, it is argued, will end abruptly because the continuous expansion of credit will lead to accelerating inflation which will threaten the collapse of the monetary system.

Haberler feels that the explanation of the crisis in the monetary over-investment theories is incomplete and that the theory of the depression is not as fully elaborated as the theory of the boom. The theories vary in the weight attached to monetary and non-monetary factors, such as the need to adjust the over-elongated process of production. Some (e.g. Strigl 1934) argue that after the breakdown of the boom, banks will not merely halt credit expansion but will go further and contract credit in order to restore their liquidity. Influenced by widespread insecurity and pessimism, firms will also seek to strengthen their cash reserves. The general struggle to increase liquidity will induce hoarding. Prices will begin to fall, and the incentive to invest will be further reduced. Following the collapse of the boom, the money rate of interest will tend to rise above the natural rate but, as the banks' liquidity position improves, the price fall comes to an end, pessimism gives way to a more optimistic outlook, the natural and market rates converge, and a state of equilibrium is approached. No special stimulus from outsiders, such as innovations or other shocks, is required. Haberler observes that the new upswing starts smoothly and imperceptibly out of the ashes of the last boom.

The behaviour of the banking system is crucial to the recurrence of such cycles of prosperity and depression. Mises (1928, pp. 56–61) argues that if the banks did not push the money rate below the natural rate by expanding credit, equilibrium would not be disturbed. It is therefore necessary to explain why the banks keep repeating their mistake. Mises contends that the root cause is an ideological preference for interest rate reduction and credit expansion among businessmen and politicians. He further argues that the banking system's ability to expand credit relies on central bank support, which in turn is reliant on its monopoly over the issuance of banknotes. If banks issued their own notes, unsound banks would be eliminated and sound banks would not indulge in imprudent credit expansion for fear of bankruptcy. Other exponents of the theory tend to believe that the solution is not this simple[11] because the problem is not always that banks reduce nominal rates below the natural rates. Instead the natural rate may rise above the prevailing nominal rate. Machlup (1931, pp. 167–78), for example, assumes a more passive role for banks, especially in the boom phase of the cycle, while trying to explain the recurrence of the cycle.

Haberler also considers over-indebtedness as a cause of the recurrence of economic depressions. He concentrates on the work of Fisher (1933), who argues that over-indebtedness and deflation tend to reproduce and reinforce one another, deflation swelling the burden of debts and over-indebtedness leading to debt liquidation, which in turn leads to a contraction in the money stream and a fall in prices. As noted in section 1.2, Fisher regarded the business cycle as a myth, in the sense that there is no regular periodic movement. He stresses the differing periods and amplitudes of the so-called cycles, regarding each one as a historical event. Nevertheless, he accepts that the economic system is subject to spirals of expansion and contraction. His description of the downward spiral which follows the onset of a depression is essentially similar to that of the purely monetary and monetary over-investment schools. Debts and over-indebtedness, however, play a crucial and destructive role in his theory. Large debts tend to intensify the deflation and over-indebtedness may be the cause that precipitates the crisis, Haberler observes.

The burden of debts aggravates depressions because it becomes heavier as prices fall and leads to distress selling and further falls in prices. Fisher argues that over-indebtedness occurs when debts are too large in relation to other economic factors and commonly occurs when opportunities to invest at large prospective profits appear, perhaps due to innovations and the opening of new markets. Easy money is seen as the main cause of over-borrowing. Haberler observes that there is, therefore, a close connection between over-investment, which implies investment that later turns out to be unprofitable, and over-indebtedness. However, he stresses the fact that over-investment has relied on borrowed money. Fisher's theory consequently adds to the monetary over-investment theory only to the extent that it stresses that debt can intensify the depression that would be expected in an over-investment cycle which relied entirely on internally generated funds, Haberler argues. But monetary over-investment theories tend to assume a role for bank credit in the funding of over-investment anyway.

Haberler next turns to the discussion of 'psychological' theories, noting that there is no fundamental difference between these theories and other economic theories, which all make assumptions about human behaviour. The distinction he draws, however, is the following:

> The 'psychological' theories introduce certain assumptions about typical reactions, mainly on the part of the entrepreneur and the saver, in certain situations; and these reactions are conventionally called psychological, because of their (in a sense) indeterminate character. (1958, pp. 142, 143)

But the distinction is one of emphasis rather than of kind, he notes. The psychological factors are used to supplement monetary and other economic determinants of business cycles and not as alternative elements of causation. They often feature less prominently, however, in other theories. The main channel through which psychological factors have an influence is that of expectations formation under uncertainty which, Haberler argues, is pervasive. But it does feature prominently in such activities as investment. He observes that the psychological theories essentially introduce optimism and pessimism as additional, intensifying determinants of the prosperity and depression phases of the cycle respectively, and the turning points are marked by a switch from optimism to pessimism and vice versa.

Haberler notes that the psychological factor will reduce the stability of the relationship between investment and the rate of interest and can stimulate or encourage investment independently, as Keynes (1936) argued. Further, the optimism can become infectious, leading entrepreneurs into irrational herd behaviour. Lavington (1922, pp. 32-3) likens businessmen who infect each other with optimism to skaters on a pond, whose confidence in their own safety is reinforced by the presence of other skaters on the ice despite the rational judgement that the greater the number of skaters on the ice the higher the risk of it breaking. Haberler observes that psychological theories also direct attention to the fact that following a period of rising prices and demand economic agents come to expect further rises in the future and this conditions their behaviour. This 'psychological fact' features prominently in the discussion of price bubbles and the financial instability hypothesis (FIH) in the subsequent sections of this chapter. Haberler also notes that theorists stressing psychological factors, especially Keynes (1936) and Pigou (1929, for example), point out that the discovery of 'errors of optimism' gives birth to the opposite 'error of pessimism'. Reviewing Pigou's work, Hawtrey (1928) argues that optimism and pessimism are wholly dependent on the policy of banks. They are optimistic when credit is rising and pessimistic when it is falling. This ignores the fact that reactions of investment to changes in interest rates may vary according to the circumstance, particularly in accordance with Keynes's 'animal spirits' (1936, p. 162); and the banks' behaviour also needs to be explained, perhaps in terms of infection by optimism and pessimism from businessmen.

Having reviewed the above and other theories of the business cycle, in which the financial system plays no major role, Haberler presents a synthetic exposition of the nature and causes of business cycles which basically incorporates money and the banking system in a Keynesian model in which the multiplier and accelerator are operative. He concludes that:

> ... a large part of contemporary economic theory has laid undue stress on 'real' factors and that 'monetary' factors ... have been neglected and their importance grossly underestimated. (1958, p. 455)

By contemporary theory he means the Keynesian multiplier–accelerator literature in particular. He notes that not only have purely monetary theories become increasingly unpopular but also that, despite the fact that most current theories are mixed in the sense that monetary and real factors interact, the monetary factor has been increasingly de-emphasised and relegated to a passive or permissive role. He cites Hicks (1950) as an example. In contrast he believes that monetary factors and policies play an important role in generating economic instability and that speculative excesses occur, in both the real and financial spheres, which are not possible on the large and disturbing scale on which they actually occur without excessive credit expansion. By 'monetary factors' he means not just active policies of inflation and deflation but also the monetary repercussions of financial crises which frequently mark the upper turning point of the cycle. He asserts that:

> ... the acceleration principle plus multiplier, unless combined with and reinforced by monetary factors, psychology and rigidities would hardly produce more than mild inconsequential fluctuations. (1958, p. 481)

He further argues that the propagation problem is more important than the impulse problem[12] and that in the propagation mechanism, which describes how the economy reacts to shocks, monetary factors play a decisive role. With regard to the impulse problem, innovations are regarded as a particularly important source of shocks. Haberler (1958) also warned prophetically that in an environment with a low tolerance for unemployment and a fear of depression, policies based on the Keynesian models of the 1940s and 1950s might ultimately lead to a secular inflation.

The pre-Keynesian literature is therefore replete with theories that attach a major role to money and the banking system in the cycle generation process. In the next section more recent work, which attempts to develop some of these themes, will be discussed. The financial instability hypothesis, in particular, develops the idea that bank behaviour encourages over-expansion in the upswing. This leads to its eventual termination by a crisis which ushers in a more severe recession, and perhaps even a depression, than might otherwise have occurred.

3.3 THE FINANCIAL INSTABILITY HYPOTHESIS (FIH)

3.3.1 Minsky on financial instability

Minsky has written at length and on numerous occasions,[13] since the early 1970s, on the FIH. No attempt will be made to analyse the evolution of his theory, which appears to have increasingly stressed the endogeneity of the process and thereby reduced its reliance on external shocks. Kindleberger's influential book (1978) develops a theory of financial crises based on Minsky's earlier work, in which shocks are important, and this will be discussed later. Minsky's more recent expositions (1982a, b, 1986) will be considered first in order to outline his hypothesis.

Minsky builds on Keynes (1937), which attempted to highlight the General Theory's essential ingredients and explain why output and employment are so liable to fluctuations. Like Shackle (1938, 1974) and others, Minsky regards Keynes (1937) as the ultimate distillation of Keynes's thoughts on money and finance and as providing a source for an alternative – to the ISLM[14] and neoclassical synthesis – interpretation of the GT.[15] Classical and neoclassical economists tend to regard financial crises and serious fluctuations in output and unemployment as anomalous and offer no theoretical explanation of them.

Keynes (1937) implies that the GT is a theory of the capitalist process able to explain financial and real sector instability as a result of market behaviour in the face of uncertainty. Investment decisions are seen as the key determinant of aggregate economic activity and can be understood only within the context of capitalist financial practices. Both investment and financial decisions are made on the basis of uncertain outlooks, and disequilibriatory forces therefore operate in financial markets where investors must raise finance. These forces affect the price ratio between capital assets and current output which, along with financial market conditions, determine investment. The two sets of prices in the ratio are determined in separate markets, which are influenced by different forces; consequently the economy is prone to fluctuations.

One interpretation of Keynes's work is that shocks emanate from financial markets and are spread by way of investment decisions. Because investment and financial decisions are made under uncertainty they can undergo marked changes in short periods of time. Changing perspectives affect the relative prices of various capital and financial assets as well as relative prices of capital assets and current outputs. 'Money enters into the economic scheme in an essential and peculiar manner' (Keynes 1936, p. vii), as a 'financing veil' (Minsky 1982a, p. 61) interposed between the real asset and the wealth owner. Wealth owners frequently have claims on money, rather than real, assets. The banking system plays a major role in the financial system by collecting deposits and lending them to finance the purchase of real assets. The 'financing veil' encompasses bank credit and other short-term financial instruments and does not correspond to a narrow or base money concept. This contrasts with the neoclassical synthesis in which money does not affect the essential behaviour of the economy (see Patinkin 1965).

Minsky (1982a, Ch. 3) builds on his interpretation of the GT to present the FIH as a theory of the business cycle. He views financial crises as systemic, endogenously generated events rather than accidents. To support his view he cites pre-Second World War history and the post mid-1960s period in which he believes financial instability is amply illustrated. This leaves the twenty post-war years, in which financial crises were notably absent, to be explained. Minsky attributes the stability in this period to a recovery from the deep depression of the 1930s and to the favourable conditions created by the need for post-war reconstruction. Others would argue that it represented the upswing of a long wave[16] and/or the fruits of post-war economic co-operation which created the IMF, the IBRD and GATT.[17] Since the mid-1960s, however, he argues that the historic, crisis-prone behaviour of economies with capitalist financial institutions has reasserted itself. Until now the Federal Reserve (Fed), the US central bank and lender of last resort (LOLR), has aborted embryonic crises which, he argues, are in any event unlikely to be similar in magnitude to previous crises because the government sector, which acts as borrower of last resort (BOLR)[18] and which has introduced automatic stabilisers,[19] is immensely larger. The Fed has acted as LOLR both domestically and, as issuer of the major international reserve currency, internationally, along with the IMF.[20] Minsky further argues that the side-effects of aborting financial crises have been bouts of accelerating inflation.

Minsky observes that economies with modern financial systems are built on commitments to pay cash today and in the future. Money today is exchanged for money in the future by contracts and commitments to pay and cash in the future is exchanged for cash today. The viability of such relations rests upon cash flows received as a result of income-generating activities. Minsky focuses particularly on business debt, which is an essential characteristic of capitalist economies. To service business debts, firms must generate sufficient net reserve to meet gross payments due or to permit refinancing, which takes place only if expected future revenue is deemed to be sufficient. The net revenue is in turn largely determined by investment. Thus ability to debt-finance new investment depends on the expectation that new investment will be sufficient to generate cash flows large enough to allow current debts to be repaid or refinanced. An economy with private debt is, therefore, especially vulnerable to changes in the pace of investment, which is an important determinant of both aggregate demand and the viability of debt structures. In an economy in which debt finance is important, instability follows from the subjective nature of expectations about the future level of investment and returns from it and the subjective determination by banks and their business clients of the appropriate liability structure for the financing of positions in different types of capital assets. Uncertainty becomes a major determinant of cycles.

In analysing the relation between debt and income, Minsky starts with an economy that has a memory of a recession, which is regarded as a disequilibrium phenomenon. Outstanding debt reflects the recent history so that acceptable liability structures and contractual debt payments are based on margins reflecting the risk that the economy may not perform as well as expected. As the period over which the economy performs well lengthens, the margins for safety decline and leverage increases because views of acceptable debt structures change. Increasing leverage raises the market price of capital assets and increases investment, and boom conditions emerge. Minsky argues that the fundamental instability of capitalist economies is upward, beyond stable growth. Periods of steady growth are transformed into speculative investment booms. This process is reinforced by financial innovation, including the introduction of new financial instruments which appear at times when the economy is thriving. The quantity of relevant, broad money increases and so too does the incidence of speculative finance.

Speculative economic units expect to fulfil their obligations by raising new debt and are vulnerable on a number of fronts. They must return to the markets to refinance debt and are particularly vulnerable to rises in nominal interest rates – which increase their cash repayments relative to their expected future receipts, whose discounted present value may well decline. Further, they are subject to sudden revaluations of acceptable financial structures. Not all units will engage in speculative finance. The more risk-averse will, for example, normally continue to operate with hedge finance, which takes place when cash flows from operations are expected to be large enough to meet payments commitments on debts as they fall due. This contrasts with speculative finance, in Minsky's usage, which occurs when anticipated capital flows are not expected to be sufficient to meet payments commitments and refinancing will be required. In addition to hedge and speculative finance there is what Minsky calls Ponzi finance, which is a sort of super-speculative finance which takes place when payments on debt are met by increasing the debt outstanding.

High and rising interest rates can force hedge finance units into speculative finance and speculative finance units into Ponzi finance, Minsky argues. Ponzi finance cannot carry on for long because feedback from the revealed financial weakness of some units affects the willingness of banks and businessmen to debt-finance others. Unless offset by government spending, the decline in investment that follows from the curtailment of finance will lead to a decline in profitability and ability to sustain debt. Quite suddenly a panic can develop as pressure builds to reduce debt ratios.

Minsky's FIH, therefore, attempts to explain how capitalist economies endogenously generate a financial structure which is susceptible to financial crises and how the normal functioning of the financial system in a recovery period will lead to a boom and a financial crisis. As the crisis approaches, the LOLR and BOLR must act to abort it and prevent debt deflation. Nevertheless, debt-financed investment and perhaps consumption expenditure will normally fall after the aborted debt deflation as a result of a reappraisal of the economic outlook, and a recession will follow. The government's expansionary fiscal activities and built-in stabilisers lead to an increase in the government deficit as income falls or growth slows down. The deficits sustain income and corporate profitability and feed secure negotiable financial instruments into portfolios hungry for safe and secure assets. The recovery from the recession can be quite rapid and can soon result in an inflationary boom if the government deficit financing persists. The implication of the FIH for policy in a financially sophisticated capitalist economy is that there is a need to curb the tendency of businesses and banks to engage in speculative and Ponzi finance while the economy is thriving and profits are seemingly validating the decision of lenders and borrowers.

The upper turning point becomes completely endogenous if it is accepted that interest rates rise in an investment boom and that the successful functioning of the economy induces profit-seeking bankers and their customers to engage in speculative and Ponzi financial arrangements and to economise on holdings of cash and liquid financial assets (Minsky 1982b). For the interest rate not to rise in an investment boom, the supply of finance must be infinitely elastic, which implies that a flood of financial innovation is taking place or the central bank is supplying reserves on demand (Minsky 1982b, 1957a). This in turn implies that investment is an ever-increasing proportion of output and accelerating inflation is tolerable (Minsky 1982b, 1957b).

The extent of the recession/depression following the crisis depends on the effectiveness of LOLR and BOLR intervention in restoring confidence. The FIH described by Minsky (1982a,b) is, therefore, a semi-endogenous investment theory of the cycle based on a financial theory of investment. The full cycle is not endogenous unless the BOLR and LOLR are activated by policy rules or substantial built-in stabilisers are in place and are sufficient to abort the crisis and terminate the recession. Consumption is regarded as a stable function of income and plays a minor role, except implicitly via a stable multiplier. Investment, however, depends on finance, and sudden changes in expectations, which are likely under uncertainty, can both influence investment decisions and lead to a collapse in the financial relationships supporting investment. The FIH explains how a sustained expansion can be endogenously converted into a speculative boom which will ultimately lead to crises even in the absence of shocks. Adverse shocks might, however, be expected to terminate a boom prematurely in an economy where decisions are made under uncertainty. If they do not, however, short- and eventually long-term interest rates can be expected to rise and the discounted present value of future profit flows will be reduced. Speculative and Ponzi units will have to sell assets to meet their payment commitments but will find that the revenue from asset sales does not cover their debts; they may also incur 'fire sale' losses.[21] Even if the LOLR and BOLR avert the crisis, long-run expectations are likely to be adversely affected, risk premiums will increase and speculative finance will decline.

The FIH has been accepted by a number of economists, some of whose work is discussed below, and derided by others. A sample of the latter work is provided by comments on Minsky's (1982b) paper in Kindleberger and Laffargue (1982). Flemming (1982) argues that Minsky's FIH is based on the assumption that economic agents cannot distinguish between a run of good luck and a structural shift in their environment. The crisis results from reductions in risk premiums and increases in speculative and Ponzi finance because economic agents incorrectly believe that there has been a structural improvement in economic performance. The implication of Flemming's remark is that, under rational expectations, the instability would disappear. In section 3.4 some of the literature on rational speculative bubbles, which demonstrates that this is not necessarily the case, will be reviewed.

Flemming also observes that LOLR and BOLR intervention to abort the crisis and the ensuing recession creates a moral hazard which will itself increase risk-taking and is apparently inconsistent with the post-war stability which Minsky attributes to the enlarged role of government. This argument can, however, be turned round to support Minsky. The moral hazard may have increased the potential for a buildup of risky positions in the post-war period but the buildup may have been slow or held in check by regulations imposed on the US banking and financial system following the 1929 stock market crash and the rash of bank failures in the early 1930s. This buildup may have become critical by the mid-1960s; and/or competition in banking of finance, which increased from the mid-1960s onwards due to deregulation and internationalisation, may have increased the level of financial instability. It is a widely held view that subsequent developments, through the 1970s and early 1980s, have resulted in an increased riskiness in bank portfolios supported by relatively lower capital holdings.[22] Flemming concludes his critique[23] by calling for a more explicit and quantitative development of the theory of financial instability, which he finds to be ambiguous.

Goldsmith (1982) entirely agrees with Minsky's plea for an integration of the theory of the financial system with that of the real economy and the need to understand financial development in any analysis of the modern economic process, but that is where his agreement ends. He is concerned by the absence of a definition of financial crisis in Minsky's and Kindleberger's work. Goldsmith therefore provides his own, which will be discussed in section 3.3.3. He argues, appealing to the evidence of economic history and the absence of crises, in terms of his definition, since the 1930s, that financial crises are a childhood disease of capitalism and not an affliction of old age. This is because, in his view, as capitalism has aged the financial system has not only become more complex but also more stable. The absence of major crises could of course be attributed instead, as implied in Minsky's work, to a better understanding of the capabilities of LOLR and BOLR intervention, improved automatic stabilisers and the existence of the FDIC[24] in the United States. Goldsmith also takes exception to Minsky's use of the terms speculative and Ponzi finance. He believes that the former is a prejudicial term for an activity that is widespread and essentially sound because it is based on the law of large numbers and forms the foundation of the business of banks and other financial institutions that legally hold assets of longer maturity than liabilities. (See McCulloch (1986) for a contrary view.)

Melitz (1982) also argues that so-called speculative finance is basically sound and goes on to question the general applicability of Minsky's FIH to all capitalist economies. He notes that the basic examples are derived from US experience, while Kindleberger (1978) draws attention to a wide range of historical and international examples of financial crises. He doubts whether Minsky's arguments are applicable under alternative institutional arrangements, such as those prevailing in countries where banks have ready access to the LOLR, and calls for a fully specified financial fragility model with a plausible application somewhere. It is to be noted, however, that Kindleberger (1978) takes Minsky's work as a basis for his analysis of crises and seems happy with its widespread applicability.

3.3.2 Financial instability and the banking sector

In the course of an analysis of the relationship between competition and regulation in banking, Revell (1986) briefly surveys some of the literature on financial crises associated with the work of Minsky and Kindleberger. He argues that aggressive competition in the financial sector tends to lead to financial crises and provides a motivation, beyond that of the desire to form a cartel to secure supernormal profits, for banks to form agreements to avoid taking on unduly risky business and adopting risky practices. Such agreements to suspend interbank competition can be regarded as a primitive form of self-regulation to preserve the safety of the financial system and the continued existence of established institutions. He acknowledges the paucity of empirical backing for Minsky's statements.[25] The main evidence presented by Minsky (1977), for example, is the deterioration of a few financial ratios between 1950 and 1974. However, despite the lack of evidence, Revell declares a 'gut feeling' that Minsky is right and goes on to suggest a method that might be used to verify the FIH (see below).

Revell draws attention to a little-known study by Barclay (1978) in which nineteenth century financial crises in Britain are compared with the 1973–4 secondary banking crisis. Barclay develops a sort of cobweb model of crises in which surplus profits in one sector of the economy, perhaps resulting from technological innovation or government regulatory changes, attract a large entry which is dangerous to the banking sector. The economic system is regarded as unstable and highly competitive so that a large entry is attracted and profits are forced below normal levels. The new entrants do not all know about each other's intentions, and there is a time lag before they can start production. Assuming that all firms do not have identical cost structures, some will leave the industry as profits fall, some will stay and some will go to the wall.

The model can be applied directly to the banking sector, where self-imposed or government-imposed regulations lead to supernormal profits. Established banks will have qualities of reputation and reliability. New entrants must offer differentiated products, leading to a tendency towards innovation, or price more cheaply. They may therefore attract more risky business without fully compensating by adding appropriate risk premiums to their charges. The profits derived from risky business will be higher as a rule, in the absence of failure, so that imprudent bankers will do better than prudent ones. Competition leads to a lowering of the quality of banking products and this increases the potential for crises since depositors are interested primarily in the security of their deposits rather than the profitability of the bank. However, at the first sign that deposits are not secure, withdrawals will occur, and these can have domino effects which reverberate around the system. Influxes of producers attracted by high profits are, therefore, potentially more serious for the banking sector than for other sectors, while the inherent instability creates regulatory conditions that are likely to result in excess profits and encourage established banks to innovate.[26] When a shock hits the system profitability declines and capital, which is commonly run down relative to assets and risks taken in the euphoria of boom markets, proves inadequate. This is because past failures come to be regarded as anomalous as memory of them decays and regulators adopt more liberal attitudes.

Fringe banks are commonly allowed to fail and many fringe banks leave the system as a result of an overreaction abetted by the regulators. The profitability of the remaining 'core' banks will eventually be restored, and the process could be cyclical. Recent banking history furnishes numerous examples, including the Latin American debt crisis, of established banks tapping into new and profitable lines of business only to find that competition from smaller banks gradually erodes margins and encourages mispricing of risks.

Barclay argues that the preconditions for attracting new entrants, namely surplus profitability, existed prior to the UK fringe banking crisis of 1973–4 because banking was organised as a cartel supported by the Bank of England. He suggests that the banking cycle could be grafted on to the general economic cycle as innovations in the nonbank sector, leading to supernormal profits, attract new entrants which require bank finance for their ventures in the manner described by Schumpeter (1939) – whose work is discussed in section 4.2. The banks then have a tendency to become over-exposed to the sector with supernormal profits and can face bad debts in the future as a result. The involvement of the UK fringe banks in the property sector can be seen as a combination of both these themes. Government regulations created pockets of excess profitability in the property markets and attracted entry. This led to a property boom and stimulated the growth of the fringe banking sector, which became over-exposed and provided speculative finance to companies in the property sector.[27] The 1987-8 Texas property market collapse and its effects on the banking sector leading to the bail-out of the state's largest bank holding company, First Republic Bank, is another example of the potentially damaging effects that the tendency towards over-exposure to excessively profitable sectors can have.

The Barclay model, Revell claims, can be developed to show that increases in competition in banking lead in almost all cases to growth of bad banking practices involving excessive risk-taking. Such practices are likely because retribution only follows in the next crisis, which might be caused by an adverse shock but is unlikely to occur until the banking system is in a state of what Minsky would call fragility. Losses and failures resulting from bad banking are, therefore, likely to be bunched. Before the crisis, the profit advantage lies with the aggressive banks that indulge in unsound and speculative practices, but established banks are likely to be drawn into bad banking in order to boost their profitability. A sort of Gresham's Law of banking holds in the sense that bad banking drives out good.

Particular features of boom periods that draw banks into unsound practices can be identified, Revell argues. The general price level will be rising, and prices of equities and properties will rise with it so that capital gains will be an important component of financial calculations. Banks not only speculate on rising price levels themselves but also issue loans that can only be serviced if the price of borrowers' output, and that of their collateral, rises continuously. During the boom, Revell argues, the yield curve usually implies that financing long-term assets with short-term deposits and liabilities yields high profits. The importance of these factors is magnified when, as in the post-war period and particularly the 1970s, accelerating inflation is superimposed on the business cycle. He further argues that risk varies over time and that his analysis implies that the probability of loss increases with each year that has passed since the previous crisis. The behaviour of bank managements, however, ignores this factor.

Provisions for loan losses and assessments of capital adequacy by banks are normally based on the averaging of losses over the immediate past; consequently, what might be regarded as in-house bank insurance[28] declines once the cyclical upswing is under way. This tendency is reinforced, Revell argues, by the fast growth of asset values, which usually outstrip the provisions for bad debts and additions to capital, and by the growing feeling of euphoria as speculation continues to be rewarded with profits. He observes that the next step in the argument has not been documented satisfactorily. It consists of the hypothesis that one of the reactions of the established banks, which have by definition survived one or more crises, is to face the continuation of the boom (in which increased risk and competition went hand in hand) by banding together to restrain bank competition. It is necessary, he notes, to examine the history of interbank agreements or 'cartels' in a number of countries to see if wider support for the hypothesis, which relies heavily on UK experience in the way that Minsky's FIH does on US experience, can be found.

The shift from primitive self-regulation to regulatory involvement by the authorities becomes necessary as soon as it is demonstrated that the former can break down (Goodhart 1985, Ch. 4). Revell suggests that this point was not reached in most countries until the 1930s. The 'cartels' proved inadequate because they lacked the means to enforce behaviour (Goodhart 1985, Ch. 4), especially once threatened by a competitive fringe. It is significant, Revell feels, that many of the agreements were continued with official blessing after the 1930s, and it was not until the mid-1960s that there were significant developments leading to increased competition in many banking systems around the world that involved disbandment or modification of the cartel agreements. This process is particularly evident in the United Kingdom and has continued in the 1970s and 1980s (Llewellyn 1985, 1986). Competition in the US banking system also began to increase in the 1960s and accelerated in the 1970s and early 1980s (Mullineux 1987c,e). The latter development was led by the broadly defined banking industry, which successfully exploited regulatory loopholes, and permissive legislation followed later. Also in the United States, and then elsewhere, financial innovation was stimulated in the 1970s and 1980s by advances in information technology, improved telecommunications networks, high inflation and volatile exchange and interest rates.

Revell draws attention to the fact that changes in regulatory regimes in Europe since the late 1960s were designed to increase competition in the broadly defined banking sector and were followed in a very few years by the most significant financial crisis since the War. He infers that the authorities in many countries thought competition would lead established banks to drive out fringe operators. This idea seemed to lie behind the Competition and Credit Control arrangements introduced in the United Kingdom in 1971 (see Bank of England 1971). The clearing banks were instructed to abandon their interest-setting cartel and in return were released from certain controls, allowing them to compete more effectively with the fringe banks. The result, Revell argues, was the fringe banking crisis which erupted in the United Kingdom in 1973 and, as a result of similar structural changes elsewhere, particularly in Europe, failures in other countries. Revell attributes the failures to bad banking. A number of failures in the early 1970s were associated with losses on foreign exchange markets,[29] but closer inspection, Revell concludes, demonstrates that these banks were tempted to speculate on the foreign exchange markets in order to recoup losses made on domestic banking operations.

The UK secondary banking crisis is a classic example of bad banking. The fringe banks raised short-term wholesale funds and invested them in long-term loans to finance speculative ventures, particularly in the property market. These ventures yielded no immediate income so that interest due had constantly to be added to the principal. In Minsky's terminology, they therefore participated in Ponzi finance. In addition to speculative banking, there were many cases of fraud and embezzlement. A worrying feature of the buildup to the crisis was that the fringe banks were able to raise finance from the established banks, which were prevented by the regulatory authorities from participating in the binge directly. The euphoria of the period was such that few saw the dangers – possibly because bank managers had no personal experience of the previous crisis in the 1930s, regarding it as an anachronism, Revell postulates. The period of euphoria came to an abrupt end with the acceleration of inflation, the freezing of the property market and the drop in equity prices. After the first hint of bank failure, the supply of wholesale funds to the fringe banks, via the interbank market, dried up, and the Bank of England's 'lifeboat' operation was launched.[30] Subsequent examples of widespread bad banking can be found in the United States, where many savings and loan associations got into trouble in the late 1970s, for example; and, on an international scale, in connection with the Latin American debt problem. When the Mexican crisis broke in 1982 it was realised that the country risks involved in sovereign lending to developing countries, which needed to refinance their debts continuously to meet interest payments, had been severely underestimated.

Revell also examines other bank failures in Europe and the United States in the early 1970s and is struck by the similarity of the business undertaken by the failed fringe banks, most of which were linked in some way with the property market. The fact that there were incidences of bad banking in many countries suggests the possibility of a common cause. Revell believes this to be the relaxation of structural controls over banking systems with a view to making them more competitive and the association of these developments with accelerating inflation and the general euphoria that accompanied it. He postulates that there might have been no ill effects if liberalisation had taken place at a time of financial stability, but the combination of greater competition with inflation and euphoria proved lethal. This begs the question of why inflation increased in the first place. In terms of Minsky's FIH, it could have been a result of a rise in government deficit financing to head off a perceived increase in the risk of crises as the economic expansion in the early 1970s built towards a euphoric boom and financial instability increased.

Revell is troubled by the fact that failures occurred even in countries with the strictest prudential regulatory regimes, since this implies that competition may not be able to ensure sound banking and that increased prudential regulation cannot be relied upon to contain the tendency of increased competition to generate bad banking practices. He feels that the prevalence of bad banking might, however, be attributable to widespread euphoria. All regulatory systems, he observes, even the most formal statutorily backed ones, leave a lot of discretion to the supervisor. If supervisors are also influenced by the euphoria, they will not act to prevent the development of unusual practices which do not contravene the rules. This implies that regulators and supervisors should not relax their vigilance in times of euphoria and that the regulatory and supervisory system must be sufficiently flexible to deal with rapid structural changes.

Metcalfe (1982) shares Revell's view that crises are a recurrent phenomenon in banking systems and feels that the generic characteristics have been succinctly described in Kindleberger (1978). He argues that crises originate with events that significantly increase profit expectations in one sector of the economy and stimulate an increased demand for finance. Innovations could play an important role here, as Barclay (1978) observed.[31] The extension of bank credit then increases the money supply and self-exciting euphoria develops in the manner described by Minsky and Kindleberger. More and more firms and households are tempted into speculative finance and are led away from rational behaviour, and manias or bubbles result. As Kindleberger observed (1978, p. 17), the term mania emphasises the irrationality and the term bubble foreshadows the bursting. Even the suspicion that the tissue of expectations is weakening can spark a crisis. Only a small incident is needed to transform manic behaviour into panic behaviour, which inflicts widespread damage. Metcalfe argues that banks exemplify a general characteristic of all organised social systems, which is that of the management of a system of expectations under conditions of risk and uncertainty.[32] Like other social systems, the effective functioning of the banking system depends on a fabric of co-ordinated expectations. Mutual expectations guide the behaviour of participants and are modified in a process of interaction. To form their own expectations, individuals must draw on assumptions and beliefs about the rules and values of others.[33] Value consensus cannot be assumed but values do coalesce into more or less coherent doctrines, myths or ideologies, which provide the intellectual rationale and moral basis for legitimate actions. This feature of social organisation, he argues, is particularly prevalent in banking where the extension of credit creates webs of rights and obligations spread over time.

The fulfilment of expectations depends on confidence in the continuing viability of the whole system and vice versa. As Hicks (1967) observed, however, stability of the banking system cannot be taken for granted because it is potentially unstable in two directions. Performance will fall short of potential if there is a lack of confidence; but overconfidence, as in the buildup to a crisis, will produce unrealistically high expectations. Because expectations are never precisely fulfilled in any complex social organisation, there is a continuous management problem of avoiding the extremes of mistrust and overconfidence. The maintenance of balance requires an institutional framework or regulatory system that encourages confidence while restraining constituent organisations.

Before leaving the topic of instability in the banking sector, Diamond and Dybvig's (1983) contribution should be considered. In their model, the illiquidity of assets provides the rationale for both the existence of banks and their vulnerability to runs. It is assumed that even if assets are traded on competitive markets with no transactions costs, low returns are received by agents forced to 'liquidate' early. Agents are, therefore, concerned about the cost of being forced into early liquidation and will write contracts reflecting these costs. Investors face private risks which are not directly insurable because they are not publicly verifiable, due to the existence of information deficiencies and asymmetries. Banks serve the function of indirectly transforming illiquid assets by offering highly liquid liabilities, such as demand deposits which are redeemable at their nominal value; they thereby provide indirect insurance that allows agents to make payments when they want or need to and, in so doing, share the risks. Efficient risk-sharing can result if confidence is maintained but if agents lose confidence and panic, incentives are distorted and a bank run results. To prevent loss of confidence, Diamond and Dybvig advocate comprehensive, government-backed deposit insurance. Its provision is, however, likely to create moral hazard problems, which must be dealt with if an optimal bank regulatory regime is to be developed. Risk-related deposit insurance premiums or capital adequacy requirements would appear to be needed, but such issues are beyond the scope of this book.

3.3.3 Kindleberger's model and the international dimension

Minsky's work provides the basic framework for the Kindleberger (1978) analysis of historical financial crises. He notes that some crises have a minor economic impact but concentrates on crises of major size and effect, normally with an international scope. He regards speculative excesses, or bubbles, as irrational events or manias which are followed by revulsion from the excesses and a crisis, crash or panic which can be shown to be common, if not inevitable. He notes that by no means does every upswing lead to a mania or panic but that the pattern occurs with sufficient frequency and conformity to merit renewed study. Initially some event changes the economic outlook. New opportunities for profit are seized and overdone in ways so resembling irrationality as to constitute mania. In the manic phase people of wealth and credit switch out of money or borrow to buy real or illiquid financial and capital assets. In the panic phase the reverse takes place, and the excessive characteristics of the upswing are realised.

In Kindleberger (1978), the background to speculation and crisis is discussed in terms of the classical ideas of overtrading followed by revulsion and discredit.[34] He acknowledges Minsky as the most recent exponent of such ideas and feels that even if it did not apply to the United States at the time, the FIH provides a useful framework for analysing past crises. Kindleberger's model of crises (1978, Ch. 2) is based on Minsky's earlier writings, which relied more heavily on shocks than the later writings, reviewed above, which attempt to develop an endogenous theory of financial crises.

As in Minsky's earlier work, the events leading up to a crisis start with a shock or displacement to the macroeconomic system, and Kindleberger tries to identify historical examples of such displacements (1978, Ch. 3). He finds that the source of displacement varies from one speculative boom to another and in that sense historians are correct in arguing that each speculative boom or cycle is unique. Economists, who argue that cycles are a repetitive process, are also correct since the reaction to the shocks and the subsequent evolution of the economy are similar. The shock alters the outlook by changing the opportunities for profit in at least one important sector of the economy. Displacement occurs as businesses switch from unprofitable to profitable lines of business and there are new entrants to the perceived high profit markets. If this process leads to a net increase in production and investment then a boom ensues. The boom is fed by an expansion of bank credit which enlarges the money supply and if the urge to speculate is present, euphoria develops and overtrading and excessive gearing can result. As speculation spreads to members of the population normally aloof from such ventures, who abandon their normal behaviour, then a mania or a speculative bubble develops. In the latter phases of the mania, speculation detaches itself from really valuable objects and turns to delusive ones, and swindlers and fraudsters flourish.

As the manic boom continues, interest rates, the velocity of circulation and prices all rise and at some stage a few insiders decide to take profits and sell out. It should be noted that the periodic taking of profits could explain the saw-toothed progress of asset prices and is likely to result if individuals hold sufficiently diverse expectations[35] and periodically hedge their bets on the continuation of the boom by taking profits and refinancing. This may explain the finding that stock market prices follow a random walk with drift, discussed in the next section. Kindleberger argues that at the peak of the boom, there is often a pause as new recruits to speculation balance those selling out. Prices level off, and there may be an uneasy period of financial distress. The probability of a flight to liquidity increases in the eyes of a segment of the speculative community, and risk increases. When it is widely accepted that the market price will go no higher, the balance will tip in favour of selling out. There will be a race to withdraw, which may develop into a stampede, in order to maximise existing capital gains and minimise prospective capital losses.

Kindleberger notes that the special signal that precipitates the crisis could be one of a number, but it is often a bank failure or the revelation of fraud or defalcation. Prior to the crisis a state of revulsion against certain commodities or securities is often observed, and banks cease lending on the collateral of such assets. This is sometimes called discredit in the classical literature. Once crisis arrives and panic sets in, it feeds on itself, as did the speculation, until one or more of the following occurs:

1. Prices fall so low that investors are again attracted by less liquid assets.
2. The exchange on which the asset, in which there has been speculation, is traded is closed or trade is otherwise inhibited.
3. The LOLR intervenes to stem flight to liquidity by guaranteeing an ample supply of money.

Kindleberger argues that his Minsky-inspired model describes the nature of financial crises under capitalism and rejects the view that each crisis is unique because he is able to identify certain common features in crises, despite the existence of differing individual features. He also rejects the view that it is no longer applicable to modern capitalism. He supports Minsky's view that Keynesian ISLM and neoclassical synthesis models missed an important point contained in Keynes's writing. As a result Hansen (1951), a leading proponent of Keynesian multiplier–

accelerator business cycle analysis, incorrectly dismissed previous theories of business cycles, based on uncertainty, speculation and overtrading, as inapplicable to the twentieth century because industry had become the main outlet for funds seeking a profitable return from savings and investment. Kindleberger argues that room for speculation in commodities and securities remains, and prices and credit continue to be unstable. Hansen concentrated on savings and investment but ignored uncertainty, speculation and instability, which featured prominently in Keynes's work.

Kindleberger then considers whether an active LOLR can forestall crises, making it possible to eliminate them altogether. The counterview that the existence of LOLR cover on a reliable basis might actually increase risk-taking and, therefore, the likelihood of bubbles is acknowledged by Kindleberger, but he observes that since 1930 the greater willingness to undertake LOLR intervention has apparently increased stability. This view would tend to be confirmed by the rapid response by central banks to the October 1987 stock market crashes around the world and the absence of their significant impact on the performance of the economies in which they occurred. With the benefit of hindsight, the supply of liquidity by LOLRs appears to have been excessive and slightly inflationary. It should also be noted that the FDIC, established in the 1930s, has probably increased stability in the United States. In fact the period of stability seems to date back further in countries such as the United Kingdom, where the LOLR established credibility following the 1866 banking crisis. (See Gilbert and Wood (1986) for further discussion.) Kindleberger also draws attention to the fact that despite the decline in domestic crises in the post-war period, there has been an increase in the incidence of international crises implying the need for an international LOLR (ILOLR) or credible contingency plans for co-ordinated LOLR intervention by national central banks.

Like Minsky, Kindleberger fails to provide a definition of crises. He merely replaces old words, such as overtrading, revulsion and discredit, with new ones, such as manias, speculative bubbles, panics and crashes. Goldsmith (1982), in his comments on Minsky (1982b), suggests the following definition: a sharp, brief, ultracyclical deterioration of all or most of a group of financial indicators, such as short-term interest rates and asset (stock, real estate, land) prices, commercial insolvencies and failures of financial institutions. This would exclude several of Minsky's so-called crises, Goldsmith observes, and particularly the minor ones in the United States in the 1960s and 1970s, to which Minsky attaches such importance. His definition achieves the goal of discrediting Minsky's thesis but is merely a description of an event which might be termed a widespread financial crisis. Unlike the FIH, it does not attempt to identify the cause of crises.

Like Kindleberger, Eichengreen and Portes (1987) are particularly interested in the generation and propagation of crises in an international setting. They define a financial crisis as a disturbance to financial markets, associated particularly with falling asset prices among debtors and intermediaries, which spreads through the financial system, disrupting markets' capacity to allocate capital. The definition implies a distinction between generalised financial crises and isolated bank failures, debt defaults and foreign exchange market disturbances. It is, therefore, in a similar vein to Goldsmith's definition. Such distinctions are clearly important, since while it is clear that the economy should be protected from the negative externalities resulting from systemic crises, it is not obvious that individual bank failures should be prevented. Such prevention might even increase the risk of systemic failures by creating a moral hazard problem.

Eichengreen and Portes (1987) observe that capital flight[36] plays a role in international financial crises similar to that played by bank runs in domestic crises and argue that institutional arrangements in the financial system are critical determinants of the system's vulnerability to destabilising shocks, which emanate primarily from macroeconomic events rather than events limited to the financial system. Their point about institutional arrangements is similar to that made by Melitz (1982) and discussed above. It implies that capitalist economies are not necessarily prone to financial instability if they adopt the appropriate institutional arrangements. Their analysis involves a comparison of the 1920s and 1930s with the 1970s and 1980s. In both the 1920s and 1970s institutional arrangements were drastically altered by changes in foreign exchange markets, international capital markets and the structure of domestic banking systems. There are certain similarities in these changes, but Eichengreen and Portes believe that the changes in the 1920s on balance increased vulnerability and the crisis in the 1930s was the consequence, while the changes in the 1970s worked in the opposite direction so that events such as the 1982 Mexican debt crisis and the subsequent October 1987 stock market crash proved containable.

Eichengreen and Portes argue that macroeconomic shocks can cause a rapid change in the credit regime, from high lending to rationing, by conveying new information to lenders. They note that Guttentag and Herring (1984) postulate that an extended period without adverse shocks creates conditions in which such a shock will provoke discontinuous market behaviour. They find this hypothesis more specific and rigorous than Minsky's FIH, although it appears to be based on a similar premise: that as time elapses since the last major shock or crisis, the lenders become more disposed to greater risk-taking. In the case of the 1982 Mexican crisis the 'disaster myopia' emphasised by Guttentag and Herring, which had led to inadequate 'spreads' or risk premiums on sovereign lending and what Minsky would call speculative finance – because the Latin American (LA) debtors were not expected to be able to service the interest payments on their debts in the short or medium term except through further loans – was dispelled, and this changed the banks' overall perception of LA debtors in an environment of imperfect information. Capital flight significantly increased the disaster probability. When the disaster scenario suddenly took on a non-negligible subjective probability, lenders reacted by pulling out of the market as fast as the IMF and their central banks would allow. Rather than gradually tightening the terms attached to loans, the banks suddenly shifted to credit rationing, which the IMF tried to offset through 'forced lending'.

The LA debt problem[37] of the 1980s differed significantly from the one in the 1930s because banks had assumed credit risks formerly borne by purchasers of sovereign bonds. There was consequently a need to contain any menace the crisis posed for the banking and wider financial system in the 1980s. This was done by the US Treasury and the Fed in conjunction with the IMF and the Bank for International Settlements, which launched a rescue operation.[38] Banks now appear to have been protected long enough to build up provisions and capital sufficient to withstand a reversion of the LA debt problem to crisis proportions. While no formal ILOLR exists, it seems that contingency arrangements are in place.[39] The key weakness of current policy, Eichengreen and Portes contend, is the failure to block capital flight in a time of increasing international capital mobility. Other problems emanate from sustained exchange rate misalignments and consequent protectionist pressure.

Eichengreen and Portes argue that the shift from bank lending to borrowing on the capital markets, or securitisation, evident in the 1980s should in principle reduce systemic vulnerability, but the Cross Report points to countervailing aspects. (See Bank for International Settlements 1986.) They acknowledge that the trade-offs are complicated but believe that the developments are on balance positive from the viewpoint of financial stability. They argue that imperfect information favours the generalisation of adverse shocks into full crises and that macroeconomic instability is the main source of shocks, but that the appropriate action by the regulatory and monetary authorities can block the most dangerous linkages. Co-ordinated action, embodied in the 'Third World debt strategy', has avoided defaults and widespread bank failures, but action should have been taken earlier to prevent the expansion of bank lending to sovereign borrowers leading to the accumulation of excessive debt burdens. Eichengreen and Portes believe that securitisation will get more information into the market-place, reduce adverse selection and remove from the banking system the heavy burden of acting as a buffer when shocks do occur.

The Eichengreen and Portes analysis implies that the real dangers lie not in disturbances originating from the financial market but in the malfunctioning of the real economy. To reduce the latter, greater economic co-operation and co-ordination are required, which might lead to a new international monetary constitution. This would provide rules on exchange market intervention and choices of international reserve assets, constraints on fiscal and monetary policy, and a well defined responsibility for ILOLR intervention. On both imperfect information and externality grounds, they feel that there is a rationale for government intervention in financial markets in general and the regulation of the banking system in particular, since it is the latter that acts as a buffer when shocks to the real economy impact on the financial system. Regulatory policy should, they argue, channel financial innovation in directions that leave the world economy less vulnerable to financial collapse. The downside risk is that the trend towards greater co-operation and co-ordination will evaporate when the world economy enjoys a period of sustained stability. Disaster probabilities may be reassessed and reduced to negligible levels as the last shock or crisis recedes into the distant past and disaster myopia or euphoria will again prevail, bringing the next crisis closer.

Further analysis and evidence on crises in economic and financial structures is presented in a collection of papers edited by Wachtel (1982). Wachtel himself observes that market bubbles or speculative explosions in one market could potentially lead to widespread crises. He notes that although there are numerous examples of crises, the economics profession does not have a framework for dealing with the topic and the problem of definition is consequently an important one. He feels that the basis for such a framework is provided by Meltzer (1982), who draws on Knight's (1921) distinction between risk and uncertainty and suggests that economic crises should be associated with uncertainty of outcomes (see also sections 2.1 and 3.2). A crisis may emerge when there is a shift in the underlying distribution of outcomes of the economic events. Meltzer treats uncertainty as a shift in expected value following a shock to either aggregate demand or aggregate supply and claims that this is consistent with the usage of Knight and Keynes. However, papers dealing with rational bubbles, such as Flood and Garber (1982) and Blanchard and Watson (1982), deal with a world of risk in which outcomes often differ from their expected value but with a known or calculable probability, rather than uncertainty, which is due to unpredictable changes in the distribution of outcomes. Economic units can prepare themselves for the consequences of risky outcomes but not for uncertain ones.

3.4 RATIONAL SPECULATIVE BUBBLES

Flood and Garber (1982) show that price bubbles can arise in models in which the current market price depends on expected future price changes. Under rational expectations, such models tend not to yield a unique expression of agents' expectations. The indeterminacy arises out of trying to solve for two endogenous variables[40] from one equilibrium market condition. As a result, arbitrary, self-fulfilling expectations of price changes may drive actual price changes independently of market fundamentals, causing price bubbles. The fundamentals are described by the precise model of market operation. Some models preclude rational bubbles and others do not; consequently it is not possible to prove that they exist at the theoretical level. They observe that empirical work attempting to identify bubbles has turned up mixed results and is, therefore, inconclusive.

They also note that the previous literature has attributed runs and panics to mass hysteria rather than to rational behaviour. Salent and Henderson (1978) regard runs as predictable events, however. They are regarded as events which terminate price fixing schemes. The viability of such schemes requires the economic agents running them to hold stocks and stand ready to buy and sell at a fixed price. If other agents perceive the scheme to be temporary and expect prices to rise, yielding a capital gain, they will draw down the stock backing the scheme. If stocks are depleted entirely in one final discrete withdrawal, then a run has occurred. Flood and Garber note that systemic bank collapses are the most famous examples of runs. Banks fix the price of deposits in terms of government currency and hold reserves of the currency as backing. If a capital loss on deposits is feared, then depositors deplete the bank's reserves forcing the bank to cease fixing the price of its deposits. Similarly, currency crises are associated with runs on government foreign exchange reserves which are held to fix the price of the domestic currency against other currencies.

Following the rational expectations (RE) revolution in the mid-1970s, it was a widely held view, Blanchard and Watson (1982) observe, that asset prices must reflect market fundamentals in the sense of depending on information on current and expected future returns on assets. Deviations from market fundamentals were viewed as evidence of irrationality. Market participants, however, often believe that fundamentals are only part of what determines the price of a security.

Extraneous events will influence asset prices if other participants believe they will do so, and crowd psychology becomes an important determinant. Meltzer (1982) suggests that the two views can be reconciled if rational expectations under risk is replaced by decision-making and expectations formation under uncertainty, since under uncertainty extraneous events or shocks can cause fundamental and sudden reappraisals of expected future returns.

Blanchard and Watson (1982) demonstrate that economists have overstated their case because rationality in behaviour and expectations formation does not prevent asset prices from deviating from fundamentals or rational bubbles occurring. They observe that there is little doubt that most large historical bubbles, such as those investigated by Kindleberger (1978), contained elements of irrationality and that such bubbles are much harder to deal with theoretically. They therefore concentrate on the analysis of rational bubbles. Their model assumes maximising behaviour, RE and continuous market clearing and implies that, given private information and information revealed by prices, assets are voluntarily held and there is no incentive to reallocate portfolios. With additional assumptions, including common and current information sets, the efficient market or no arbitrage condition can be derived from it. Their model is typical of a class in which expectations of future variables affect current decisions and does not have a unique solution. As a result the market price can deviate from the present value of the asset, without violating the no arbitrage condition. If a deviation occurs, the structure of the model implies that it can be expected to grow over time and constitute a bubble. Using examples they show that the bubble can take various forms. They also demonstrate that bubbles can occur even when agents are risk-averse and are no longer assumed to have identical information sets. They are not, however, able to make much progress on such issues as whether differential information permits a wider class of bubbles or whether some aspects of real world bubbles involve differential information. They also note that, while the efficient market condition itself does not preclude bubbles, there may be other conditions imposed institutionally or from market clearing, or implicit in rationality that rule them out.

Further, standard analysis assumes that bubbles themselves do not affect market fundamentals, but Blanchard and Watson feel this is unlikely. The rise in price associated with bubbles may well encourage an increase in the supply of assets affected. When the bubble bursts, prices will fall below the pre-bubble level because of the increased supply. Additionally, a price bubble in one asset will increase its price relative to other assets not subject to bubbles, and this will lead to portfolio redistribution. It should be noted that this may be a mechanism by which non-speculators are drawn into speculation because if they do not redistribute their portfolios, their relative returns will decline.

Because of the potential for real effects, it is important to ascertain whether bubbles are theoretical constructs of little relevance or whether they are witnessed frequently in the real world. Blanchard and Watson therefore turn to a review of the empirical literature. They observe that testing for bubbles is not easy because rational bubbles can follow many types of process. They show that certain bubbles will violate the variance bounds implied by a certain class of RE models and present empirical evidence that demonstrates such violations. They note that irrational bubbles would also cause such violations. Runs and tails tests are suggested when only price data is available, but it is demonstrated that such tests have low power.

Despite Blanchard and Watson's misgivings, Garbade (1982) argues strongly that bubbles are unlikely to occur in the New York Stock Exchange (NYSE). This is attributed largely to the Fed's margin requirements, which limit the amount of credit that can be used to purchase stocks. The margin requirements were introduced for the specific purpose of inhibiting speculative bubbles following the 1929 crash. (See Galbraith (1954, Ch. X) for further discussion.) In addition the Securities and Exchange Commission (SEC) has encouraged the provision of broader and more detailed information, and empirical evidence implies that stock prices are efficient in the sense of reflecting publicly available information, Garbade observes. Greater and more accurate information, he believes, should reduce the likelihood of bubbles. Empirically, he finds little evidence of bubbles. The stock market should demonstrate a run of increases as the bubble builds and a run of decreases as it collapses. On average, he finds a stock price increase is equally likely to be followed by another increase or a fall. It is implicit in Garbade's discussion that the 1929 crash could have been the collapse of a bubble and that this prompted the Fed to introduce margin requirements in 1934 to inhibit the development of bubbles in the future. The NYSE crash of October 1987 is also viewed by many analysts as the bursting of a bubble. It is argued that stock prices lost touch with fundamentals in the speculative bubble that preceded the crash.[41]

Santoni (1987) notes that the 1924–9 NYSE bull market is widely accepted to have been a speculative bubble[42] and that the same theory of stock market price formation has been used to describe the 1982–7 bull market. They are normally regarded as irrational rather than rational bubbles. He challenges the view that these events were speculative bubbles, arguing instead that stock prices reflected fundamentals in each period and presenting empirical support for his hypothesis. He accepts that current stock prices depend on forecasts of future outcomes and the expected returns derived from them, which are subject to changes as new information becomes available and which do not depend on current dividends observed. Consequently, relatively small changes in forecasts can lead to large changes in the fundamental price. Fundamentals cannot be observed directly, however, and proxies must be used that are believed to provide information on fundamentals, though they can only give a rough guide to the behaviour of fundamentals. When the market crashed in October 1987, commentators pointed to the proxies and claimed that stock prices were overvalued prior to the crash. An alternative explanation, he notes, is that the proxies gave a misleading impression of the fundamentals.

To examine the proposition that stock prices in the 1920s and 1980s were driven by factors extraneous to fundamentals, it is necessary to derive alternative hypotheses from the competing theories and test them. Santoni considers three different hypotheses:
1. The efficient market hypothesis.
2. The irrational bubble hypothesis.
3. The rational bubble hypothesis.

The efficient market or no arbitrage hypothesis assumes that stock prices are determined in efficient markets so that relevant known information is reflected in them. Prices change only in response to new information, which cannot be predicted ahead of arrival and is just as likely to be good or bad. If it is correct that past information on price changes contains no useful information about future changes, then the observed changes in stock prices should be uncorrelated,[43] and price changes should exhibit no long sequence of successive changes that are greater or less than the median change for the sample. This proposition should hold even if the level of prices appears to drift up or down. The fact that prices drifted up in both bull markets does not imply that price changes are correlated or that market participants were able to predict future changes by observing past changes. The irrational bubble hypothesis argues that self-feeding expectations drive up prices. Fundamentals are regarded as largely irrelevant. Stocks are bought in the belief that they can be sold at a higher price in the future for capital gain. Extrapolating from past price rises, speculators expect the rise to continue.[44] The hypothesis implies that there are times when past changes matter. There should therefore be positive correlation in past sequences of price changes and long runs of positive changes that exceed the median change for the sample period, Santoni argues. The rational bubble hypothesis also postulates that there will be occasions when stock prices deviate from the fundamental price and that deviations will tend to persist and explode leading to bubbles that cannot be negative. Santoni concludes that the efficient markets hypothesis implies that stock price changes should follow a random walk while both the rational and irrational bubble hypotheses imply that stock price changes should not follow a random walk but should instead be positively serially correlated.

Despite the growing literature on rational bubbles, Santoni is concerned about the absence of a well specified theory. Following Brunner and Meltzer (1987), he argues that a complete theory of bubbles should identify their cause in terms of phenomena that can be observed, separately from the bubbles themselves. On occasions when a bubble was observed then so too would be the causal event. This would allow a direct test of the theory and could explain why bubbles are observed on some occasions and not on others. In the case of irrational bubbles, the unusual behaviour is attributed to euphoria and manias, which do not identify the cause of the bubble but merely give it another name, he argues. Brunner and Meltzer (1987) go further and argue that bubbles are inconsistent with the rational exploitation of information invoked by the analysis demonstrating their existence. It is clear that they are criticising the rational bubble literature. Their argument may well be true for rational bubble models which assume a risky environment, although Blanchard and Watson (1982) were unable to prove that RE prevents bubbles. It is not so clear that it applies to the so-called irrational bubble hypothesis which, as Meltzer (1982) observed, is more likely to hold in an environment of uncertainty. Kindleberger (1978) in fact attempts to identify events that generated fundamental re-evaluations of expectations of future returns leading to bubbles and also tries to identify events that lead to their bursting. The irrational bubble and FIH literature is much richer because it attempts to explain the creation and bursting of bubbles and provides some insight into how to prevent them in the future by regulating the financial system. The rational bubble literature, which attributes crashes to bursting bubbles without adequately explaining why they burst, is of little help to the policy-maker.

Santoni (1987) concludes with an examination of the evidence to see if it supports the efficient markets or the bubbles hypotheses. He uses samples of more than 400 observations from each of two periods, the 1920s and the 1980s. In each period there was rapid price advance. Autocorrelation coefficients were estimated for price changes, and the Box–Pierce test was applied, but no significant autocorrelation was evident. The data was, therefore, consistent with the efficient market hypothesis. The upward drift was undeniable but at the time, he argues, it was not something that investors could have bet on with confidence. He also applied the runs test, which Blanchard and Watson noted has low power, and this too rejected the bubble hypotheses.

Despite these results, and others like them, the so-called upward price drift in these periods remains a cause for concern to some economists.

The price levels, rather than changes, were clearly positively correlated, and a trend term would have contributed strongly to any equation explaining price levels without lagged price terms. It may be that this is the important feature, implicit in calling such periods bull markets, and that the random walk in price changes can be readily explained. For example, speculators could, and probably did, bet on the medium-term rise in the trend price. But because of diverse expectations,[45] which might be the result of non-homogeneous information and differing perceptions, speculators might take profits periodically and refinance their positions. It is after all the rising price levels that deliver the capital gains. A detailed analysis of the behaviour of speculators during the bull markets appears to be called for. In this case daily fluctuations in prices would not necessarily lead speculators to assume that the medium-term trend had altered. Further, if the stock prices were not overvalued, why did they drop so precipitously in 1929 and 1987? If the no arbitrage hypothesis holds, how was it possible that the government bond markets got so out of line with the equity markets prior to the 1987 crash? It is also notable that regardless of whether or not stock markets are subject to bubbles, other markets seem to demonstrate speculative behaviour consistent with the bubble hypothesis. This is particularly true of the property market, possibly as a result of the long gestation periods and potential for oversupply. There are numerous examples of property market bubbles and crashes,[46] the most recent being the Texan crisis of the mid-1980s, which led the largest bank holding company in the state, First Republic Bank, to seek a capital injection from the FDIC in March 1988 and left many office blocks empty.

Recent literature on rational bubbles has not confined itself to stock market prices. It has also featured applications to the analysis of exchange rates, which many analysts believe have shown excessive short-run fluctuations and sustained periods of misalignment, neither of which are consistent with the fundamentals. Brunner and Meltzer (1987) argue that neither the efficient asset market approach of the 1970s nor the theories based on balance of payments fundamentals that preceded them can explain the exchange rate behaviour observed in the post-1973 floating exchange rate period. The natural approach in the 1980s was to return to the analytical framework of the efficient markets approach and extend it. This resulted in the literature on bubbles and sunspots. As in asset markets, the theories of bubbles in exchange markets exploit the non-uniqueness of solutions in RE equilibria. Standard RE models relate the exchange rate (y_t) to fundamentals (f_t), which are determined by a linear combination of exogenous variables. But $y_t = f_t + b_t$ will also be a solution where b_t follows a possible stochastic time path imposed on the system. The bubble term (b_t) is determined by extrinsic information and refers neither directly nor indirectly to any observable phenomena.

The choice of extrinsic information is entirely arbitrary and is difficult to reconcile with the rationality and information postulates used in the analysis, Brunner and Meltzer argue. The basic model provides a continuance of convergent equilibrium paths while the supplementary, and arbitrary, specification of information extrinsic to the basic model determines the specific path taken by the exchange rate. They find this unsatisfactory because it offers no explanation of the volatility of exchange rates or the serially noncorrelated changes in exchange rates discovered in empirical analysis. The problem arises, they argue, from attempting to explain phenomena crucially conditioned by a pervasive uncertainty with an analysis incorporating RE that assumes that the probability distribution of shocks is known and, therefore, that risk rather than uncertainty prevails.

Previous attempts to explain exchange rates in terms of purchasing power parity (PPP),[47] which postulate rational expectations in the context of complete and homogeneous information among agents, also eliminate all manifestations of the pervasive uncertainty. They argue that, with such an analysis, an explanation of volatility is inaccessible. Singleton (1987) examines the consequences of replacing complete and homogeneous information among agents with imperfect and heterogeneous information. This captures some of the dimensions of uncertainty and radically changes the implications. It allows for much greater volatility than standard exchange rate models but fails to settle the remaining major question: the integration of the observed random walk behaviour of exchange rate changes into the analysis. If, as seems undeniable, speculators are present in the exchange markets, then the explanation could lie in non-homogeneous information and perceptions among agents and the tendency for individual agents to take profits periodically and refinance positions, as a method of hedging, as outlined earlier.

Singleton (1987) provides a critical review of the burgeoning literature on the potential importance of speculative bubbles and sunspots for explaining the time series behaviour of exchange rates. He expresses doubts about such explanations of exchange rate behaviour and argues that speculation has not had a stabilising effect in exchange markets as previously argued by proponents of floating exchange rates. (See, for example, Friedman 1953, pp. 157–203.) Singleton notes that bubble and sunspot models adopt fairly simple, and inadequate, specifications of the interplay between and the information of agents by commonly imposing current and homogeneous information and assuming that the distribution of shocks is known. This, as Brunner and Meltzer (1987) observed, eliminates uncertainty in the sense of Knight (1921). There is a strange incoherence in models that imply that past price changes are no guide to future price changes and yet future shocks will follow the distribution of past shocks. These bubble and sunspot models abstract entirely from the dynamics introduced by incomplete information and heterogeneous beliefs and/or information, he observes. The rejection of the PPP and economic fundamentals theories, based on balance of payments analysis, has led to the development of bubbles and sunspot theories; but, he argues, changes in fundamentals can easily generate exchange rate behaviour that resembles a rational bubble.

Agents may believe, with time-varying degrees of confidence, that major changes in the stochastic processes governing fundamental economic variables, such as the money stock or income, may occur in the future. It is unlikely that all the fundamentals are observed by econometricians conducting empirical analysis, and consequently there may appear to be bubbles in the misspecified models being investigated. With the addition of some of the features of uncertainty, this misspecification explanation of broad swings in exchange rates can be extended to explain their short-term volatility, Singleton argues. If agents believe that changes in the environment will occur with some small probability, then misspecifying the model by ignoring this possibility may lead to an underestimation of volatility. He argues that the probability attached to such events is also likely to change over time, adding to the swings.

Further, incorporating nonlinearities into the model will create a much more important role for informational problems. To illustrate this point, he extends his basic model to include risk aversion. He also demonstrates that reducing the information available to agents can increase volatility relative to the full current information model. When he allows risk aversion to vary across agents, volatility also increases. Singleton demonstrates in addition that by altering the information structure so that shocks and real variables are observed at discrete time intervals while trading in continuous, current and past shocks can have persistent effects on exchange rates, which again become more volatile. Heterogeneous information further magnifies the reaction of the exchange rate to shocks. He argues that it is likely that some traders will be more interested in hedging, importers and exporters for example, while others may take uncovered, speculative positions. With imperfect competition of this sort, volatility may be further increased.

Singleton's examples employ models in which PPP holds. He concludes that to develop an alternative fundamental interpretation of the dollar's appreciation up to 1985, which is generally regarded as an overvalued position, it is necessary to identify credible sources of uncertainty which, when combined with risk aversion, explain the appreciation. One source of uncertainty might have been the growing budget deficit which could have led to a rise in the real rate of interest, and he considers others as well. He argues that a fundamentalist explanation of the dollar appreciation cannot be easily dismissed while doubts remain about the correct specification of current PPP-related models. He concludes that volatile exchange rates do not constitute evidence of inefficient trading or justify central bank exchange intervention. Rather they reflect decision-making in an uncertain environment which may be enhanced by uncertainty about future government policies leading to medium-term swings and increased day-to-day movements in exchange rates. This implies that these features of exchange rate movement could be reduced if the uncertainty regarding future government policies, especially those relating directly to exchange rates, was removed and policy rules were announced instead.

Singleton therefore rejects bubbles and argues that correctly specified models of the fundamentals will be able to explain medium-term movements in exchange rates and their short-term volatility under uncertainty. The latter is approximated by relaxing the current and homogeneous information assumption while the medium-term movements are attributed to omitted variables, including government policy stances, whose future evolution is also uncertain. While some of the medium-term movements may be explicable by omitted variables, the perception that they have frequently led to sustained misalignments is hard to dispel. This implies that better-specified models of the fundamentals may not be sufficient, and irrational bubbles based on speculative euphoria, which are more likely to occur under uncertainty than risk (as Meltzer (1982) observed), may still be present. The problem may be that the so-called fundamentals are not immutable in the complex social organisation[48] we call the economy but depend themselves on the interaction of the perceptions of the economic agents at a specific time. The fashions and myths evident in dominant economic doctrines at various times and their tendency to change over time, perhaps even cyclically, may be a reflection of this problem. It is also highly likely that individual economic agents hold perceptions of the set of fundamental variables and their future evolution, and attach weights to them that vary at least as much as those infamously held by members of the economic profession.

3.5 CONCLUSION

Behaviour consistent with bubbles, namely a shock followed by a rapid fall, a slow change and then a rapid recovery can be described by catastrophe theory. (See discussion at end of section 2.3.) Cusp catastrophe models, Varian (1979) demonstrates, can be used to explain cycles containing recessions, and also cycles containing depressions, in which the return from the crash is gradual and drawn-out. The path followed is dependent on the severity of the shock. The shock examined by Varian is a wealth shock which might, for example, emanate from a stock market crash. The links between financial market crashes and economic recessions and depressions remain uncertain, however, as Galbraith's (1954) analysis of the possible links between the 1929 New York Stock Exchange crash and the subsequent depression demonstrates. In contrast, the October 1987 crash appears to have had relatively minor effects, which suggests that the impact of financial crashes depends on the underlying condition of the economy at the time and the distribution and proportion of wealth-holding in the form of stocks and shares at the time.

If bubbles exist, then plans to save and invest may be subject to erratic change because, in a world of uncertainty, the expectations on which decisions are based are liable to change rapidly and over-optimism or euphoria can build up. As a result, Keynes argued (1936, p.322), misguided over-optimistic expectations can lead to investment that would normally be deterred at the prevailing rate of interest.

The identification of the cause of the buildup to euphoria, which encourages the speculation that underlies bubbles, remains a problem. Even in the most notorious case of the speculative orgy of 1928–9, Galbraith (1954) finds it difficult to pin down the exact cause. He notes that easy money was not the cause because interest rates were relatively high. He observes, however, that speculation on a large scale requires a sense of confidence and optimism and a feeling of trust in the intentions of others. Savings must be plentiful in aggregate, but speculation can rely on borrowed funds. If people feel well off, then they may be willing to 'have a flutter' and take more risks in the hope of enhanced return. He postulates that speculation is, therefore, likely to follow a long period of prosperity which leads to rising expectations of future incomes. He cites the South Sea Bubble of 1720 as an example. Savings had grown rapidly and domestic returns had declined. The collapse of the bubble destroys the mood that fosters speculation but, with time and the dimming of memory, immunity to speculation wears off and a recurrence becomes possible, he argues.

Minsky's FIH and related work[49] imply that bubbles entail elements of irrationality, but bubbles can apparently also occur under rational behaviour. The rational bubble models, however, add little to our understanding of the phenomena, and some of those who have demonstrated the possibility of their existence believe that irrationality is displayed in historical accounts of bubbles. The irrational bubble theories imply that financial markets provide vehicles for speculative excesses. Minsky views the financial system itself as basically unstable. Others, such as Eichengreen and Portes (1987), see the financial system as potentially sound, once appropriately regulated, but as playing a significant role in generalising the effects of shocks emanating from the real sector.

If the financial system is fundamentally unstable, then regulation is clearly required. Minsky (1986), however, argues that it will not be possible to assure financial stability through regulation since instability laid to rest by one set of reforms will eventually emerge in a new guise. Those that do not share Minsky's views have a greater belief in the potential for regulation to prevent speculative excesses and the resultant crises. Nevertheless, the rapid financial innovation in the 1970s and 1980s ensures that regulators and supervisors must be ever-vigilant and develop flexible systems to contain the speculative urge and associated risks. In this vein the Brady Report[50] recommended that margin requirements in the US futures markets should be tightened following the October 1987 crash. In addition, should a financial crisis occur, the LOLR and BOLR should act swiftly to prevent it leading to a multiple credit contraction and recession or depression.

Eichengreen and Portes (1987) postulate that the banking system serves as a buffer between the real sector and the wider financial system. As a result of deregulation, however, banks are becoming increasingly integrated with the wider financial system (Mullineux 1987b, c). This has a number of regulatory and supervisory implications. The risk of 'contagion' is increased, in the sense that banks are more likely to be adversely affected by depositors' reactions to losses in securities markets in which banks are known or believed to be participating. To the extent that securities markets, as well as the real sector, are a source of shocks, then the banking system's buffer role will be expanded. The LOLR cover provided by central banks to support the banks' buffer function, and thereby to protect the payments system and the credit relationships it entails, will implicitly have to be extended to cover the wider financial system in order to protect banks from 'contagion'. (See Dale 1988 for further discussion.)

The discussion of the role of money and finance in pre-Keynesian business cycle theories in section 3.2, and of the FIH in section 3.3, revealed a tendency to concentrate on the behaviour of banks rather than the wider financial system. The implication appeared to be that there is something special about banks. It has been asked,[51] however, if banks differ from other financial intermediaries because they are more heavily regulated or if the regulatory strictures are applied because they are different. We have no space to explore such issues here but, to the extent that the financial system increases the ability of the economy to bear risks and in so doing allows more investment and faster growth to take place,[52] then it has a key role and its ability to absorb and manage risk must be assured. This provides a rationale for regulation. In most financial systems banks continue to play a key role, despite the apparent shift away from traditional bank loan finance towards funding through marketable securities. By virtue of their risk-bearing or insurance[53] role, they probably remain the most important shock absorbers or buffers in the financial system. This implies that in order to ensure that their buffer role is not impaired, it is particularly important to regulate banks.

If the banks do indeed perform a key buffer function, then the role of the banking sector in the economy is more complex than envisaged by Schumpeter (1939) and Shackle (1938), whose work will be discussed in the next chapter, and Minsky. Schumpeter and Shackle assumed that banks provided finance for innovatory investment and a secondary wave of expansion, while Minsky argues that banks engage in speculative and Ponzi finance. It may well be that financial fragility develops as the expansionary phase is sustained, as Minsky argues, and that this creates conditions that ensure a more severe downswing than would otherwise have occurred, as Schumpeter (1939) argued. If this is the case then bank regulation, aimed at curbing speculatory excesses and maintaining the banking sector's ability to perform its buffer function, would be an essential component of anticyclical policy.

NOTES

1. See Friedman and Schwartz (1963b), for example.
2. See Friedman and Schwartz (1963a), for example.
3. See Knight (1971, originally published 1921).
4. There is, however, a growing literature on economic decision-making under uncertainty; see for example McKenna (1986), Hey (1979, 1981) and Ford (1983, 1987).
5. Except in so far as they help to explain the determination of the rate of interest and savings and investment.
6. Not to be confused with John Stuart Mill cited above.
7. See Hawtrey (1913, 1919, 1928, 1932, 1933, 1937).
8. Which was particularly important under the gold standard.
9. Including Machlup (1931), Mises (1934), Robbins (1934), Röpke (1936) and Strigl (1934).
10. In the Fisher (1930) sense of the money rate corrected for inflation.
11. Although Hayek (1976a, 1976b) has since become an advocate of competing monies.
12. As posed by Frisch (1933). See Chapter 2 and Mullineux (1984) for further discussion.

13. The more recent contributions are Minsky (1982a, b, and 1986), but see also Minsky (1972) and Sinai (1977) for a detailed list of Minsky's writings.
14. On ISLM models see Hicks (1937) and Hansen (1941).
15. On neoclassical synthesis see Patinkin (1965).
16. See for example Mandel (1978a, b, 1980) and Van Duijn (1983).
17. The International Monetary Fund, the International Bank for Reconstruction and Development or 'World Bank', and the General Agreement on Tariffs and Trade.
18. By expanding the budget deficit when domestic demand slackens.
19. Such as income-related taxes and transfer payments, including unemployment benefits.
20. See Kindleberger (1978, Ch. 10) and Eichengreen and Portes (1987, pp.69–71).
21. Which derive from having to sell illiquid assets at short notice under adverse market conditions.
22. See Pecchioli (1987) and the Bank for International Settlements (1986).
23. In common with the other commentators on Minsky's (1982b) paper (Goldsmith (1982) and Melitz (1982)), Flemming also criticises Minsky for making inappropriate use of the Kalecki (1933) model (see Kalecki (1971, Part I)) by converting identities into structural equations.
24. The Federal Deposit Insurance Corporation was established in 1933 to protect depositors from the consequences of bank failures and to reduce the likelihood of resulting 'bank runs'.
25. See also comments on Minsky's paper in Altman and Sametz (1977).
26. Onado (1986) argues further that regulation will enhance confidence, reduce the innovation lags discussed by Kane (1981), and lead to increased efficiency in the financial system.
27. See Reid (1982) and Channon (1977) for accounts of this process.
28. See Chapter 4 for further discussion of capital as a component of banking system insurance.
29. The West German Herstatt Bank and the US Franklin National Bank failures, for example; see Channon (1977) and Dale (1985) for further discussion.
30. See Reid (1982), Channon (1977) or Bank of England (1978) for full accounts of the 'lifeboat' operation, or Mullineux (1987a, Appendix A) for a brief account.
31. See Chapter 4 for further discussion of the role of innovations in cycle generation.
32. See Deutsch (1966) and Parsons (1963) for further discussion.
33. Keynes (1936, p.136) used the analogy of a 'Beauty Contest'.
34. See Hansen (1951, Chs. 13 and 15) and section 3.2 for further discussion.
35. As Keynes (1936, Ch. 15) postulated in his analysis of the speculative demand for money.
36. See Lessard and Williamson (1987a, b) for definition and analysis and Mullineux (1987a, Ch. 5) for brief discussion.
37. See Mullineux (1987a, Ch. 5) for a brief discussion.
38. See Kraft (1984) for a detailed account of the Mexican rescue.
39. See Mullineux (1987a, Chs. 4 and 8, and 1988) for further discussion.
40. The market price and the expected rate of market price change.
41. See, for example, Clive Woolman, 'Efficient market theory stumbles', the *Financial Times*, 5 April 1988, p.16.

42. See Santoni (1987) for references, which include Galbraith (1954), Schumpeter (1939) and Shiller (1981).
43. Under additional assumptions, see Santoni (1987).
44. See Galbraith (1954) and Malkiel (1981) for further discussion.
45. As postulated by Keynes (1936, Ch. 15), for example.
46. Including that associated with the UK secondary banking crisis discussed in section 3.3.2.
47. See Dornbusch (1980, pp.150–5), for example.
48. See earlier discussion of Metcalfe (1986).
49. See, for example, Eckstein and Sinai (1986, sections 1.3 and 1.5), who suggest a more elaborate classification of business cycle stages than the NBER one. They include 'credit crunches', or financial crises, as a specific stage of the cycle and lay emphasis on the 'reliquification', or financial restructuring, that occurs in the recession and early recovery. The upturn is difficult to achieve or sustain until reliquification is complete. See also Sinai (1976, 1978 and 1980) and Eckstein (1983, Ch. 4).
50. The Report of the Brady Commission on 8 January 1988. The report was commissioned by the President of the United States following the October 1987 NYSE share price collapse.
51. By Tobin (1963) and Black (1970), for example.
52. See Rybczynski (1985) and Tobin (1984).
53. See Lewis and Davis (1987) for a discussion of the insurance function of banks.

4 · TOWARDS A THEORY OF DYNAMIC ECONOMIC DEVELOPMENT

4.1 A BRIEF OVERVIEW OF CYCLE MODELLING

Like Marx, Keynes failed to formalise a complete theory of dynamic economic development or of its components, growth and business cycles. It is a testament to the magnitude of the problem that these two great economic and social thinkers were unable to formulate such a theory. The consequence has been numerous attempts by their disciples to complete their work.[1] Keynesians have tended to seek separate theories of growth and the business cycle while Marxians have attempted to move beyond their initial preoccupation with crises towards an integrated theory of cycles and growth, but they have failed to agree on a common theory.[2] Meanwhile the work of Schumpeter (1934, 1939), who came much closer to developing a complete theory of dynamic economic development, has largely been ignored in post-war business cycle literature. It has not, however, been ignored in the long-cycle literature that has proliferated since the early 1970s (see note 31). There is no space to review this literature here, but Schumpeter's contribution will be discussed in the next section and Shackle's related work will be discussed in section 4.4. Both of these great economists stressed the role of innovations in the generation of business cycles.

Having seen early drafts of Keynes's General Theory, Harrod (1936) produced a Keynesian theory of the trade cycle in the same year as Keynes's book was published. His theory was based on multiplier–accelerator interaction. Harrod (1948) went on to concentrate on growth theory but his work on cycles was developed by Samuelson (1939), who demonstrated the various dynamic paths that could be derived from a linear deterministic multiplier–accelerator model. Earlier work by Frisch (1933) and Slutsky (1937) had shown the possibility of converting a series of random shocks or impulses into a cycle using a linear propagation model that displayed a damped monotonic or cyclical path in response to a single disturbance (see section 1.4). If linear stochastic models are to be employed, the basic choice is between Frisch–Slutsky models and explosive paths constrained by ceilings and floors, such as Hicks (1950), which also employed multiplier–accelerator interaction to give the essential dynamics.

In the 1950s a number of nonlinear deterministic models were developed.[3] Goodwin (1951), for example, employed a nonlinear accelerator to generate a limit cycle solution (see section 2.3 on limit cycles). The Hicks (1950) model can also be regarded as a nonlinear model which incorporates what Samuelson (1947) dubbed 'billiard table' nonlinearities and what we have called 'type I' nonlinearities.[4] Other examples of such models are Smithies (1957) and Minsky (1959), which employ Duesenberry-type ratchet effects (Duesenberry 1949) on consumption expenditure within a basic multiplier–accelerator framework. Goodwin (1951), however, employed a nonlinear accelerator function, or 'type II' nonlinearity to generate cycles.[5] These nonlinear models were capable of producing cycles that repeated themselves in the absence of shocks and consequently introduced the possibility of developing models in which the cycle was endogenously generated. They also allowed for the possibility of asymmetric expansionary and contractionary phases, which are not permitted in linear formulations (see section 1.3). Further, in the case of stable limit cycle solutions, shocks can be added to explain the observed irregularity in business cycles.

Also in the 1950s, Goodwin (1955) and Kaldor (1954), among others, became concerned about the separation of cycle and growth theory. The Hicks (1950) assumption of a trend in autonomous investment seemed artificial. They felt that the role of innovation in stimulating growth, as stressed by Schumpeter (1934, 1935, 1939), had been overlooked and that undue stress had been placed on investment induced via the accelerator process. The Schumpeterian bunching of innovatory investment had been ignored. Goodwin and Kaldor expressed the view that a theory of dynamic economic development was required and that it was incorrect to decompose economic time series into a linear trend and cyclical fluctuations and to try to explain them separately, because they were part of the same process.

The Keynesian structural econometric models built between the late 1950s and the early 1970s tended to display extreme monotonic, rather than cyclical, dampening. Adelman and Adelman (1959) found that autocorrelated, rather than random, shocks were required to generate realistic cycles.[6] 'Type I' and 'type II' nonlinearities were largely ignored in these models and by the end of the 1960s the very existence of business cycles was being questioned.[7] Others, following Fisher (1925) (see section

1.2) argued that it had never really existed because it represented the summation of random events with no propagation model transforming them into regular and repeated cycles.

Interest in the business cycle was rekindled as a result of the response of OECD countries to the 1973 oil price shock and in the mid-1970s two papers were published, Nordhaus (1975) and Lucas (1975),[8] which stimulated renewed academic interest in the subject. Lucas's work seems to have had the more lasting impact and has led to numerous attempts to model the cycle as an equilibrium phenomenon (see section 2.2). Most of the work is in the Frisch–Slutsky tradition with a linear model propagating cycles in response to a series of random shocks. The cycle so formulated is, therefore, not endogenous and self-sustaining. This period also saw a resurgence of interest in long waves with speculation that the long post-war upswing had given way to the downswing of the long wave in the 1970s. (See Mandel (1980) and Van Duijn (1983).)

The major debate in the 1980s was not over whether the Frisch–Slutsky modelling strategy was correct but over the most important sources of shocks. Lucas (1975) had stressed the importance of monetary shocks but in the 1980s attention turned to real shocks as the major source of impulses. More recently Lucas (1987) has suggested a synthesis of the real and monetary equilibrium business cycle approaches which he feels should build on the Kydland and Prescott (1982) contribution (see section 2.2). The latter generates cycles using a stochastic derivative of the neoclassical growth model and as such marks a renewed attempt to integrate cycle and growth theory.

A parallel development in the 1980s was the attempt by New Keynesians to derive microeconomic theories to explain wage stickiness and the various other planks on which Keynesian macroeconomic theory was built and, in so doing, to provide a rationalisation for disequilibrium theories of the cycle inspired by Keynes. Greenwald and Stiglitz (1987) assess the progress of the New Keynesian approach to business cycle modelling,[9] which they note is in the Frisch–Slutsky tradition. External and internal shocks, in the form of shifts in Keynesian 'animal spirits' that arise from modelling under uncertainty rather than risk,[10] drive the cycle, which is propagated by a Keynesian disequilibrium model with wage and price stickiness and information imperfections. No endogenous theory of the cycle has been developed and no theory of cyclical growth or dynamic economic development is presented in line with the theory towards which Keynes was groping.

The stochastic linear multiplier–accelerator, the linear equilibrium business cycle and the emerging New Keynesian models are all, therefore, based on the Frisch–Slutsky approach and do not attempt to provide an endogenous theory of the cycle. They all utilise essentially linear propagation models to convert random or serially correlated shocks into cycles. Nonlinearities can, however, be used to generate endogenous cycles which can be regarded as the equilibrium motion of the economy. Recent demonstrations of this fact are due to Chiarella (1986) and Grandmont (1985), who uses nonlinearity to derive a truly equilibrium, in the sense that the cycle is the equilibrium motion and markets clear continuously, theory of the cycle (see section 2.3). Normally, however, the nonlinear models employ time trends to explain the movement of the point around which the limit cycle occurs. Even with nonlinear models, the full integration of cycles and growth remains a problem. In an attempt to achieve such an integration, numerous economists have extended the Goodwin (1967) predator-prey model (see section 2.3), which relied on trends in technical progress and the working population to generate growth. Some have, for example, tried to introduce endogenous technical progress. Goodwin himself has stressed the need for a more disaggregated approach and in section 4.5 his recent work, published in Goodwin and Punzo (1987), will be discussed.

In order to develop an integrated theory of cycles and growth it may be necessary to look to Schumpeter for inspiration, as Goodwin and Kaldor suggested in the 1950s and as long-cycle theorists have done since the early 1970s. Shackle (1938) had already developed a theory which integrated Keynesian and Schumpeterian ideas with a Duesenberry-type 'ratchet effect' on consumption. Shackle's work on the cycle has been largely neglected. In order to rectify this, his work on the business cycle will be reviewed in section 4.4. First, however, Schumpeter's contribution to business cycle theory will be briefly discussed to provide a background for the discussion of Shackle's work and the more recent contribution of Goodwin (section 4.5).

4.2 SCHUMPETER ON ECONOMIC EVOLUTION

No attempt is made here to survey in depth Schumpeter's work on business cycles. Fels (1964) provides a short summary and cites references to other surveys, and innovatory assessments of Schumpeter's work continue to be produced. Instead, a brief sketch of the essentials will be provided to form a background to subsequent sections of this chapter.

Schumpeter (1934, Ch. II) distils the essential features of his theory of capitalist economic development and explains why innovations might be expected to occur in 'swarms'. This theory is embellished in Schumpeter (1934, Ch. VI) in an attempt to explain the Juglar, or business cycle, rather than minor, or Kitchen cycles and long, or Kondratieff waves. The embellishment includes discussion of secondary expansionary waves, which spread as a result of the burst of innovatory investment that sets the cycle in motion. Schumpeter (1939, Chs. III and IV) reconsiders the previous analysis and presents three approximations to a theory of the business cycle.

The first approximation is a two-phase cycle which is the result of stripping the Schumpeter (1934, Ch. VI) model back to basics, by ignoring the secondary wave of expansion and developing the ideas of Schumpeter (1934, Ch. II) to explain the fundamental cause of capitalism's cyclical evolution. The second approximation involves the examination of the effects of introducing the secondary wave of expansion and consists of a four-phase cycle in which financial crises and depressions become possibilities. Concluding his analysis of the secondary approximation, Schumpeter acknowledges that due to their historical uniqueness, observed cycles will be irregular in period and amplitude. The third approximation postulates that the process of evolution may well give rise to more than one wavelike motion. A three-cycle schema is adopted to facilitate theoretical, statistical and historical analysis of cycles of various lengths. The basic idea is, however, that innovations may vary in importance and that the more important they are the longer the periods of gestation and absorption are likely to be. This reflects a relaxing of the assumption that swarms of innovatory investment can only occur once the economy has completed its adjustment to a new equilibrium following a previous burst of innovatory investment.

Schumpeter (1939, Ch. VI) concludes his theoretical analysis by considering the impact and causes of external shocks and special cycles, such as agricultural and 'hog' cycles. He argues that external shocks elicit a responsive adaptation from the economy which is fundamentally different from the evolutionary adaptation that results from internal shocks caused by bursts of innovatory investment.

Schumpeter therefore aims to describe both why the economy evolves cyclically, rather than evenly, and why business, and perhaps other longer and shorter cycles, take their observed form. His first approximation attempts to identify the fundamental cause and nature of dynamic economic development or evolution. His second and third approximations, and the discussion of 'other fluctuations', attempt to explain the observed business and other cycles and reconcile them with alternative theories of the business cycle. The latter tend, in his view, to concentrate on secondary aspects rather than on the primary cause of fluctuations, which is the bunching of innovatory investment.

The proposition that the bunching of innovatory investment is the primary cause of the cyclical development of capitalism is utilised by Shackle (1938), whose contribution (discussed in section 4.4) was to employ Keynesian and Myrdallian insights to develop Schumpeter's analysis of the secondary wave of expansion. Goodwin, like many other economists, remains unconvinced by Schumpeter's explanation of bunching[11] and prefers to explain the apparent bunching of innovatory investment as a rapid secondary response, illustrated using his multi-sectoral input–output approach, involving what Schumpeter would call induced investment and multiplier–accelerator interaction. Shackle's explanation of the bunching is weak and it appears to be used as a *deus ex machina*. Fels (1964) notes that the clustering of innovations in Schumpeter's analysis is not due to the rarity of innovatory genius *per se*. Instead it is a reflection of the fact that innovation is difficult. Untried combinations must be tested and financiers must be persuaded to back the potential new ventures. Not all will get finance and few of those that do will be successful. Once a breakthrough is made, however, other entrepreneurs will copy or improve upon it and the credibility of ventures, in the eyes of banks, will increase. Induced innovatory investment will occur, resulting in clustering.

The point of departure for Schumpeter's theory of economic development is an equilibrium state in which there may be growth but no evolution, in the sense that no new products are coming on to the markets and no new methods of production are being tried. The underlying cause of growth in equilibrium is not analysed in depth but is attributed to population growth among other things. The equilibrium is then disturbed by an internal shock in the form of a swarm of new entrepreneurs successfully introducing a cluster of innovations. The result is a bunching of innovatory investment. Even in the absence of secondary effects a new equilibrium must be sought, for which factors of production must be redeployed. The banks are assumed to be the main source of finance for the 'new combinations'.[12] They are seen as venture capitalists which sponsor new combinations, rather than as broking intermediaries. They play a key role by expanding credit and creating new purchasing power to meet the additional demands of the new enterprises. In the first approximation, the entrepreneurial function is completely separated from the capitalist function, which is performed by banks. Entrepreneurs are not capitalists; they are innovators who draw on the stock of new possibilities being offered as a result of additions to the stock of knowledge resulting from inventions and other discoveries. Clearly, in a modern financial system entrepreneurs often need to look to specialist venture capitalists, rather than banks, for start-up and development capital.

The swarm-like appearance of entrepreneurs necessitates a special and distinctive process of absorption, which involves incorporating new products and technologies and adapting systems to them, and also a process of liquidation of outmoded enterprises, which must make way for the new. This process is the essence of Schumpeter's recessions, in which the economy struggles towards a new equilibrium.

The disturbance, to which old enterprises must react, manifests itself in various ways. As the new enterprises bid for means of production, their price is bid up and this raises the cost of the old enterprises. As the new products enter the market to compete with old ones, the old enterprises face a fall in demand for their products and a decline in revenue. The seeds of recession are sown. The length of time between the formation of new enterprises and the appearance of new products, also *en masse*, is a fundamental determinant of the length of the boom in Schumpeter's model. As new enterprises begin to receive revenue, they begin to extinguish debts, and the purchasing power created by banks begins to disappear. The reduced profitability of the old enterprises and the increased uncertainty that follows rapid change will make banks wary about diverting credit to old enterprises. The new enterprises enter a highly competitive environment with differentiated products and earn monopoly profit for a period, but it is gradually eroded by competition.

Eventually the period of prosperity gives way to a recession. Businessmen must learn to adapt to the new situation in which new competitors have become established, old customers and lines of credit cannot be relied upon, and production levels must be adjusted to prevent the accumulation of stocks of commodities that have become more difficult to sell. Schumpeter therefore regards the recession as a process of adjustment and 'resorption'. Old businesses must adjust and new ones must survive their first test. The next boom cannot start until the adjustment is nearly complete and a new equilibrium is approached. This is because the high level of uncertainty that is present while adjustment is taking place discourages new investment. Given the assumed separation of the entrepreneurial and capitalist functions, this must be due to the unwillingness of banks to lend.

The fundamental process of economic development described above is embellished in Schumpeter (1934, Ch. VI and 1939, Ch. IV) by the introduction of a secondary wave of expansion. The banking sector also plays a key role in the financing of the secondary wave, which is based on a sort of multiplier-accelerator expansion. As a result of the secondary wave, excesses can occur and there is likely to be significant overshooting of the new equilibrium. Financial crises can occur as a consequence and the ensuing recession can develop into a depression if overshooting in the downward direction results. A problem of explaining the lower turning point then arises and Schumpeter argues that government economic policy should aim to terminate depressions because, unlike recessions which entail a movement towards a new equilibrium, they serve no useful purpose. Policy-makers are not told, however, how to identify the point at which recession turns into depression and the new equilibrium is overshot. Once terminated, the depression gives way to a recovery or revival, which is also a motion towards equilibrium. The new equilibrium is unstable in an upward direction and following another burst of innovatory investment, a new expansionary phase, with its primary and secondary waves, begins. The depression phase, it is argued, is not a necessary part of economic development but may feature in some business cycles and so too might financial crises. Institutional reform and macroeconomic policy should, therefore, concentrate on the elimination of depressions and financial crises, but it should be accepted that cyclical evolution is the norm for capitalist economies. By deciding which innovations to sponsor and, in pursuit of profit, allocating capital as efficiently as they can, banks in capitalist economies essentially play the role that the planning agency plays in centrally planned economies.

Each cycle, Schumpeter argues, is a historical individual in the sense that it will depend on the nature of the particular innovations that provide the initial shock starting the cycle and the prevailing structure of the economy and the financial system. These factors are in turn clearly influenced by the evolution that has preceded the cycle in question. Given the uniqueness of each cycle, there is no need to expect regularity of period or amplitude (see section 1.2). Further, Schumpeter argues in his third approximation, there is no reason to expect that the cyclical evolution will consist of only one wavelike motion because innovations have different periods of gestation and absorption. It is more likely, he concludes, that there is a multiplicity of cycles which may or may not be related in some way.

The internal shocks caused by the bunching of innovatory investment, Schumpeter argues, give rise to a primary tendency to cyclical evolution, which is the manifestation of the economy's adjustment to these shocks and which Schumpeter calls economic development. Because of the diverse nature of the shocks, the primary cycles can vary in period and amplitude. The capitalist economic system is organised in such a way that these internal shocks are likely to be amplified by secondary waves of expansion which give rise to the possibility of financial crises and depressions. The government's role should be to regulate the capitalist system to prevent excesses leading to crises and to utilise monetary and fiscal policy to attenuate depressions. The economic system is also hit by external shocks which will themselves create a need for economic adjustment. This is not regarded by Schumpeter as being part of the development process, but it will clearly add to the irregularity of cycles and assure their historical uniqueness. The shocks are also likely to add to the amplitude of cycles in the way that the secondary waves of expansion and other factors, discussed in Schumpeter (1939, Ch. IV), are assumed to do. Before a discussion of the related work of Shackle (1938), the next section will consider the hypothesis that there are longer cycles than the business cycle, and related issues.

4.3 THE LONG SWING HYPOTHESIS AND THE GROWTH TREND

4.3.1 The long swing hypothesis

There have been recurrent suggestions in the literature on business cycles that as well as minor and major cycles, there may exist longer swings or waves. Long waves are usually investigated using an economic historical analysis of a few series that display only a small number of complete cycles.[13]

The long swing hypothesis is that long waves flow through economic life with shorter waves, including business cycles, superimposed upon them. As noted in the previous section, Schumpeter (1939) postulated the existence of numerous cycles but adopted a three-cycle schema, involving Kitchen (minor), Juglar (major) and Kondratieff (long) cycles, as an approximation. Using US data, Adelman (1965) undertook a statistical test for the existence of long swings. The question raised by Adelman was whether these cycles were independent of, though perhaps interacted with, the business cycle. The answer, Adelman observed, hinges on two issues: the cause of long swings, and the extent to which smoothing procedures themselves are responsible for the cycles.

As far as statistical backing for the various approaches is concerned, Adelman refers to her own work on the shocked Klein-Goldberger (K-G) model, which was found to perform quite well for long cycles.[14] The implication is that the lead-lag structure imposed by the model weights the shocks to produce long cycles in the manner suggested by the Frisch I hypothesis. Adelman draws attention to another possible interpretation, namely that the lead-lag relations are accidental or reflective of shorter cycles and that random causes explain the long cycle. In addition, smoothing to eliminate short cycles, which is common in the analysis of long cycles, may introduce systematic bias via the Slutsky-Yule effect so that the long cycles might be illusory.

Adelman tries to determine whether smoothing biases are sufficient to explain the existence of long cycles. Spectral analysis is used because it enables the simultaneous determination of cycles of all durations without the need to eliminate shorter cycles. The traditional approach to analysis of cycles of ten to twenty years, as exemplified by Kuznets (1937) and

Burns (1934), has been to use moving averages to smooth shorter cycles. Adelman points out that unless the period chosen for the moving average (MA) corresponds to the frequency of the short cycle exactly, spurious cycles will be introduced. This is, of course, likely since the short (business) cycles do not display regular period or amplitude. It is evident from Slutsky (1937) that the spurious cycles are likely to be of longer duration (see section 1.4).

Adelman (1965) calculated power spectra for detrended consumption, investment, output, employment, labour productivity, productivity of capital, and the wholesale price index, with many series being used for each variable. The filtered spectra displayed no evidence of long swings since 1890. Adelman claims that the entire variance in the long swing frequencies is attributable to leakages from power at low frequencies. When the effects of random fluctuations are smoothed out, using spectral techniques, the power that remains in the long swing domain appears to be traceable to the difficulty of removing the entire trend from the data. An alternative view is that the difficulty of removing the 'entire' trend implies long-run structural or systematic change or a stochastic trend (see section 4.3.2). Adelman seems, therefore, to have shown that the trend is unlikely to be cyclical and if it is, the cycle is weak. It is also possible that the trend removal may have eliminated more than just the trend. It is consequently necessary to look at Adelman's method of deriving deviations from trend. Adelman used deviations from log linear rather than MA trends. There seems to be little danger, therefore, that non-trend variation was removed but still the data could have been distorted.

Adelman concludes that long cycles have largely been introduced by smoothing techniques, although large exogenous shocks, and possibly structural shifts, have led to changes in trend which have not been adequately allowed for. To the extent that it exists, the long swing is not endogenously determined but is the result of exogenous shocks.

Howrey (1968) tests the hypothesis that there are swings of between fifteen and twenty-five years, a period which covers various versions of the long swing hypothesis. He first examines the effects of filtering on time series and then applies spectral analysis to various economic time series. He notes that the method commonly used to isolate long swings is to filter the data with an MA process to attenuate short-term fluctuations. The chronology of peaks and troughs is then used to test whether the original series contains a long swing component. Howrey notes that this method is subjective and arbitrary and demonstrates that inference about the original series from filtered series can be misleading. He finds that a major cycle of eight to eleven years in the original series could be converted to a cycle of fifteen to twenty-five years by use of an MA filter, giving further confirmation of the Slutsky-Yule effect.

Howrey estimates the spectral density functions of a number of economic time series. To abide by the stationarity assumption in applying the spectrum analysis, the growth rates are used. The trend introduces nonstationarity and so the growth rate sequence is more likely to be stationary. Adelman used deviations from log linear trends to test the long swing hypothesis. Howrey points out that the series used by Adelman display nonstationarity and so the applicability of spectral analysis and the validity of Adelman's results are questionable. Howrey notes that nonstationarity in the growth rates series is less conspicuous in most instances, but perhaps no less real.

The long swing hypothesis is interpreted as stating that the contribution of the band of frequencies corresponding to the average period of twenty years is significantly greater than that of neighbouring bands. The hypothesis would be rejected if no peak in the spectrum occurs near the long swing frequency. Howrey finds that the long swing seems to be absent from the production series while five to nine and three to five year cycles are present. Two of the consumption series show a peak in the long swing band but the peak is not significant. Investment series show no peak in the long swing frequencies but a significant peak in the five to nine year band. A long cycle is found in nonfarm residential construction, indicating a building cycle of eleven to twelve years, which is shorter than previous estimates. Inventories show a significant peak indicating a four year period, which is about half a year longer than in other series showing peaks in the three to five year period. This is interesting in view of the association of inventories with minor cycles. He notes that the result may be due to the inadequacy of the series.

Howrey finds that his results are inconclusive but they do nothing to dispel scepticism about the existence of a Kuznets cycle. The spectrum peaks that occur in long wave frequency bands are in most cases weak and in no case statistically significant. The results indicate relatively regular fluctuations which are longer than the three to five year, approximately forty month, average of NBER cycles and which fit conveniently into the major cycle category of nine to fifteen years. Howrey's results imply that by virtue of Burns and Mitchell's (1946) definition of business cycles as being of one to ten or twelve years in duration, the NBER may be missing some of the major cycles and that a better test of the Monte Carlo hypothesis (see section 1.2) may be derived by splitting reference cycles into major and minor categories. Nevertheless, this is a strong set of evidence contradicting the Monte Carlo hypothesis.

Burns and Mitchell (1946, Ch. 11) also tested for the significance of the long swing hypothesis. They were aware that the hypothesis that business cycles are subdivisions of longer cycles raises some fundamental questions about their use of averages to expose the typical characteristics of cyclical behaviour and to establish a base from which wide variations in duration can be explained. If the business cycle differed radically according to its position in a long swing then, Burns and Mitchell acknowledge, they would not be justified in using simple averages. In comparing cycles of different activities it would be essential to ensure that they covered like periods within long swings; otherwise bias would occur. The problem, for Burns and Mitchell, was not so much to decide whether or not long cycles exist but whether they are strong enough to command attention at the early stage of the study of business cycles that they felt they were in.

To test the importance of the long swings, seven US series,[15] with their accompanying NBER measures, were used. Little indication is given as to why these series were chosen. Burns and Mitchell's procedure was to test a number of hypotheses regarding long swings in order to gauge whether there was any marked change in cycles during the periods indicated. They found that building activity displayed a remarkably regular cycle, with duration between fifteen and twenty years and large amplitudes. They investigate whether business cycles vary in intensity according to whether the economy is experiencing an upswing or a downswing in a building cycle. The averages of reference and specific cycles during the upswing of a building cycle are compared with those occurring in a downswing. Little difference is found and their variance ratio tests show that any differences are not significant. Tests were made for variability in duration and amplitude.

Burns and Mitchell next explore the hypotheses of Wardwell (1927) (major cycles), Kuznets (1930) (secondary secular variations), Kondratieff (1935) (long waves) and Burns (1934) (trend cycles). The general approach of these studies was to fit lines of intermediate trend (usually moving averages) that are supposed to eliminate specific cycles. The deviations of these intermediate trends from the primary trend are supposed to expose long cycles. The studies of Kuznets and Burns are most extensive but the cycles cannot be tested directly because their chronology is either non-existent or too coarse for NBER monthly analysis. Similarly Wardwell's annual chronology is not sufficiently accurate.

Burns and Mitchell first test for Kondratieff waves of fifty to sixty years, pointing out that long waves in prices had been frequently postulated. Since NBER data is post-1850, no serious test of the hypothesis, as it stands, can be made since only two complete cycles are observable. Burns and Mitchell therefore consider a simpler question: is there evidence that business cycles in the upswings of long cycles (waves) in commodity prices differ substantially from those occurring in downswings? They find no significant difference. They then test whether cycle measures vary during periods of opposite price trends. They find a significant difference in the case of durations but not amplitudes. They reserve judgement on the direction of causation.

Next Burns and Mitchell consider Schumpeter's (1939) hypothesis, that Juglar cycles (nine to ten year major cycles) contain three (minor) cycles of approximately forty months. Howrey's (1968) results seem to support this hypothesis. A test is performed by grouping the first and third cycles, according to their position in the alleged Juglar cycles. One would expect the rise in the first cycle to be larger, and the fall smaller, than that in the third cycle. Evidence is favourable towards the hypothesis but Burns and Mitchell note that the trough dates of Juglars correspond to severe depressions so that one would expect a substantial difference between cycles occupying opposite ends of the particular Juglar periods examined. If some internal regularity characterised cycles separated by troughs of severe depressions the hypothesis would be on sounder footing, they argue. They find no support for this, however, but do regard Schumpeter's suggestion as a valuable one warranting further research.

Burns and Mitchell next examine the Kitchen (1923) hypothesis. Kitchen's major cycles are aggregates of two, and sometimes three, minor cycles each lasting forty months on average. The limit of each major cycle is distinguished by a maximum of exceptional height, by a high bank rate and sometimes by a panic. Kitchen's chronology of cycles differs markedly from the NBER chronology. Burns and Mitchell believe that this is due to Kitchen's concentration on financial variables, which show extra cycles. Kitchen's chronology is closest to that of the NBER for US data. Burns and Mitchell explore the possibility of differences between first and last business (minor) cycles occurring within Kitchen's major cycles. The two groups of cycles, they find, are basically the same although the average duration of the first group of cycles is greater. This difference is not significant and, in fact, of the five major cycles explored, three of the first cycle groups were shorter. One would also expect smaller amplitude for the first group than the second group of cycles. This was true for eleven out of eighteen cases but the difference was found not to be significant. Burns and Mitchell feel that major cycles may exist but their existence does not produce systematic bias to business cycles and so the averaging procedure used in their work is an acceptable approximation.

Burns and Mitchell observe that trends make it easier to mark off depressions than booms. They therefore rerun the above tests, but with major cycles marked off by severe depressions, due to the unsatisfactory chronology provided by Kitchen's work. This also provides a test of the

Schumpeter and Wardwell hypotheses that major cycle troughs coincide with major depressions. Burns and Mitchell mark out a list of major depressions, which they regard as highly tentative. The cycles are distributed into three groups: reference cycles marked by troughs just following a severe depression; reference cycles within which a major depression falls; and the rest of the cycles. Specific cycles are grouped in a similar manner. Tests for differences in duration and amplitude were made. They found no significant difference in duration, but a significant difference in amplitude was discovered. This is attributed to the method of classification. They conclude that the hypotheses need further investigation, but there is insufficient evidence to accept the major cycle marked off by severe depression hypothesis. Their tests are to be understood in the light of the tentative datings of severe depressions.

In summarising their results, Burns and Mitchell draw attention to the fact that they used only a small sample of series (seven in all). In addition, these series are not the ones normally chosen by long-cycle theorists to demonstrate their theories. Further, they have made no allowance for leads and lags and their significance tests are approximate at best. They regard themselves as being in no position to say whether cycles have varied systematically but they are satisfied that these long-run effects are sufficiently small to allow them to use their averages as a first approximation.

The tests of the various hypotheses usually proceed by dividing cycles into groups and using F-tests to determine whether there is a significant difference, either in measures of average duration or average amplitude, between groups of cycles. The probability tables used in the F-tests are derived from a theoretical population distributed according to the normal curve. Burns and Mitchell point out that because definite evidence exists that the frequency distribution of their cycle measures is often skewed, the tests they make are in some degree inexact. A second problem is that the probability tables are based on the assumption that the observations entering the sample are independent. Burns and Mitchell feel reasonably sure that cyclical measures do not fulfil this condition, although they come closer to doing so than the original time series data. Thus there is a second source of bias to the tests. They feel that these biases in the testing procedure have not seriously hampered their analysis since they are only interested in testing whether the effects of cyclical changes in cycles are substantial, rather than whether they exist.

The renewed interest in long cycles since the early 1970s was noted in section 4.1. There is no space to review this literature here. If, however, cycles with periods longer than that normally associated with the business cycle exist, then (log) linear trend removal will not isolate the business cycle. Instead it will be necessary to remove the influence of the long swing on the data. This presents a difficult problem, given the risk that moving average smoothing will severely distort the data.

4.3.2 The growth trend

Perhaps anticipating the contribution of Nelson and Plosser (1982), discussed below, Blatt (1980) points out that the Frisch–Slutsky hypothesis implies that business cycles are caused by shocks and that any attempt to include business cycle-like oscillations as part of the trend curve produced by the model runs directly counter to the Frischian view. Nevertheless, he notes that the trend does not have to be strictly linear to be consistent with the Frisch–Slutsky hypothesis. If nonlinear, however, it should be stable with smooth curvature. It should not itself display fluctuations in the business cycle time-scale because otherwise detrending would remove part of the business cycle phenomena to be explained. In the light of the discussion of section 4.3.1, it should be added that the trend should not display regular cycles of longer duration either, because these would instead be consistent with the various long swing hypotheses.

In section 1.2 it was noted that there is a growing tendency, even at the NBER, to analyse cycles in detrended data.[16] In many analyses (log) linear trends are assumed and elsewhere moving average trends are estimated. The presumption in favour of (log) linear trends is a natural extension of the linearity hypothesis, but the data should at least be examined to see if it is appropriate; otherwise detrending will distort the series. It was noted in section 4.3.1, however, that the more sophisticated approach of estimating a moving average trend introduces its own distortions which often show up as spurious cycles of longer duration than the business cycle, as defined by the NBER. Detrended data used for business cycle analysis is, therefore, highly likely to be distorted and in the absence of better methods of trend estimation, which take account perhaps of the structural changes that occur during long runs of data, it is hard to escape Burns and Mitchell's (1946) conclusion that it is better to work with non-detrended data.

Nelson and Plosser (1982) challenge the Frischian view, as expressed by Blatt (1980), that macroeconomic time series are best characterised as stationary fluctuations around a deterministic trend. They argue instead that they should be viewed as nonstationary processes that have no tendency to return to a deterministic (trend) path. They see no reason why the secular movement in economic time series should not itself be stochastic and observe that if it is, then models based on deterministic time trend residuals will be misspecified. They illustrate the types of misspecification that can arise from inappropriate detrending by considering the properties of residuals from a random walk on time, which are known to display drift, similar to secular movements, which is stochastic rather than deterministic in nature (see section 3.4). They show that the autocorrelation function of the deterministic time trend residuals is a statistical artifact which is determined entirely by sample size. The autocorrelation function displays strong autocorrelation at low lags and pseudo-periodic behaviour at long lags. Empirical investigations that ignore the possibility that a stochastic trend is the source of the autocorrelation might, therefore, be led to overestimate both the persistence and variance of the business cycle. Further, to the extent that the stochastic nature of the trend can be associated with real shocks, the use of a deterministic trend will underestimate the influence of real shocks.

Since the basic statistical issue is the appropriate representation of nonstationary economic time series, Nelson and Plosser (1982) consider two fundamentally different classes of nonstationary processes as alternative hypotheses. One class consists of deterministic function of time plus a stationary stochastic process with zero mean, referred to as the trend-stationary (TS) process. It is judged that such processes are most appropriately applied to the natural logs of economic time series, and deviations from trend, the so-called cyclical components of the series, are represented as invertible ARIMA processes.

The second class of nonstationary process considered is that in which first, or higher order differences, are a stationary and invertible ARIMA process. This is referred to as a difference-stationary (DS) process and the first order case is used to explain the natural logs of the economic time series examined. The DS class is purely stochastic and the TS class is fundamentally deterministic.

Various historical time series from the United States, including measures of output, spending, money, prices and interest rates, are examined and the relationship of the analysis to McCulloch's test of the Monte Carlo hypothesis is noted (see section 1.2). In particular McCulloch (1975) finds some evidence of periodicity in the logs of real income, investment and consumption after fitting a linear trend but finds no periodicity in their first differences, a finding consistent with their results. The sample autocorrelation structures for the series are found to be consistent with those expected from a random walk.[17] The exception is the unemployment rate series, which exhibits autocorrelation properties consistent with a stationary series. The autocorrelation structures of real, nominal and per capita GNP, real and nominal wages and common stock prices display positive autocorrelation at lag one only. This is characteristic of first order MA processes and inconsistent with the TS model. The GNP deflator, consumer prices, the money stock and the bond yield exhibit more persistent autocorrelation in first differences but do not show evidence of having been generated by a differenced TS process. In sum, Nelson and Plosser find their evidence to be consistent with the DS representation of nonstationary economic time series. They do, however, recognise that their tests have little power against the alternative hypothesis of a TS process with an AR root close to unity. This alternative implies little tendency to return to trend and could be indicative of a stable limit cycle produced by a nonlinear model.[18]

Their results, therefore, suggest that economic time series contain stochastic trends of the DS type rather than deterministic time trends. In this case, if (the log of) output is viewed as the sum of a secular or growth component and a cyclical component, and the latter is assumed to be transitory (stationary), then any underlying nonstationarity must be attributed to the secular component. Thus if actual output is in the DS class then so too must be the secular component. The separation of the secular component from the observed data can, they note, be thought of as a problem of signal extraction when only the information in observed series itself is used. Using, as an example, Friedman's permanent income model they show that it is not always possible to identify the cyclical and secular components. However, if the cyclical component is stationary and, as they discover, the autocorrelations in the first differences of output are positive at lag one and zero elsewhere, then they demonstrate that the variation in actual output changes will be dominated by changes in the secular, rather than the cyclical, component. They acknowledge that they cannot prove empirically that cyclical fluctuations are stationary or transitory but feel that their evidence is strongly supportive of the hypothesis that the business cycle is a stochastic process of the DS class.

The hypothesis that the cycle is stationary is implicit in the Frisch I hypothesis (see section 1.4), which assumes that cyclical fluctuations dissipate over time and the cycle is the result of hitting the propagation model with repeated random shocks. Long-run or permanent movements (nonstationarities) are attributed to the secular (trend) component and are the result of real factors. Nelson and Plosser believe most economists accept both the Frisch I hypothesis and this view of the trend and, therefore, that the cyclical component is stationary. Finally, they observe that assigning a major portion of the variance in output to innovations in the nonstationary component gives an important role to real factors in output fluctuations and places limits on theories of the business cycle that stress the importance of unanticipated monetary disturbances, such as the Lucas (1975) model. The debate between proponents of real and monetary causes of the business cycle is reviewed in section 2.2.

Nelson and Plosser (1982) therefore provide another strong warning against using residuals from fitted deterministic trend lines for the empirical analysis of business cycles. If the trend follows a nonstationary stochastic process, a possibility that cannot be discounted, then the residuals will contain both cyclical and stochastic trend variation and the magnitude and duration of the supposedly cyclical component will be overstated. They also warn that first differencing will not remove the stochastic growth component but may render the time series stationary, and the problem of inferring the behaviour of each unobserved component from the observed sum, the signal extraction problem, will remain.

4.4 SHACKLE ON THE BUSINESS CYCLE

Shackle (1938) regards his theory as being more like the cycle Keynes was moving towards than the 'Keynesesque' neoclassical multiplier–accelerator interaction models (see Shackle 1967, p.266). He attempted to provide an integrated theory of the multiplier and the investment process in a model with interdependent markets and sectors. Later Shackle (1967, Ch. 14) drew a strict distinction between the income–expenditure (Kahn) multiplier, the accelerator and the input–output multiplier. He stressed that underlying the Kahn multiplier is the interdependence of all sectors and components of the economy and that this entails a less mechanical multiplier–accelerator interaction than that expounded in Keynesesque models. Goodwin's recent work, which develops these ideas, is discussed in the next section. By combining the Kahn multiplier with a Schumpeter-like clustering of innovations and a Duesenberry-type consumption ratchet effect, Shackle (1938) is able to derive an essentially endogenous theory of the cycle.

Like many other cycle theorists, Shackle was primarily concerned with explaining the major or Juglar cycle, which seemed to be prevalent in the United Kingdom, and implicitly accepted that the minor or Kitchen cycle was an inventory cycle. At the outset he makes it clear that economic decisions are made under uncertainty, rather than risk, in the sense of Keynes (1936) and Knight (1921). Consequently economic conduct is not completely rational but, he argues, this does not imply that economists cannot theorise rationally about it. Nevertheless, he notes that there is a tendency to draw the opposite conclusion and that this has led to a preference for the Walrasian equilibrium framework. We might add that latterly it has led to the widespread adoption of the rational expectations hypothesis and equilibrium business cycle modelling. In the Shackle tradition, the New Keynesian school is making renewed efforts to develop disequilibrium business cycle models in which decisions are made under uncertainty.

Shackle (1938) in fact presented two theories of the cycle. One is a theory, closely related to the work of Schumpeter, in which a bunching of innovatory investment initiates a cycle in which the income–expenditure multiplier and induced investment also figure prominently as a result of the interdependence of sectors of the economy. The other is an attempt to develop the General Theory's insights using what Shackle calls Swedish sequence analysis. The General Theory had concentrated on explaining underfull employment equilibrium. It had not proceeded to develop a dynamic theory of the cycle, though Keynes believed that he had laid the foundations for one by developing Kahn's income–expenditure multiplier idea.

In 1936, fired by the Myrdallian idea of *ex ante* and *ex post* and a belief in the vital role of expectations, Shackle tore up a year's work on the Austrian theory of capital and began to study the new (post-General Theory) Keynesianism in the light of the new Wicksellianism. The resulting doctoral thesis formed the basis of Shackle (1938). Shackle did not regard the two theories contained therein as being mutually exclusive.

Shackle viewed Keynesesque multiplier–accelerator theory as retrograde because it incorrectly attempted to replace the concept of an equilibrium point with an equilibrium trend or cycle and to dispense with the use of outside influences to explain the cycle. However, in a stochastic world, which Shackle clearly believed in, nonlinearities are required to generate an endogenous cycle. What Shackle was probably trying to highlight with the above observation was that the essence of the General Theory was the instability of investment that resulted from its dependence on unexplainable expectational variables. He stressed that Keynes's system was essentially open in the sense that it was subject to both exogenous shocks and internal shocks which affected functions and parameters. The investment decision was regarded as nonrational (not irrational) because of its dependence on expected profits and the unknowable future, even to the extent that investment can be expressed as a function of the interest rate. Shackle noted that the rate of interest itself is a function of the expected interest rate (1967, p.247) because of the speculative motive for holding money. The General Theory itself, Shackle observed, has little to say about how expectations are formed under uncertainty, regarding them as a free autonomous variable.

Shackle concentrates on investment as the key to understanding the business cycle and stresses the importance of expectations formation under uncertainty as an influence on investment decisions. In this respect his work is consistently Myrdallian. It is a world where:

> People must find out, compare and decide before they act; then register results and make fresh plans and decisions. (1967, p.270)

Shackle's Schumpeterian theory is based on the bunching of innovations and its impact via the income–expenditure multiplier. Shackle observes that businessmen are less confident and exact in their expectations following a large scale change wrought by a major investment. Past experience provides little guidance and consequently, following a new investment, businessmen need a learning period to explain new possibilities and develop new plans. In this period they are essentially involved in ensuring that the new system is managed efficiently. Monetary influences are also important. Having undertaken new investment, firms will be highly geared and face financial constraints on further expansion. Individual businesses are, therefore, likely to show alternating periods of growth and constancy of physical equipment, an improvement phase being followed by a testing phase. If the phases of the majority of businesses 'cluster' then cyclical variation of aggregate investment will follow. To explain the clustering, Shackle invokes the interaction of multiplier and induced investment. The latter is not based on a fixed coefficient accelerator, which Shackle rejects as unrealistic, but is influenced by input–output interaction. The clustering of investment activity leads to a rise in construction costs and the price of capital which eventually chokes off the boom.

Shackle believed his Myrdallian theory to be more interesting. Following a rise in autonomous investment, perhaps due to a burst of innovatory investment, there is a multiplier-based expansion leading to induced investment which has further multiplier effects and so on. The process can only continue, Shackle argues, as long as the multiplier effect is unexpected, for once it comes to be expected net investment will have reached a maximum because there will be no further unexpected increase in aggregate income to induce an increase in it. The failure of net investment to accelerate will eliminate the multiplier effect and, with growth reduced, investment will fall and a downswing will ensue. The whole cycle is explained by changes in expectations which are generated continuously by the effects of former changes. Investment is again the key variable. The multiplier-induced expansion, which follows the rise in autonomous investment, causes an unexpected improvement in business outlook and induces a further increase in investment. The accelerator effect therefore does not mechanistically depend on the capital–output ratio, as did Harrod's (1936) 'Relation', but is the consequence of business psychology.

Even though Shackle is not seeking a fully endogenous theory of the cycle, he states:

> The business cycle is much more akin to fatigue than to disease in that it is not an exceptional or accidental occurrence but part of the nature of a modern industrial economy. (1938, p.5)

The theory is, however, endogenous in the sense that the most important shocks are the internal ones that lead to shifts in businessmen's psychology, rather than the external or exogenous shocks that drive Frisch–Slutsky-type cycle models.

Shackle's Schumpeterian theory is based on the idea that there is a 'leaping fountain' of investment opportunities due to a continuous stream of inventions which provide innovatory opportunities. At some point some entrepreneurs will act to take advantage of these opportunities because of a shift in their expected profitability. Once autonomous investment increases the multiplier comes into play and causes bunching and the cycle follows. There does seem to be a risk that the cycle could stick at the floor for some time if expectations concerning profitability remain depressed. The Wicksellian theory requires an initial rise in autonomous investment and, to the extent that this is a result of a burst of innovatory investment, the two theories can be integrated. Shackle is more optimistic than Keynes, who sees a 'stagnating pool' of investment opportunities (Keynes 1936, Ch.17). There may, however, be some stagnation in times of recession, when pessimism prevails, and this may lead to a protracted depression.

Expanding on his theory, Shackle identifies two types of industry: one producing consumption goods and the other investment equipment. The expansion phase is initiated by a shift in expectations leading to investment. Workers are taken on, consumption expenditure rises and there is a multiplier effect. This leads to induced investment by the consumption industries and a secondary multiplier effect and then to increased demand for the products of the equipment industries and induced investment by them. A third multiplier effect results and so on. In the Schumpeterian theory the upswing ends when the price of capital rises as a result of bunching and the process goes into reverse, causing a downswing. Alternatively the multiplier loses its impact once it comes to be expected, as in the Wicksellian theory.

Shackle postulates that the downswing is unlikely to witness an equiproportional decrease in the activity of the equipment and consumption industries because a Duesenberry-type ratchet effect will prevent consumption falling as fast as income. Investment will, therefore, fall more rapidly than consumption. He notes that because of the ratchet effect the expansion and contraction phases are likely to be asymmetric. Shackle therefore identified, at an early stage, the importance of nonlinearities for explaining the observed asymmetry of business cycles (see also section 1.3).

As the recession persists two processes are ongoing. Entrepreneurs are gradually overcoming the disappointment of their expectations in previous crises, and foreseen and unforeseen events are changing their economic outlook. To the extent that they influence business outlook, the unforeseen events or external shocks play a role in Shackle's theory. With the accumulation of new apparent opportunities and the return of the desire to exploit them there is an increase in investment and the recovery gets under way. The foreseeable events include demographic changes, improvements in infrastructure, and innovation. The unforeseeable events include political crises, disasters and windfalls, and inventions. Inventions are seen as the primary source of the fountain of continually changing opportunities. Shackle identifies two types of invention: new consumables and technology changes.

Shackle's integrated Schumpeterian–Wicksellian theory, therefore, consists of a boom generated by the interaction of induced investment with the income–expenditure multiplier and the clustering of inventions. It comes to an end as the price of capital rises due to the clustering, the most profitable investment opportunities are exhausted, and the multiplier comes to be expected. The interaction of the multiplier and induced investment, through input–output interaction, can explain the clustering. The Wicksellian theory, Shackle feels, needs help to explain the upturn, while the Schumpeterian theory may need help to explain the downturn. The integration of theories helps to overcome their weaknesses.

Shackle concludes by presenting a number of alternative (to the consumer-expenditure ratchet effect) explanations of asymmetry. One is based on the idea that the marginal propensity to consume will decline during the boom and that as the peak approaches the multiplier will be small for increases in income but large for decreases, with the reverse holding in the trough. Another explanation revolves around the behaviour of the banking system which will have a strong incentive to reduce its outstanding loans when the boom busts. As a consequence banks are likely to raise their interest rates and put pressure on debtors to reduce their expenditure. This will further discourage investment. The boom starts with a return of courage and desire for entrepreneurial activity. During the depression, technical progress will have rendered some capital obsolescent. The equipment industries will initially have spare capacity and the supply of capital goods will be elastic. Individuals will have increased their monetary balances as a result of the speculative motive and banks will be looking for lending opportunities. Credit will, therefore, be cheap and the price of capital will be low and expected to remain so, at least in the short run, and modernisation will be required. Cumulative recovery and boom, based initially on cheap bank credit pending the issue of new securities, can therefore be expected.

4.5 GOODWIN'S MACRODYNAMICS

Goodwin[19] explores similar ground to Shackle (1938). In so doing he employs modern mathematical techniques to develop ideas which he had previously explored[20] using more primitive mathematical tools. Influences on Goodwin's work include Keynes, Harrod, Schumpeter, Sraffa, von Neumann, Kalecki and Marx. The result is a magisterial attempt to analyse the process of capitalist economic development.

Goodwin adopts a multi-sectoral approach in order to emphasise the high degree of interdependence of various sectors of the economy, which he views as a 'system' in the sense that it is a structure in which the interaction of the parts is as important as the nature of each part. Further, it is a system which is continuously changing, although not at a uniform rate, and which is inherently nonlinear. This creates a problem because it is not currently possible to solve a general n-equation system of nonlinear equations. It is difficult enough to solve systems of two or three nonlinear equations and Goodwin notes that limit cycle theorems cease to hold when there are more than two equations. Linear approximations must therefore be employed, but this need not be too damaging if linearisation is done with caution, Goodwin argues. He is not therefore advocating general linearisation and accepts that, as a result of the approximation, his results have limited validity. They will only be applicable in the short run, rather than the long run: which, in the tradition of Keynes and Kalecki, is regarded as a series of short runs.

Goodwin draws attention to the inability of linear models to explain the generation of limit cycles (see section 2.3). In spite of this, he demonstrates that piecewise linear analysis can be employed to explain the existence and persistence of oscillations. He provides an illustrative example in which a two-sector model has two distinct regimes, one stable and one unstable, and shows that such a system can generate a limit cycle.[21] Although piecewise linear, the overall model essentially contains type I nonlinearities[22] because there are bifurcation points at which qualitative changes in economic behaviour occur with movements from stable to unstable regimes.

Goodwin's method of analysis is then to apply systems theory to multi-sectoral macroeconomic models to facilitate analysis of qualitative changes in the behaviour of economic models. Catastrophe theory and the theory of bifurcations[23] are employed to explain why the economy moves between qualitatively different regimes and to examine the effects of moving backwards and forwards between such regimes. To make use of catastrophe theory (see section 2.3), the piecewise linear systems include variables with fast and slow adjustment speeds.

The general objective of Goodwin's analysis is to develop the observation of Marx and Schumpeter that capitalism grows in fits and starts. He argues that the driving force of the evolutionary dynamics of the capitalist economic system is the relentless search for profit. The Schumpeterian view that innovation is the root cause of cyclical growth is viewed as central to the understanding of dynamic economic development or the evolution of the economy. The continuous drive for profits forces technical change but the morphology is not smooth. Rather than through steady growth, the economy evolves by way of a series of rapid expansions followed by recessions, and occasionally depressions.

Goodwin argues that the major constraints on economic growth are the inputs that cannot be produced by the economy, namely 'labour' and 'land', and that until now the 'land' constraint has not been binding. The rate of extraction of raw materials has proved to be fairly elastic, and synthetic substitutes have often been produced as part of the innovatory process. The binding constraint has usually, therefore, been the size of the working population. Goodwin discusses the possibility that the land constraint may become binding in the future if a concerted attempt is made to eliminate the unemployment that has persisted in the 1980s by stimulating significantly faster growth. In his model this could be brought about by an increase in government expenditure. The sustained high level of unemployment might reflect, he feels, the widespread adoption of computer- and robot-based technology. In the same way that innovatory investment has enabled production of synthetic substitutes for raw materials, it has now made a major breakthrough in replacing human brain and muscle power and co-ordination.

The coefficients of the technology matrix employed in his multi-sectoral analysis may have changed substantially from those prevailing in previous periods, to which his analysis is perhaps more applicable. An alternative view is that Goodwin's assumption that the growth of the working population is steady is unrealistic and that a fluctuation in population growth contributed significantly to the rise in unemployment in the 1970s and 1980s. Under this view it is perfectly possible that the labour constraint will reassert itself, as it appeared to be doing, especially where skilled labour is concerned, in a number of OECD countries towards the end of the 1980s following a sustained period of growth. It is also likely that population growth itself is influenced by economic growth.

Goodwin's analysis is based on the assumption that growth is unstable in an upward direction in the sense that, once started, the expansion phase develops into a boom period of exponential growth. The exponential growth reduces the reserve army of the unemployed, which is the available trained and disciplined workforce not currently employed. The fall in unemployment leads to an excess demand for labour, which encourages firms to bid up wages and bestows greater bargaining power upon the trade unions. Once the labour constraint begins to bite, the rise in real wages will lead to a reduction in profits. Firms will explore cost reducing, labour saving innovatory investment opportunities. Nevertheless, growth will eventually slow and the optimistic expectations, on the basis of which the investment was undertaken, will be disappointed. The upper turning point will have been reached and declining aggregate demand and output will lead to recession and a decline in employment. The boom is thus terminated as the growing economy bumps up against a Hicksian ceiling imposed by labour shortages (see Hicks 1950).

The rise in unemployment leads to a reduction in the rate of growth of wages and it is assumed that labour saving investment will continue in an effort to reduce labour inputs and restore profitability. The possibility of getting stuck in a depression is acknowledged and it is stressed that the problem of explaining the lower turning point is harder than that of explaining the upper one. But if the stimulus of autonomous innovatory investment proves insufficient to lead the economy out of the depression, then Goodwin feels that the government has the option of expanding autonomous expenditure by increasing its own expenditure. Goodwin does, however, assume that autonomous innovatory investment will generally lead the economy out of a recession and essentially provide a Hicksian floor (Hicks 1950). The cycle model described is clearly also related to the Goodwin (1967) model (see section 2.3), which examines the symbiosis of capital and labour, and to the Kalecki (1943) model, which has spawned a literature on political business cycles.[24] Kalecki considers how the state might be expected to behave in a capitalist system. In Kalecki's model its role is essentially to ensure that the 'reserve army' remains disciplined and prepared for work. This is done by allowing booms to be terminated, rather than sustaining them using Keynesian policies, and attenuating slumps by stimulating demand. Developing these ideas, Boddy and Crotty (1975) have pointed out that periodic employment of members of the reserve army is essential to prevent loss of skills, just as periodic unemployment is necessary to maintain discipline. This would imply that the long-term unemployed of the 1980s have effectively ceased to be members of the reserve army and have become an 'underclass' of unemployables instead. This may explain why high unemployment levels appear to have little influence on wage bargaining while the rate of change of unemployment has a more significant impact. According to this view, governments may have found it necessary to encourage a sustained increase in unemployment to discipline workers after the excesses of the 1970s and now need to introduce retraining schemes to bring the long-term unemployed back into the reserve army.

In Goodwin's model, the lower turning point occurs because even though profits are low and there is abundant excess capacity, innovatory investment will be spurred by the ceaseless search for increased profitability. He suggests that rather than being lumpy, as postulated by Schumpeter and Shackle, technical change may in fact progress fairly smoothly by virtue of being the result of many small independent events. Nevertheless, it is capable of giving rise to cyclical output growth. Innovatory investment in the slump may not be directed towards labour saving, as it is in the boom, but towards cost reduction and the creation of new products. Innovatory investment is regarded as the source of autonomous as opposed to induced investment; and because it is assumed to grow relatively smoothly, it effectively establishes a floor, in the Hicksian manner, and helps to explain the lower turning point. The size of the ensuing expansion will depend on the technological significance of the innovations. If they are of major importance, Goodwin postulates, then long waves may be generated. If they are of lesser importance, then they will not give such a large impetus to growth.

Thus Goodwin employs what he regards as Schumpeter's key insight: that new processes lower costs and restore profitability, even in conditions of excess capacity. He attaches less importance to the bunching of innovations, which Schumpeter and Shackle regard as so important. He attributes the apparent bunching to multiplier–accelerator interaction, which is analysed using a multi-sectoral model. The trend increase in autonomous innovatory investment leads to a change in the parameters of the technology matrix as well as an increase in the level of investment. Via input–output relationships and the interaction between consumption and investment, a matrix multiplier–accelerator interaction generates exponential growth. Using the multi-sectoral approach, he is able to formalise ideas that seem to underlie Shackle's (1938) description of the multiplier–accelerator interaction process.[25]

The multi-sectoral approach employed by Goodwin is a stark contrast to the market islands scenario discussed in section 2.2, but Goodwin does employ a Lucasian limited information assumption. Producers are assumed only to observe information in their own markets. Each market or sector, however, directly or indirectly depends on every other; therefore shocks to one sector will eventually affect all other sectors in the system. The transmission mechanism described by the input–output relationships can be regarded as fixed in the short run. All sectors will nevertheless change at different rates, though normally in the same direction, Goodwin argues. Because shocks are unlikely to hit the same set of sectors with the same magnitude twice and technological events will have changed in the improbable event that they do, economic development is likely to be highly irregular and historically unique. Thus the problem for analysts of economic dynamics is, Goodwin argues, to discover the response of a slowly changing structural system to a series of external shocks. This makes it particularly intractable and suggests that catastrophe theory might be a useful tool for the analysis of economic systems.

Goodwin's adoption of the multi-sectoral approach is enlightening and appears to be consistent with the model Shackle (1938) had in mind. His decision to model innovatory investment as a smooth trend, rather than as appearing in swarms as hypothesised by Schumpeter and Shackle, is consistent with the analysis of Hicks (1950) and Goodwin's earlier work on the business cycle. This is perhaps the least satisfactory aspect of his important contribution to the theory of dynamic economic development. In Shackle (1938), the bunching of innovatory investment is essentially a *deus ex machina*. Goodwin finds that it is unnecessary to use such a device in his more sophisticated multi-sectoral model. Neither Goodwin nor Shackle appears to get to grips with what Schumpeter was attempting to do. This was to explain how autonomous investment is generated. This and the wider issue of technological diffusion is being examined in the long swing literature. There is no space to review this literature here but clearly the insights employed by Goodwin, that diffusion can be described by changes in the coefficients of the technology matrix, must be developed further. It is simply not sufficient to assume that these changes occur smoothly, as if described by some simple time trend.

4.6 CONCLUDING REMARKS

Shackle therefore attempted to synthesise Keynes's insights into the implications of decision-making under uncertainty, especially with regard to investment, with ideas, normally associated with Schumpeter, concerning the effects of the bunching of innovations. He also considered the implications of nonlinearities, in the form of ratchet effects and an implied nonlinear consumption function, for the asymmetry of the cycle. Finally, he considered the implications of introducing a banking system into the model. His work could be extended using New Keynesian insights, such as wage contracts and implicit price contracts. The mechanism for the diffusion of innovations and the role of input–output interactions clearly require further examination. Long and Plosser (1983), and others working with real business cycle (RBC) models, have also begun to explore the implications of input–output interactions for the business cycle, while work on the diffusion of technical progress has so far been mainly associated with long-cycle analysis.[26] However, using a multi-sectoral model Goodwin and Punzo (1987) make a major contribution to the analysis of the role of technical change in dynamic economic development. Goodwin ignores the bunching of innovations stressed by Schumpeter and Shackle in explaining the lower turning point, and also the role of the financial sector in general and the banking sector in particular, although he acknowledges that financial instability may contribute to the upper turning point. There is, therefore, still some way to go, but they point us in the right direction.

By stressing the importance of real as opposed to monetary shocks, the RBC approach has neglected the role of the banking and the wider financial sector in cycle propagation. Lucas (1987) and Eichenbaum and Singleton (1986) have suggested a synthesis of real and monetary shock-induced equilibrium business cycle theories. The Keynesian econometric models of the 1960s and the early 1970s also tended to have underdeveloped monetary and financial sectors. Further work clearly needed to be done to develop a model in which money and banking played an important part in the propagation of cycles. Some progress has been made in modelling the monetary transmission mechanism since the mid-1970s and numerous non-Keynesian models have been developed, but the essential role of the financial sector in cycle generation is perhaps still not fully understood.

More generally, greater attention needs to be paid to the propagation model. The tendency has been to adopt the Frisch–Slutsky approach without question and, if the propagation model cannot generate realistic cycles from random impulses, to assume that the shocks are themselves serially correlated. Convincing explanations of why shocks should in fact generally be serially correlated have yet to be presented. This approach begs the question of whether an endogenous theory of the cycle, or a theory which at least relies less heavily on shocks, should be sought. The existing endogenous theories utilise nonlinearities but a systematic attempt to identify the nonlinearities that form the basis of such theories has not been undertaken. As Zarnowitz (1985) concludes, following a sifting of the evidence derived from confronting the various testable hypotheses with economic data, a synthesis of competing business cycle theories is required.

The synthesis model will have to be a structural one. It will, therefore, be necessary to move away from the quasi-reduced form vector-autoregressive models (VAMS) that have been prevalent in the literature since the mid-1970s. More complex econometric models, in the spirit of those abandoned in the face of the 'Lucas critique' (Lucas 1976) and Sims's (1980) warnings concerning 'incredible identification' restrictions, will have to be built. Such models will need to pay more attention to microfoundations than their predecessors and will perhaps incorporate

New Keynesian insights and sectoral analysis based on input–output relationships. They will also need to pay more attention to the role of money and the modelling of the banking and financial sector and its interaction with the other sectors. Additionally they should exploit the profession's improved understanding of time series analysis. The over-identifying exclusion restrictions should be analytically and empirically justified. Finally, the models should aim to explain dynamic economic development as a combined process of growth and the business and perhaps other cycles. In order to take account of the 'Lucas critique', the game-theoretic context of economic decision-making will need to be given further consideration[27] and the implications of the uncertain environment for decision-making will have to be considered further. In the presence of uncertainty, as opposed to risk, the rational expectations hypothesis is inadequate (see section 2.1) and alternative expectations formation mechanisms and their implications must be considered.

Finally, developments in the field of open economy macroeconomics[28] must be acknowledged in the modelling of dynamic economic development. It is widely accepted that the world's economies are becoming increasingly interdependent and that the greater capital mobility permitted since the early 1970s has accelerated this process. There seems to be a growing international synchronisation of cycles among OECD countries and this has major implications for North–South relationships. In the pre-war period there was also evidence of an increased synchronisation of cycles. In the post-war period there was little evidence of synchronisation but it has emerged again since the early 1970s.[29] The causes and implications of this require further investigation. Eichengreen and Portes (1987) have made a start by attempting to identify the most important international linkages and the major similarities and differences between the 1920s and 1930s and the 1970s and 1980s. The re-emergence of synchronisation appears to have been combined with the return of the 'classical' business cycle, in place of the 'growth cycles' of the 1960s,[30] and a decline in the growth rate. This suggests a clear link between cycles and growth which requires further investigation. An explanation of why shifts in the revealed statistical growth trend occur from period to period is also required. Students of long cycles may well have a contribution to make here.[31]

NOTES

1. See Rau (1974) for a survey of Keynesian business cycle literature. There is also a voluminous literature on Marxist and Marxian theories of economic crises and the cycle. See for example Kühne (1979, vol. II).

2. See Goodwin *et al.* (1984), which was discussed briefly in section 2.3, for recent attempts to utilise Goodwin's (1967) model as a basis for a Marxian model of dynamic economic development.
3. See Mullineux (1984, section 2.5) and Ichmura (1954).
4. See Mullineux (1984, section 2.5) and section 1.4.
5. See Mullineux (1984, section 2.5) for further discussion and a brief review of other contributions to the nonlinear business cycle literature.
6. See also Hickman (ed.) (1972).
7. See Bronfenbrenner (ed.) (1969), and section 1.5.
8. See Mullineux (1984, Ch. 3) for a discussion of these contributions.
9. See section 2.3 for a brief discussion.
10. The equilibrium business cycle models normally assume rational expectations formation in an environment subject to risk, rather than uncertainty, in the sense of Knight (1921).
11. See Goodwin and Punzo (1987, p.130).
12. The term 'new combinations' is used by Schumpeter to cover not only the formation of new firms to produce new products but also the opening up of new markets, in the geographical sense, *inter alia*. See Schumpeter (1934, p.66).
13. See for example Abramovitz (1964), Kuznets (1937), Kondratieff (1935), Garvy (1943), Isard (1942) and Lewis and O'Leary (1955).
14. See Adelman (1960).
15. Railroad bond yields, deflated clearings, pig-iron production, railroad stock prices, shares traded, call money rates and freight car orders.
16. See, for example, Bodkin (1969), Lucas (1973), Barro (1978), Sargent (1978), Taylor (1979), Hall (1980) and Kydland and Prescott (1980), who all use residuals from linear or quadratic time trends as the basis of their analyses.
17. According to formulae due to Wichern (1973).
18. See section 2.3 and Mullineux (1984, Ch.2).
19. In Goodwin and Punzo (1987).
20. See Mullineux (1984, section 2.5).
21. See also Klein and Preston (1969), who use a piecewise linear system to proxy Kaldor's (1940) nonlinear trade cycle model, which is discussed in Mullineux (1984, section 2.5).
22. See section 1.4 and Mullineux (1984, section 2.5).
23. See Goodwin and Punzo (1987, pp.377–83).
24. See Mullineux (1984, section 3.3).
25. See also Shackle (1967, Ch.17).
26. See for example Metcalfe (1984).
27. See Mullineux (1984, Ch.5), Rogoff (1987) and Tabellini (1987) for further discussion.
28. See for example Dornbusch (1980).
29. See Zarnowitz (1985, pp. 530 and 532).
30. At least in the 1970s and early 1980s, although the subsequent sustained expansion since the early 1980s recession, particularly in the United Kingdom and the United States, has again cast doubt upon this.
31. See Freeman (1984), Van Duijn (1983), Goldstein (1988) and Solomou (1987), for example.

5 · THE UNFINISHED RESEARCH AGENDA

There are a number of important questions about business cycles which remain to be answered conclusively. They include the following:
1. Are there long cycles coexisting with the business cycle? If there are, then the practice of treating business cycles as 'growth cycles' (i.e. fluctuations around a linear or log linear growth trend) will be misleading. This practice is also dubious if the trend itself is stochastic or nonlinear, as noted in section 4.3.2.
2. Is the cycle endogenously or exogenously generated or, alternatively, what are the relative roles of the economic propagation mechanism and exogenous and internal shocks in cycle generation?
3. Have major structural, institutional or policy changes, or shocks, made it necessary to analyse business cycles pertaining to different historical periods separately?
4. Is the business cycle real or monetary in origin, or is it caused by a complex interplay of real and monetary factors?
5. Is the cycle the result of the process of capitalist development?
6. What role has the growth of the government sector, which may be seen as a natural result of capitalist development, played in attenuating, and perhaps even generating, post-war cycles?
7. Are there key nonlinearities in the economic system or can linear propagation models be employed for cycle analysis?

The major conclusions of the 1967 conference, reviewed in section 1.5, were that post-war cycles had become 'growth cycles' and were different in nature from pre-war cycles. It was also accepted that as a result of alternation between inflation and unemployment policies, in response to political considerations, governments had aggravated cycles but that stabilisation policy was feasible and may have been responsible for the change in the nature of the cycle in the post-war period.

The conference papers reported in Hickman (ed.) (1972) aimed to test the cyclical properties of quarterly models of the US economy. There was some testing of whether cycles were endogenous or exogenous, but it was of limited scope since all the competing hypotheses were really based on the Frisch I or the Slutsky hypothesis (see section 1.4). There was no systematic testing of endogenous cycle theories. The only business cycle theory incorporated in the essentially Keynesian models reflected multiplier–accelerator interaction and inventory considerations and, therefore, concentrated on the goods market. Despite the presence of nonlinear parameter restrictions, there were no major functional (type II) nonlinearities or 'billiard table' (type I) nonlinearities[1] in the models. The systematic econometric testing of cycle theories envisaged by Tinbergen (1942) and Koopmans (1947) was not evident in the papers in Hickman (ed.) (1972). No attempt was made to incorporate alternative cycle hypotheses into the models and test their validity. Tinbergen (1942, p.129) believed that the ultimate scope of econometric testing of cycle theories:

> . . . would be that we could state for any theory: (1) whether or not it is in accordance with the facts; and (2) if it were true, to what extent it explains the course of events. The decision that a theory is true can only be taken on economic arguments, but provided that the statistician has not found it to be contrary to the facts. That decision once taken, the statistician may again take over the job and tell (c.f. point (2) above) to what extent it influences the course of events.

Given the nascent state of the art of econometrics, Tinbergen was unable to achieve his ideal. With the larger amount of data available, the higher technical ability of the profession, the much improved computer capabilities and the larger number of competing hypotheses, the time has now come to attempt what Tinbergen suggested. The approach advocated by Tinbergen (1951) was to set up cycle-generating models for each sector of the economy and to link them in an overall model. It would then be possible to see if the sectoral models were in accordance with the facts and measure the contribution to cyclical variation of each sector.

The Hickman (ed.) (1972) conference papers were lacking in this respect because the models were taken as adequate and concentration was trained on the required external influences to generate cycles that mimicked those observed. Random shocks did not do the job in most cases but autoregressive (AR) shocks did. This set a dangerous precedent because it looked to exogenous cycle generation without adequate testing of endogenous cycle theories. Further, AR shocks are difficult to interpret without a coherent theory of shock generation, which was not presented. Despite the fact that the AR shocks might represent misspecification errors, the approach, if followed to its conclusion, would lead us to search for the shock generation process that provided the best simulations, taking the propagation model as correct. The analysis would be purely statistical and would not advance our understanding of the economy. In the absence of good a priori reasons to expect AR shocks, it is likely that the AR shocks are the result of misspecification and indicate the need to improve model specification and our understanding of the economy. The other question touched upon at the conference was that of the role of exogenous variables in cycle generation.

The 1970 conference, reviewed in section 1.5, confirmed that business cycles were not obsolete but had changed to 'growth cycles' in the postwar period. Methods of measuring growth cycles were proposed and the forecasting and simulation results were consistent with the findings of Bronfenbrenner (ed.) (1969) and Hickman (ed.) (1972) and were derived in a similar manner to those reported in Hickman. There was no evidence of systematic testing of cycle theories.

If the need to incorporate AR shocks to simulate realistic cycles is interpreted as symptomatic of a misspecification of the lag structure, then one of two routes can be followed to improve the lag specification: further theoretical analysis; or use of data-based techniques. The latter approach was foreseen by Griliches (1967), who noted that such an approach would ask an awful lot of the data. Further, Boch, Yancey and Judge (1973a, b) warn against the biases resulting from repeated testing from the same data base. Nevertheless, this is essentially the approach taken by users of VAR models in the 1980s.

The 1984 conference, reviewed in section 1.5, tried to identify the causes of the post-war changes in the US business cycle. Attempts were made to identify the major sources and the nature of shocks and to gauge the impact of institutional, structural and policy changes. Particular attention was paid to the impacts of the growth in the proportion of government expenditure in GNP, automatic stabilisers and discretionary demand management policy. Generally, it updated information on the themes that occupied the 1967 and 1970 conferences while drawing attention to the importance of supply side shocks since the early 1970s. The Frisch–Slutsky view of a cycle driven by shocks remained unchallenged, and the abandonment of essentially linear large scale econometric models in favour of linear VAR models was illustrated by the fact that the results in only one paper were derived from a large scale econometric model.

The role of nonlinearity has largely been ignored because the size of the large quarterly econometric models of the 1970s encouraged the minimisation of problems arising from nonlinearity. The subsequently popular VAR models in turn assume linearity in order to make use of linear time series techniques. Nonlinear techniques have, however, advanced and the problem of nonlinear estimation is no longer so forbidding.

Blatt (1978) expresses concern about the econometric procedures that have been used to test the cycle specification of econometric models. He notes that because the models tested[2] are essentially linear in variables, the type of deterministic solution is severely restricted and if any cycles are produced at all, they are likely to be damped or explosive. In the linear deterministic case the third possibility is that a conservative oscillation will result, but this becomes explosive when shocks are introduced. Blatt (1986) notes that the range of possibilities is greater for nonlinear models and argues that nonlinearities are strongly indicated by the finding of asymmetry between expansion and contraction phases of the cycle,[3] which cannot be explained by stable models that are linear in deviations from trend regardless of the size or the autocorrelation properties of the shocks to the model. Blatt (1978) argues that following past econometric testing, it has been accepted that the economy is stable and the cycle must be generated by exogenous processes. There are a number of possibilities. Oscillations could be forced. Damped cycles could be produced by the propagation model and kept alive by random shocks. Finally there could be monotonic damped adjustment which converts shocks into a recurrent, but not precisely periodic, oscillation. He believes that such a view has conditioned the methods of testing and he shows some errors that can result.

Blatt (1978) considers a Hicks-type (Hicks 1950) nonlinear deterministic model with type I nonlinearities, in the form of ceilings and floors. A best fit for a linearised version of the model is derived using standard econometric techniques. Simulation experiments with the estimated model reveal it to be stable and yet the data used to estimate the linearised model was generated by the nonlinear model with assumed parameter values imposed to ensure that it generated an exact periodic cycle. Further, the nonlinear model was shown to be highly unstable. Thus Blatt started with a completely deterministic model which is highly unstable and fitted a stable linear model, in which the economy is driven through the cycle by random shocks. Blatt (1978, pp.298-9) identifies the basic source of the result as the substitution of a linear for a nonlinear equation and argues that:

> ... mathematically any linear (or nearly linear) model is fundamentally different from essentially nonlinear models. Introduce as many endogenous or exogenous variables as you wish; introduce as complicated a lag structure as can be imagined – it makes no difference. If the structural equations are linear (or nearly so), then results similar to the ones of our calculation must emerge.

Thus existing tests, in disallowing nonlinearities, are failing to consider a large and growing number of cycle hypotheses,[4] and linear econometric techniques applied to linear formulations in a nonlinear world are likely to arrive at incorrect conclusions. Nonlinear specifications should be allowed to compete on an equal basis in the testing of business cycle theories.

Verdoorn and Post (1964) provide one of the few tests of nonlinear cycle theory. Concentrating on labour as the limiting factor, they test for the existence and effects of a ceiling in the Dutch economy. They note that introducing a ceiling implies the introduction of curvilinearity into what may otherwise be a linear model, because a ceiling usually foreshadows its existence before output has reached its maximum. A continuous curvilinear relationship is, therefore, postulated and a double log transformation is selected from three alternatives considered. With the nonlinearity included, their model displays damped oscillations in expenditure variables. Cyclical fluctuations are more pronounced for value variables and prices, for which the dampening of cyclical movements takes longer. The introduction of nonlinearity, therefore, resulted in damped oscillations in the propagation model but not in a self-sustaining limit cycle (see section 2.3).

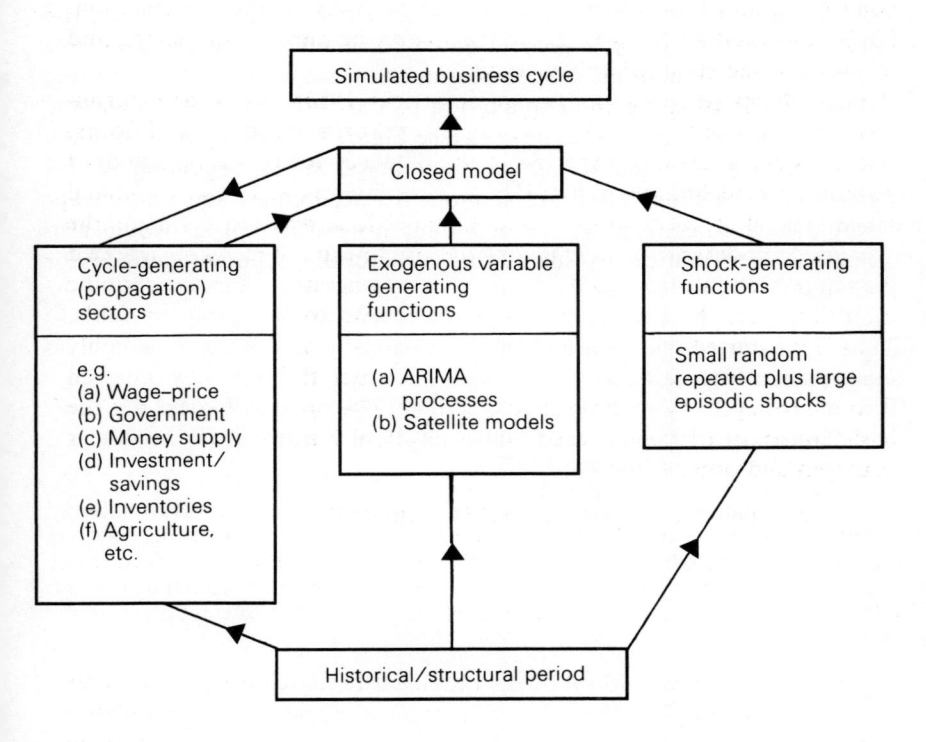

Figure 5.1 An iterative approach to business cycle modelling

The broad conclusion is that despite the increasing sophistication of the econometric and time series techniques used for analysing economic time series, very few of the cycle hypotheses implicit in the business cycle literature have been formulated and adequately tested. Too many things have been allowed to vary at once or have been precluded from testing by the linearity hypothesis. The linearity assumption may also have clouded the picture by encouraging (log) linear trend fitting and the separation of business cycle and growth analysis.

The previous discussion suggests an approach to modelling which can be outlined as follows. The model of the macroeconomy should be broken down into its main structural sectors, and shock-generating and exogenous variable generating models should be appended. The exogenous variables may themselves be cyclical or subject to shocks and might best be modelled using ARIMA generating processes or satellite models. The choice of structural sectors would be guided by the block recursive features of the model and particular attention should be paid to the potential cycle-propagating features, indicated by the theoretical business cycle literature, of each sector. As suggested by Tinbergen (1939), the different theories of cycle generation could then be tested using various combinations of alternative specifications of these sectors and evaluating their contributions to the explanation of the variance in the economic time series. Using such a framework (see Figure 5.1), an attempt could be made to answer some of the questions posed at the beginning of this chapter. Both time series and econometric techniques and approaches would have roles to play, and economic historical analysis would also make a contribution by identifying structurally different periods for analysis.

NOTES

1. See sections 1.4 and 2.3 and Mullineux (1984, Ch. 2).
2. Such as those in Hickman (1972).
3. See section 1.3 for further discussion.
4. See section 2.3 and Mullineux (1984, section 2.5).

REFERENCES

Abramovitz, M. (1961), Statement in *Hearings Before the Joint Economic Committee of the Congress of the United States*, 66th Congress, 1st Session, Part 2, pp. 141-66.
Abramovitz, M. (1964), *Evidences of Long Swings in Aggregate Construction Since the Civil War*, National Bureau of Economic Research, New York: Columbia University Press.
Adelman, I. (1960), 'Business cycles – endogenous or stochastic', *Economic Journal*, 70 (Dec), pp. 783-96.
Adelman, I. (1965), 'Long cycles: fact or artifact?', *American Economic Review*, 55 (June), pp. 444-63.
Adelman, I. and Adelman, F. L. (1959), 'Dynamic properties of the Klein-Goldberger model', *Econometrica*, 27 (4), pp. 597-625.
Aftalion, A. (1927), 'The theory of economic cycles based on the capitalist technique of production', *Review of Economics and Statistics*, 10 (Oct), pp. 165-70.
Alt, J. E. and Chrystal, K. A. (1983), *Political Economics*, Berkeley: University of California Press.
Altman, E. I. and Sametz, A. W. (eds.) (1977), *Financial Crises: Institutions and markets in a fragile environment*, New York: Wiley.
Anderson, E. E. (1977), 'Further evidence on the Monte Carlo cycle in business activity', *Economic Inquiry*, 16, pp. 269-76.
Azariadis, C. (1981), 'Self-fulfilling prophecies', *Journal of Economic Theory*, 25, pp. 380-96.
Backus, D. and Driffill, J. (1985a), 'Inflation and reputation', *American Economic Review*, 75 (3), pp. 530-8.
Backus, D. and Driffill, J. (1985b), 'Rational expectations and policy credibility following a change of regime', *Review of Economic Studies*, 52, pp. 211-21.
Balducci, R., Candella, G. and Ricci, G. (1984), 'A generalisation of R. Goodwin's model with rational behaviour of economic agents', pp. 47-66 in R. M. Goodwin *et al.* (eds.), *Nonlinear Models of Fluctuating Growth*, New York: Springer-Verlag.
Bank for International Settlements (1986), *Recent Innovations in International Banking*, Basle.
Bank of England (1971), *Competition and Credit Control*, May, London: Bank of England. Reprinted in *Bank of England Quarterly Bulletin*, 11 (June), pp. 189-93.
Bank of England (1978), 'The secondary banking crises and the Bank of

England's support operations', *Bank of England Quarterly Bulletin*, 18 (2), pp. 149-59, London.
Barclay, C. (1978), 'Competition and financial crises – past and present', in J. Revell (ed.), *Competition and Regulation of Banks*, Bangor Occasional Papers in Economics, No. 14, Cardiff: University of Wales Press.
Barro, R. J. (1976), 'Rational expectations and the role of monetary policy', *Journal of Monetary Economics*, 2 (1), pp. 1-32, reprinted in Barro (1981).
Barro, R. J. (1978), 'Unanticipated money, output, and the price level in the United States', *Journal of Political Economy*, 86, pp. 549-80.
Barro, R. J. (1981), *Money Expectations and Business Cycles*, New York: Academic Press.
Barro, R. J. (1986), 'Comment', *Macroeconomics Annual*, 1, National Bureau of Economic Research, pp. 135-9, Cambridge, Mass.: MIT Press.
Barro, R. J. and Gordon, D. B. (1983a), 'A positive theory of monetary policy in a natural rate model', *Journal of Political Economy*, 91 (4), pp. 584-610.
Barro, R. J. and Gordon, D. B. (1983b), 'Rules, discretion and reputation in a model of monetary policy', *Journal of Monetary Economics*, 12 (July), pp. 101-25.
Barro, R. J. and Grossman, H. (1976), *Money, Employment and Inflation*, Cambridge: Cambridge University Press.
Black, F. (1970), 'Banking and interest in a world without money', *Journal of Bank Research*, Autumn, pp. 9-20, reprinted in Black (1987).
Black, F. (1982), 'General equilibrium and business cycles', National Bureau of Economic Research Working Paper No. 950, August, reprinted in Black (1987).
Black, F. (1987), *Business Cycles and Equilibrium*, Oxford: Basil Blackwell.
Blanchard, O. J. and Watson, M. W. (1982), 'Bubbles, rational expectations and financial markets', pp. 295-316 (Ch. 11) in P. Wachtel (ed.), *Crises in the Economic and Financial Structure*, Lexington, Mass.: Lexington Books.
Blanchard, O. J. and Watson, M. W. (1986), 'Are business cycles all alike?', in R. J. Gordon (ed.), *The American Business Cycle*, National Bureau of Economic Research, Chicago: University of Chicago Press.
Blatt, J. M. (1978), 'On the econometric approach to business cycle modelling', *Oxford Economic Papers*, 30 (2), pp. 292-300.
Blatt, J. M. (1980), 'On the Frisch model of business cycles', *Oxford Economic Papers*, 32 (3), pp. 467-79.
Blinder, A. S and Fischer, S. (1981), 'Inventories, rational expectations and the business cycle', *Journal of Monetary Economics*, 8, pp. 277-304.
Boch, M. E., Yancey, T. A. and Judge, G. C. (1973a), 'The statistical consequences of preliminary test estimation in regression', *Journal of the American Statistical Association*, 68 (341), pp. 109-16.
Boch, M. E., Yancey, T. A. and Judge, G. C. (1973b), 'Some comments on estimates in regressions after preliminary tests of significance', *Journal of Econometrics*, 1 (2), pp. 191-200.
Boddy, R. and Crotty, J. (1975), 'Class conflict and macro-policy: the political business cycle', *Review of Radical Political Economics*, 7, pp. 1-19.
Bodkin, R. G. (1969), 'Real wages and cyclical variations in employment: an examination of the evidence', *Canadian Economic Journal*, 2, pp. 353-74.
Boschen, J. and Grossman, H. I. (1982), 'Tests of equilibrium macroeconomics using contemporaneous monetary data', *Journal of Monetary Economics*, 10 (Nov), pp. 309-34.
Box, G. E. P. and Jenkins, G. M. (1970), *Time Series Analysis: Forecasting and*

control, San Francisco, London: Holden-Day.
Bronfenbrenner, M. (ed.) (1969), *Is the Business Cycle Obsolete?*, New York: Wiley.
Brunner, K. and Meltzer, A. H. (1986), *The National Bureau Method, International Capital Mobility and Other Essays*, Carnegie-Rochester Conference Series on Public Policy 24, Amsterdam: North Holland.
Brunner, K. and Meltzer, A. H. (1987), *Bubbles and Other Essays*, Carnegie-Rochester Conference Series on Public Policy 26, Amsterdam: North Holland.
Burns, A. F. (1934), *Production Trends in the United States Since 1870*, New York: National Bureau of Economic Research.
Burns, A. F. (1960), 'Progress toward economic stability', *American Economic Review*, 30 (March), pp. 1–19.
Burns, A. F. and Mitchell, W. C. (1946), *Measuring the Business Cycle*, New York: National Bureau of Economic Research.
Carey, M. (1816), *Essays on Banking*, Philadelphia: M. Carey.
Chang, W. W. and Smyth, D. J. (1970), 'The existence and persistence of cycles in a nonlinear model: Kaldor's 1940 model re-examined', *Review of Economic Studies*, 38 (113), pp. 37–44.
Channon, D. F. (1977), *British Banking Strategy*, London: Macmillan.
Chiarella, C. (1986), 'Perfect foresight models and the dynamic instability problem from a higher viewpoint', *Economic Modelling*, October, pp. 283–92.
Clower, R. W. (1965), 'The Keynesian counter-revolution: a theoretical appraisal', in F. H. Hahn and F. Brechling (eds.), *The Theory of Interest Rates*, London: Macmillan.
Cooper, R. L. (1972), 'The predictive performance of quarterly econometric models of the United States', in B. G. Hickman (ed.), *Econometric Models of Cyclical Behaviour*, National Bureau of Economic Research, New York: Columbia University Press.
Cuckierman, A. (1986), 'Central bank behaviour and credibility: some recent theoretical developments', *Federal Reserve Bank of St Louis Review*, 68 (5), pp.5–17.
Dale, R. S. (1985), *The Regulation of International Banking*, Cambridge: Woodhead-Faulkner.
Dale, R. S. (1988), 'Financial regulation after the crash', *The Royal Bank of Scotland Review*, June (158), pp. 3–17.
Daly, D. J. (1972), 'Forecasting with statistical indicators', pp. 1159–207, in B. G. Hickman (ed.), *Econometric Models of Cyclical Behaviour*, 2, National Bureau of Economic Research, New York: Columbia University Press.
Day, R. H. (1982), 'Irregular growth cycles', *American Economic Review*, 72 (3), pp. 406–14.
De Leeuw (1972), 'Discussion', pp. 191–6, in B. G. Hickman (ed.), *Econometric Models of Cyclical Behaviour*, 1, National Bureau of Economic Research, New York: Columbia University Press.
De Long, J. B. and Summers, L. H. (1986a), 'Are business cycles symmetrical?', in R. J. Gordon (ed.), *The American Business Cycle*, National Bureau of Economic Research, Chicago: University of Chicago Press.
De Long, J. B. and Summers, L. H. (1986b), 'The changing cyclical variability of economic activity in the United States', in R. J. Gordon (ed.), *The American Business Cycle*, National Bureau of Economic Research, Chicago: University of Chicago Press.
Desai, M. (1973), 'Growth cycles and inflation in a model of class struggle',

Journal of Economic Theory, 6, pp. 527-45.
Desai, M. and Shah, A. (1981), 'Growth cycles and induced technical change', *Econometrica*, 91 (Dec), pp. 1006-10.
Deutsch, K. W. (1966), *The Nerves of Government*, London: Collier-Macmillan.
Diamond, D. and Dybvig, P. (1983), 'Bank runs, deposit insurance and liquidity', *Journal of Political Economy*, 91, pp. 401-19.
Di Matteo, M. (1984), 'Alternative monetary policies in a classical business cycle', pp. 14-24 in R. M. Goodwin *et al.* (eds.), *Nonlinear Models of Fluctuating Growth*, New York: Springer-Verlag.
Dornbusch, R. (1980), *Open Economy Macroeconomics*, New York: Basic Books.
Driscoll, M. J. and Ford, J. L. (1980), 'Real sector parameter instability and the optimal choice of monetary policy', *Journal of Macroeconomics*, 4 (3), pp. 339-48.
Duesenberry, J. (1949), *Income, Saving and the Theory of Consumer Behaviour*, Cambridge, Mass.: Harvard University Press.
Eckstein, O. (1983), *The DRI Model of the US Economy*, New York: McGraw-Hill.
Eckstein, O. and Sinai, A. (1986), 'The mechanisms of the business cycle in the postwar era', in R. J. Gordon (ed.), *The American Business Cycle*, National Bureau of Economic Research, Chicago: University of Chicago Press.
Eichenbaum, M. and Singleton, K. J. (1986), 'Do real business cycle theories explain postwar US business cycles?', *Macroeconomics Annual*, National Bureau of Economic Research, pp. 91-146, Cambridge, Mass.: MIT Press.
Eichengreen, B. and Portes, R. (1987), 'The anatomy of financial crises', pp. 10-58 (Ch. 1) in R. Portes and A. K. Svoboda (eds.), *Threats to International Financial Stability*, International Center for Monetary and Banking Studies and Centre for Economic Policy Research, Cambridge: Cambridge University Press.
Evans, M. K. (1967), *Macroeconomic Activity: Theory, forecasting and control*, New York, London: Harper & Row.
Fels, R. (1964), 'Summary of Schumpeter's theory of the business cycle', pp. 424-41 in J.A. Schumpeter, *Business Cycles: A theoretical, historical and statistical analysis of the capitalist process*, abridged ed., New York: McGraw-Hill.
Fischer, S. (1980), 'On activist monetary policy with rational expectations', pp. 211-38 (Ch. 7) in S. Fischer (ed.), *Rational Expectations and Economic Policy*, A Conference Report: National Bureau of Economic Research, Chicago and London: Chicago University Press.
Fisher, I. (1925), 'Our unstable dollar and the so-called business cycle', *Journal of the American Statistical Association*, June.
Fisher, I. (1930), *The Theory of Interest*, New York: Macmillan.
Fisher, I. (1932), *Booms and Depressions*, New York: Adelphi.
Fisher, I. (1933), 'The debt deflation theory of great depressions', *Econometrica*, 1 (4), pp. 337-57.
Flemming, J. S. (1982), 'Comment', pp. 39-41 in C. P. Kindleberger and J. P. Laffargue (eds.), *Financial Crises: Theory, history and policy*, Cambridge: Cambridge University Press.
Flood, R. P. and Garber, P. M. (1982), 'Bubbles, runs and gold monetization', pp. 275-94 (Ch. 10) in P. L. Wachtel (ed.), *Crises in the Economic and Financial Structure*, Lexington, Mass.: Lexington Books.
Ford, J. L. (1983), *Choice, Expectations and Uncertainty: An appraisal of G. L.*

S. *Shackle's theory*, Oxford: Martin Robertson.
Ford, J. L. (1987), *Economic Choice Under Uncertainty: A perspective theory approach*, Ledbury: Edward Elgar.
Freeman, C. (ed.) (1984), *Long Waves in the World*, London: Francis Pinter.
Frey, B. S. (1978), *Modern Political Economy*, Oxford: Martin Robertson.
Friedman, M. (1953), *Essays in Positive Economics*, Chicago: University of Chicago Press.
Friedman, M. (1957), *A Theory of the Consumption Function*, National Bureau of Economic Research General Series No. 63, Princeton: Princeton University Press.
Friedman, M. (1959), *A Program For Monetary Stability*, New York: Fordham University Press.
Friedman, M. (1968), 'The role of monetary policy', *American Economic Review*, 58 (1), pp. 1–17.
Friedman, M. and Schwartz, A. J. (1963a), *A Monetary History of the United States: 1867–1960*, National Bureau of Economic Research, Princeton: Princeton University Press.
Friedman, M. and Schwartz, A. J. (1963b), 'Money and business cycles', *Review of Economics and Statistics*, 45 (1), pp. 32–78.
Friedman, M. and Schwartz, A. J. (1982), *Monetary Trends in the US and the UK: 1867-1975*, National Bureau of Economic Research, Chicago, London: University of Chicago Press.
Frisch, R. (1933), 'Propagation and impulse problems in dynamic economics', in *Essays in Honour of Gustav Cassel*, London: George Allen & Unwin.
Frydman, R. and Phelps, E. S. (eds.) (1983), *Individual Forecasting and Aggregate Outcomes: 'Rational Expectations' examined*, Cambridge: Cambridge University Press.
Galbraith, J. K. (1954), *The Great Crash 1929*, London: Hamish Hamilton.
Garbade, K. D. (1982), 'Federal Reserve margin requirements: a regulatory initiative to inhibit speculative bubbles', pp. 317–36 (Ch. 12) in P. L. Wachtel (ed.), *Crises in the Economic and Financial Structure*, Lexington, Mass.: Lexington Books.
Garber, P. M. and King, R. G. (1983), 'Deep structural excavation? A critique of Euler equation methods', National Bureau of Economic Research, *NBER Technical Working Paper No. 31*.
Garvy, G. (1943), 'Kondratieff's theory of long cycles', *Review of Economics and Statistics*, 25, pp. 203–20.
Gilbert, R. A. and Wood, G. E. (1986), 'Coping with bank failures: some lessons from the United States and the United Kingdom', *Federal Reserve Bank of St Louis Review*, 68 (10), pp. 5–14.
Glombowski, J. and Krüger, M. (1984), 'Unemployment insurance and cyclical growth', pp. 25–46 in R. M. Goodwin *et al.*, *Nonlinear Models of Fluctuating Growth*, An International Symposium, Sienna, Italy, 24–27 March 1983, Berlin, New York: Springer-Verlag.
Goldsmith, R. W. (1982), 'Comment', pp. 41–3 in C. P. Kindleberger and J. P. Laffargue (eds.), *Financial Crises: Theory, history and policy*, Cambridge: Cambridge University Press.
Goldstein, J. S. (1988), *Long Cycles: Prosperity and war in the modern age*, New Haven, London: Yale University Press.
Goodhart, C. A. E. (1985), *The Evolution of Central Banks: A natural development?*, STICERD Occasional Paper No. 8, London: London School of

Economics and Political Science.
Goodwin, R. M. (1951), 'The non-linear accelerator and the persistence of business cycles', *Econometrica*, 19 (1), pp. 1-17.
Goodwin, R. M. (1955), 'A model of cyclical growth', in E. Lundberg (ed.), *The Business Cycle in the Post War World*, London: Macmillan.
Goodwin, R. M. (1967), 'A growth cycle', pp. 54-8 in C. H. Feinstein (ed.), *Socialism, Capitalism and Economic Growth*, Cambridge: Cambridge University Press.
Goodwin, R. M. (1984), 'Disaggregating models of fluctuating growth', pp. 67-72 in R. M. Goodwin *et al.* (1984).
Goodwin, R. M., Krüger, M. and Vercelli, A. (eds.) (1984), *Nonlinear Models of Fluctuating Growth*, An International Symposium, Sienna, Italy, 24-27 March 1983, Berlin, New York: Springer-Verlag.
Goodwin, R. M. and Punzo, L. F. (1987), *The Dynamics of a Capitalist Economy: A multi-sectoral approach*, Cambridge: Polity Press in association with Basil Blackwell.
Gordon, R. J. (ed.) (1986), *The American Business Cycle*, National Bureau of Economic Research, Chicago: University of Chicago Press.
Grandmont, J. M. (1985), 'On endogenous competitive cycles', *Econometrica*, 53 (5), pp. 995-1045.
Granger, C. W. J. (1966), 'The typical spectral shape of an economic variable', *Econometrica*, 34 (1), pp. 150-61.
Granger, C. W. J. and Newbold, P. (1975), 'Econometric forecasting: the atheists' viewpoint', Ch. 5 in G. A. Renton (ed.), *Modelling the Economy*, London: Heinemann.
Granger, C. W. J. and Newbold, P. (1977), *Forecasting Economic Time Series*, New York, London: Academic Press.
Greenwald, B. and Stiglitz, J. E. (1987), 'Keynesian, New Keynesian and New Classical Economics', *Oxford Economic Papers*, 39, pp. 119-32.
Griliches, Z. (1967), 'Distributed lags: a survey', *Econometrica*, 35 (1), pp. 16-49.
Grossman, S. J. (1986), 'An analysis of the role of "insider trading" on futures markets', *Journal of Business*, 57, pp. 129-46.
Grossman, S. J., Hart, O. D. and Maskin, E. S. (1983), 'Unemployment with observable aggregate shocks', *Journal of Political Economy*, 91 (6), pp. 907-27.
Grossman, S. J. and Weiss, L. (1982), 'Heterogeneous information and the theory of the business cycle', *Journal of Political Economy*, 90 (4), pp. 699-727.
Guttentag, J. M. and Herring, R. J. (1984), 'Commercial bank lending to developing countries: from overlending to underlending to structural reform', Brookings Discussion Papers in International Economics, 16, Washington, DC: The Brookings Institution.
Haavalmo, T. (1940), 'The inadequacy of testing dynamic theory by comparing theoretical solutions and observed cycles', *Econometrica*, 8, pp. 312-21.
Haberler, G. (1958), *Prosperity and Depression*, London: George Allen & Unwin.
Haitovsky, Y. and Wallace, N. (1972), 'A study of discretionary and non-discretionary monetary and fiscal policies in the context of stochastic macroeconometric models', pp. 261-310 in V. Zarnowitz (ed.), *Econometric Research Retrospect and Prospect, Fiftieth Anniversary Colloquium, Vol. 1, The Business Cycle Today*, National Bureau of Economic Research General Series No. 96, New York, London: Columbia University Press.
Hall, R. E. (1980), 'Labour supply and aggregate fluctuations', pp. 7-35 in K. Brunner and A. H. Meltzer (eds.), *On the State of Macroeconomics*, Carnegie-

Rochester Conference Series on Public Policy 12, Amsterdam: North Holland.
Hansen, A. H. (1941), *Fiscal Policy and Business Cycles,* New York: Norton.
Hansen, A. H. (1951), *Business Cycles and National Income,* enlarged edn. 1964, New York: Norton.
Harrod, R. F. (1936), *The Trade Cycle,* Oxford: Clarendon Press.
Harrod, R. F. (1948), *Towards a Dynamic Economics,* London: Macmillan.
Hawtrey, R. G. (1913), *Good and Bad Trade,* 2nd edn. 1926, London: Longman.
Hawtrey, R. G. (1919), *Currency and Credit,* London: Longman.
Hawtrey, R. G. (1928), *Trade and Credit,* London: Longman.
Hawtrey, R. G. (1932), *The Art of Central Banking,* London: Longman; 2nd edn, 1962, Frank Cass.
Hawtrey, R. G. (1933), *The Gold Standard in Theory and Practice,* London: Longman.
Hawtrey, R. G. (1937), *Capital and Employment,* London: Longman.
Hayek, F. A. (1931), *Prices and Production,* enlarged edn. 1934, London: Routledge.
Hayek, F. A. (1933), *Monetary Theory and the Trade Cycle,* London: Jonathon Cape.
Hayek, F.A. (1976a), *Choice in Currency,* Occasional Paper No. 48, London: Institute of Economic Affairs.
Hayek, F.A. (1976b), *Denationalisation of Money,* Hobart Special Paper No. 48, London: Institute of Economic Affairs.
Hendry, D. F. and Ericsson, N. R. (1983), 'Assertion without empirical basis: an economic appraisal of Friedman and Schwartz', Bank of England Panel of Economic Consultants, Panel Paper No. 22, London: Bank of England.
Hey, J. D. (1979), *Uncertainty in Economics,* Oxford: Martin Robertson.
Hey, J. D. (1981), *Economics in Disequilibrium,* Oxford: Martin Robertson.
Hickman, B. G. (1972), 'Introduction and summary', in B. G. Hickman (ed.) (1972), Vol. 1.
Hickman, B. G. (ed.) (1972), *Econometric Models of Cyclical Behaviour,* Vols. 1 and 2, National Bureau of Economic Research, New York: Columbia University Press.
Hicks, J. R. (1937), 'Mr Keynes and the "Classics": a suggested interpretation', *Econometrica,* 5 (2), pp. 147–59.
Hicks, J. R. (1950), *A Contribution to the Theory of the Trade Cycle,* Oxford: Oxford University Press.
Hicks, J. R. (1967), *Critical Essays in Monetary Theory,* Oxford: Clarendon Press.
Hines, A. G. (1971), *On the Reappraisal of Keynesian Economics,* Oxford: Martin Robertson.
Holden, K. and Peel, D.A. (1986), 'An empirical investigation of combinations of economic forecasts', *Journal of Forecasting,* 5 (4), pp. 229–42.
Howitt, P. (1978), 'Limits to stability of a full employment equilibrium', *Scandinavian Journal of Economics,* 80 (3), pp. 265–82.
Howrey, E. P. (1968), 'A spectrum analysis of the long swing hypothesis', *International Economic Review,* 9 (2), pp. 228–52.
Howrey, E.P., Klein, L.R. and McCarthy, M.A. (1974), 'Notes on testing the predictive performance of econometric models', *International Economic Review,* 15, pp. 366–83.
Ichmura, S. (1954), 'Toward a general macrodynamic theory of economic fluctuations', Ch. 8 in K. Kurihara (ed.), *Post Keynesian Economics,* New

148 REFERENCES

Jersey: Rutgers University Press.
Isard, W. (1942), 'A neglected cycle: the transport building cycle', *Review of Economics and Statistics,* 24 (4), pp. 149–58.
Jevons, W. S. (1884), *Investigations in Currency and Finance,* London: Macmillan.
Kaldor, N. (1940), 'A model of the trade cycle', *Economic Journal,* 50 (March), pp. 78–92.
Kaldor, N. (1954), 'The relation of economic growth and cyclical fluctuations', *Economic Journal,* 64 (March), pp. 53–71.
Kaldor, N. (1957), 'A model of economic growth', *Economic Journal,* 67, pp. 591–624.
Kalecki, M. (1933), 'Proba Teori Koniunktury', Warsaw. Translated from Polish and published as Ch. 1 of M. Kalecki (1966), *Studies in the Theory of the Business Cycle: 1933–39,* Oxford: Basil Blackwell. Reprinted as Ch. 1, Part I, in Kalecki (1971) below.
Kalecki, M. (1943), 'Political aspects of full employment', *Political Quarterly,* 14, pp. 322–30.
Kalecki, M. (1952), 'The business cycle and shocks', Ch. 13 in M. Kalecki, *Theory of Economic Dynamics: An essay on cyclical and long run changes in capitalist economy,* London: George Allen & Unwin.
Kalecki, M. (1971), *Selected Essays in the Dynamics of Capitalist Economies,* Cambridge: Cambridge University Press.
Kane, E. J. (1981), *The Gathering Crisis in Federal Deposit Insurance,* Cambridge, Mass, London: MIT Press.
Kendall, M. G. and Stuart, A. (1969), *The Advanced Theory of Statistics,* 3 Vols., London: Griffen.
Keynes, J. M. (1936), *The General Theory of Employment, Interest and Money,* London: Macmillan.
Keynes, J. M. (1937), 'The general theory of employment', *Quarterly Journal of Economics,* 51, pp. 209–23.
Keynes, J. M. (1939), 'Professor Tinbergen's method – a method and its application to investment activity', *Economic Journal,* 49, pp. 558–68.
Keynes, J. M. (1940), 'Comment', *Economic Journal,* 50, pp. 154–6.
Kindleberger, C. P. (1978), *Manias, Panics and Crashes,* New York: Basic Books.
Kindleberger, C. P. and Laffargue, J. P. (eds.) (1982), *Financial Crises: Theory, history and policy,* Cambridge: Cambridge University Press.
King, R. and Plosser, C. (1984), 'Money, credit and prices in a real business cycle economy', *American Economic Review,* 74 (3), pp. 363–80.
Kitchen, J. (1923), 'Cycles and trends in economic factors', *Review of Economics and Statistics,* 5, pp. 10–16.
Klein, L. R. and Preston, R. S. (1969), 'Stochastic Nonlinear Models', *Econometrica,* 37 (1), pp. 95–106.
Knight, F. H. (1921), *Risk, Uncertainty and Profit,* New edn 1971, Chicago: University of Chicago Press.
Kondratieff, N. D. (1935), 'The long waves in economic life', *Review of Economics and Statistics,* 17 (Nov), pp. 105–15.
Koopmans, T. C. (1947), 'Measurement without theory', *Review of Economics and Statistics,* 29 (Aug), pp. 161–72.
Koopmans, T. C. (1949), 'A reply to Rutledge Vining', *Review of Economics and Statistics,* 31 (May), pp. 86–91.
Kraft, J. (1984), *The Mexican Rescue,* New York: Group of Thirty.

Kühne, K. (1979), *Economics and Marxism*, Vol. 2, *The Dynamics of the Marxian System*, London: Macmillan.
Kuznets, S. S. (1930), *Secular Movements in Production and Prices*, New York.
Kuznets, S. S. (1937), *National Income and Real Capital Formation: 1919-1933*, New York: National Bureau of Economic Research.
Kydland, F. E. and Prescott, E. C. (1977), 'Rules rather than discretion: inconsistency of optimal plans', *Journal of Political Economy*, 55 (3), pp. 473-92.
Kydland, F. E. and Prescott, E. C. (1980), 'A competitive theory of fluctuations and the desirability of stabilisation policy', Ch. 5 in S. Fischer (ed.), *Rational Expectations and Economic Policy*, National Bureau of Economic Research, Chicago: University of Chicago Press.
Kydland, F. E. and Prescott, E. C. (1982), 'Time to build and aggregate fluctuations', *Econometrica*, 50 (6), pp. 1345-70.
Lavington, F. (1922), *The Trade Cycle: An account of the causes producing rhythmical changes in the activity of business*, London: King.
Leijonhufved, A. (1968), *On Keynesian Economics and the Economics of Keynes*, Oxford: Oxford University Press.
Leijonhufved, A. (1973), 'Effective demand failures', *Swedish Journal of Economics*, 75, pp. 27-48.
Leijonhufved, A. (1981), *Information and Coordination: Essays in Macroeconomic theory*, New York: Oxford University Press.
Lessard, D. R. and Williamson, J. (eds.) (1987a), *Capital Flight and Third World Debt*, Washington, DC: Institute of International Economics.
Lessard, D. R. and Williamson, J. (1987b), *Capital Flight: The problem and policy responses*, Washington, DC: Institute of International Economics.
Lever, H. and Huhne, C. (1985), *Debt and Danger*, Penguin Special, Harmondsworth: Penguin Books.
Lewis, M. K. and Davis, K. T. (1987), *Domestic and International Banking*, Oxford: Philip Allan.
Lewis, W. A. and O'Leary, J. P. (1955), 'Secular swings in production and trade', *Manchester School*, 23 (May), pp. 113-52.
Llewellyn, D. T. (1985), *The Evolution of the British Financial System*, London: Institute of Bankers.
Llewellyn, D. T. (1986), *The Regulation and Supervision of Financial Institutions*, London: Institute of Bankers.
Long, J. B. and Plosser, C. I. (1983), 'Real business cycles', *Journal of Political Economy*, 91 (1), pp. 39-69.
Lotka, A. J. (1956), *Elements of Mathematical Biology*, New York, London: Constable.
Lucas, R. E. (1972), 'Expectations and the neutrality of money', *Journal of Economic Theory*, 4 (2), pp. 103-24.
Lucas, R. E. (1973), 'Some international evidence on output-inflation trade-offs', *American Economic Review*, 63 (3), pp. 326-34.
Lucas, R. E. (1975), 'An equilibrium model of the business cycle', *Journal of Political Economy*, 83 (6), pp. 1113-44.
Lucas, R. E. (1976), 'Econometric evaluation: a critique', in K. Brunner and A. H. Meltzer (eds.), *The Phillips Curve and Labour Markets*, Carnegie-Rochester Conference Series on Public Policy 1, Amsterdam and New York: North Holland.
Lucas, R. E. (1977), 'Understanding business cycles', in K. Brunner and A. H.

Meltzer (eds.), *Stabilisation of the Domestic and International Economy*, Carnegie-Rochester Conference Series on Public Policy 5, Amsterdam and New York: North Holland.

Lucas, R. E. (1987), *Models of Business Cycles*, Yrjö Jahnsson Lectures, Oxford: Basil Blackwell.

Lucas, R. E. and Sargent, T. J. (1978), 'After Keynesian macroeconomics', in *After the Phillips Curve: Persistence of high inflation and unemployment*, Federal Reserve Bank of Boston Conference Series No. 19, Boston.

Lucas, R. E. and Stokey, N. L. (1984), 'Money and interest in a cash in advance economy', CMSEMS Discussion Paper, No. 628, Northwestern University.

Lundberg, E. (ed.) (1955), *The Business Cycle in the Post War World*, London: Macmillan.

Machlup, F. (1931), *Börenkredit, Industriekredit and Kapitalbilding*, Vienna.

Malkiel, B. G. (1981), *A Random Walk Down Wall Street*, New York: W. W. Norton.

Mandel, E. (1978a), *Late Capitalism*, London: Verso.

Mandel, E. (1978b), *The Second Slump: A Marxist analysis of recession in the 1970s*, London: New Left Books.

Mandel, E. (1980), *Long Waves of Capitalist Development: The Marxist interpretation*, Cambridge: Cambridge University Press.

Mankiw, N. G. (1986), 'Comment', *Macroeconomics Annual*, 1, National Bureau of Economic Research, pp. 139–45, Cambridge, Mass.: MIT Press.

Mann, H. B. and Wald, A. (1943), 'On the statistical treatment of linear stochastic difference equations', *Econometrica*, 11 (3 & 4), pp. 173–220.

Markowitz, H. M. (1959), *Portfolio Selection*, Cowles Foundation, New Haven and London: Yale University Press.

Marshall, A. and Marshall, M. (1879), *Economics of Industry*, London: Macmillan.

Marx, K. (1867), *Das Kapital, Volume I*, see also Vol. II (1885) and III (1894), London: Lawrence and Wishart.

McCulloch, J. H. (1975), 'The Monte-Carlo cycle in business activity', *Economic Inquiry*, 13 (3), pp. 303–21.

McCulloch, J. H. (1977), 'The Monte-Carlo hypothesis: a reply', *Economic Inquiry*, 25 (Oct), p. 618.

McCulloch, J.H. (1981), 'Misintermediation and macroeconomic fluctuations', *Journal of Monetary Economics*, 8 (1), pp. 103–15.

McCulloch, J. H. (1986), 'Bank regulation and deposit insurance', *Journal of Business*, 59 (1), pp. 79–86.

McKenna, C. J. (1986), *The Economics of Uncertainty*, Hemel Hempstead: Harvester Wheatsheaf.

McNees, S. K. (1986), 'Forecasting accuracy of alternative techniques: a comparison of US economic forecasts', *Journal of Business and Economic Statistics*, Vol. 4, no. 1, January, pp. 5–15.

Melitz, J. (1982), 'Comment', pp. 43–7 in C. P. Kindleberger and J. P. Laffargue (eds.), *Financial Crises: Theory, history and policy*, Cambridge: Cambridge University Press.

Meltzer, A. H. (1982), 'Rational expectations, risk, uncertainty and market responses', pp. 3–32 (Ch. 1) in P. L. Wachtel (ed.), *Crises in the Economic and Financial Structure*, Lexington, Mass.: Lexington Books.

Metcalfe, J. L. (1982), 'Self regulation, crises management and preventive medicine: the evolution of UK bank supervision', Ch. 8 in E. P. M. Gardener

(ed.) (1986), *UK Banking Supervision: Evolution, practice and issues*, London: George Allen & Unwin.
Metcalfe, J. S. (1984), 'Impulse and diffusion in the study of technical change', Ch. 8 in C. Freeman (ed.), *Long Waves in the World*, London: Francis Pinter.
Metzler, L. A. (1941), 'The nature and stability of inventory cycles', *Review of Economics and Statistics*, 23 (Aug), pp. 113-29.
Mill, J. S. (1848), *Principles of Political Economy*, 1st edn; new edn (1909), Longman Green & Co.
Mills, J. (1867), 'Credit cycles and the origin of commercial panics', Transactions of the Manchester Society, Manchester.
Minsky, H. P. (1957a), 'Central banking and money market changes', *Quarterly Journal of Economics*, pp. 171-87.
Minsky, H. P. (1957b), 'Monetary systems and accelerator models', *American Economic Review*, 47 (6), pp. 859-85.
Minsky, H. P. (1959), 'A linear model of cyclical growth', *Review of Economics and Statistics*, 41 (2), pp. 133-45.
Minsky, H. P. (1972), 'Financial stability revisited: the economics of disaster', pp. 95-136 in *Reappraisal of the Federal Reserve Discount Mechanism*, vol. 3, June, Washington, DC: Board of Governors of the Federal Reserve System.
Minsky, H. P. (1977), 'A theory of systematic financial instability', in E. I. Altman and A. W. Sametz, *Financial Crises: Institutions and markets in a fragile environment*, pp. 138-52, New York: Wiley.
Minsky, H. P. (1982a), *Can 'IT' Happen Again? Essays on Instability in Finance*, New York: M. E. Sharpe.
Minsky, H. P. (1982b), 'The financial instability hypothesis: capitalist process and the behaviour of the economy', Ch. 2 in C. P. Kindleberger and J. P. Laffargue (eds.), *Financial Crises: Theory, history and policy*, Cambridge: Cambridge University Press.
Minsky, H. P. (1986), *Stabilising an Unstable Economy*, New Haven, London: Yale University Press.
Mises, L. von (1928), *Geldwertstabilisierung und Konjunkturpolitik*, Jena.
Mises, L. von (1934), *The Theory of Money and Credit*, London: Jonathan Cape.
Mitchell, W. C. (1927), *Business Cycles: The problem and its setting*, New York: National Bureau of Economic Research.
Muellbauer, J. and Portes, R. (1978), 'Macroeconomic models with quantity rationing', *Economic Journal*, 88 (352), pp. 788-821.
Muellbauer, J. and Portes, R. (1979), 'Macroeconomics when markets do not clear', Ch. 16 in W. H. Branson, *Macroeconomic Theory and Policy*, 2nd edn, New York: Harper International.
Mullineux, A. W. (1984), *The Business Cycle After Keynes: A contemporary analysis*, Hemel Hempstead: Harvester Wheatsheaf; New Jersey: Barnes & Noble.
Mullineux, A. W. (1987a), *International Money and Banking: The creation of a new order*, Hemel Hempstead: Harvester Wheatsheaf; New Jersey: Barnes & Noble.
Mullineux, A. W. (1987b), *UK Banking After Deregulation*, London: Croom-Helm.
Mullineux, A. W. (1987c), *International Banking and Financial Systems: A comparison*, London: Graham & Trotman.
Mullineux, A. W. (1987d), 'Monopoly money or monopoly of money?', *National Westminster Bank Quarterly Review*, August, pp. 35-44.

152 REFERENCES

Mullineux, A.W. (1987e), 'Why is the US banking system so unstable?', *Royal Bank of Scotland Review*, March, pp. 36–52.
Mullineux, A. W. (1988), 'Do we need a world central bank?', *Royal Bank of Scotland Review*, December, pp. 23–35.
Naylor, T. H., Seeks, T. G. and Wichern, D. W. (1972), 'Box-Jenkins methods: an alternative to econometric models', *Review of the Institute of International Statistics*, 40, pp. 123–37.
Neftci, S. N. (1982), 'Optimal prediction of cyclical downturns', *Journal of Economic Dynamics and Control*, 4 (Aug), pp. 225–41.
Neftci, S. N. (1984), 'Are economic time series asymmetric over the business cycle?', *Journal of Political Economy*, 92 (2), pp. 307–28.
Neftci, S. N. (1986), 'Is there a cyclical time unit?', pp. 11–48 in K. Brunner and A. H. Meltzer (eds.), *The National Bureau Method, International Capital Mobility and Other Essays*, Carnegie-Rochester Conference Series on Public Policy 24, Amsterdam: North Holland.
Nelson, C. R. (1972), 'The predictive performance of the FRB-MIT-PENN model of the US economy', *American Economic Review*, 62, pp. 902–17.
Nelson, C. R. and Plosser, C. I. (1982), 'Trends and random walks in macroeconomic time series', *Journal of Monetary Economics*, 10 (2), pp. 139–62.
Nordhaus, W. D. (1975), 'The political business cycle', *Review of Economic Studies*, 42 (2), pp. 169–90.
Okun, A. M. (1980), 'Rational expectations with misperceptions as a theory of the business cycle', *Journal of Money, Credit and Banking*, 12 (4), pp. 817–25.
Onado, M. (1986), 'Objectives of banking regulation: the trade-offs between efficiency and stability', Ch. 9 in E. P. M. Gardener (ed.), *UK Banking Supervision: Evolution, practice and issues*, London: George Allen & Unwin.
Parsons, T. (1963), 'On the concept of influence', *Public Opinion Quarterly*, 27, pp. 37–62.
Patinkin, D. (1965), *Money, Interest and Prices*, New York: Harper International.
Pecchioli, R. M. (1983), *The Internationalisation of Banking: The policy issues*, Trends in Banking Structure and Regulation in OECD Countries Series, Paris: OECD.
Pecchioli, R. M. (1987), *Prudential Supervision in Banking*, Trends in Banking Structure and Regulation in OECD Countries Series, Paris: OECD.
Phelps, E. S. (ed.) (1972), *Microeconomic Foundations of Employment and Inflation Theory*, London: Macmillan.
Pigou, A. C. (1967), *Industrial Fluctuations*, 2nd edn, London: Frank Cass. Originally published 1929.
Prescott, E. C. (1986), 'Theory ahead of business cycle measurement', pp. 11–24 in K. Brunner and A. H. Meltzer (eds.), *Real Business Cycles, Real Exchange Rates and Actual Policies*, Carnegie-Rochester Conference Series on Public Policy 25, Amsterdam: North Holland.
Rau, N. (1974), *Trade Cycles: Theories and evidence*, London: Macmillan.
Reid, M. (1982), *The Secondary Banking Crisis: 1973–5*, London: Macmillan.
Revell, J. (ed.) (1978), *Competition and the Regulation of Banks*, Bangor Occasional Papers in Economics No. 14, Bangor: University of Wales Press.
Revell, J. (1986), 'The complementary nature of competition and regulation in the financial sector', Ch. 10 in E. P. M. Gardener (ed.), *UK Banking Supervision: Evolution, practice and issues*, London: George Allen & Unwin.
Robbins, L. (1934), *The Great Depression*, London: Macmillan.

Rogoff, K. (1987), 'Reputational constraints on monetary policy', pp. 148-82 in K. Brunner and A. H. Meltzer (eds.), *Bubbles and Other Essays*, Carnegie-Rochester Conference Series on Public Policy 26, Amsterdam: North Holland.
Romer, C. D. (1986), 'Is the stabilisation of the postwar economy a figment of the data?', *American Economic Review*, 76 (3), pp. 314-34.
Röpke, W. (1936), *Crises and Cycles*, London: Hodge.
Rose, H. (1967), 'On the nonlinear theory of the employment cycle', *Review of Economic Studies*, 34, pp. 138-52.
Rose, H. (1969), 'Real and monetary factors in the business cycle', *Journal of Money, Credit and Banking*, May, pp. 138-52.
Rotemberg, J. J. (1986), 'Is there a cyclical time unit: a comment', pp. 49-53 in K. Brunner and A. H. Meltzer (eds.), *The National Bureau Method, International Capital Mobility and Other Essays*, Carnegie-Rochester Conference Series on Public Policy 24, Amsterdam: North Holland.
Ryan, T. M. (1978), *Theory of Portfolio Selection*, London: Macmillan.
Rybczynski, T. M. (1985), 'Financial systems, risk and public policy', *Royal Bank of Scotland Review*, 148 (Dec), pp. 35-45.
Salent, S. and Henderson, D. (1978), 'Market anticipation of government gold policies and the price of gold', *Journal of Political Economy*, 86 (4), pp.627-48.
Samuelson, P. A. (1939), 'Interaction between the multiplier analysis and the acceleration principle', *Review of Economics and Statistics*, 31 (May), pp. 75-8.
Samuelson, P. A. (1947), *Foundations of Economic Analysis*, Cambridge, Mass.: Harvard University Press.
Samuelson, P. A. (1965), 'A theory of induced innovations along Kennedy-Weizäcker lines', *Review of Economics and Statistics*, 47 (4), pp. 343-56.
Santoni, G. J. (1987), 'The great bull markets 1924-29 and 1982-87: speculative bubbles or economic fundamentals', *Federal Reserve Bank of St Louis Review*, 69 (9), pp. 16-29.
Sargent, T. J. (1976), 'The observational equivalence of natural and unnatural rate theories of macroeconomies', *Journal of Political Economy*, 84 (June), pp. 631-40.
Sargent, T. J. (1978), 'Estimation of dynamic labor demand schedules under rational expectations', *Journal of Political Economy*, 86, pp. 1009-44.
Sargent, T. J. (1979), *Macroeconomic Theory*, New York: Academic Press.
Sargent, T. J. and Wallace, N. (1975), 'Rational expectations, the optimal monetary instrument and the optimal money supply rule', *Journal of Political Economy*, 83 (2), pp. 241-54.
Sargent, T. J. and Wallace, N. (1976), 'Rational expectations and the theory of economic policy', *Journal of Monetary Economics*, 2 (2), pp. 169-83.
Savin, N. E. (1977), 'A test of the Monte-Carlo hypothesis: comment', *Economic Inquiry*, 15 (Oct), pp. 613-17.
Scheinkman, J. A. (1984), 'General equilibrium models of economic fluctuations: a survey of theory', University of Chicago Working Paper.
Schinasi, G. J. (1981), 'A nonlinear dynamic model of short run fluctuations', *Review of Economic Studies*, 48 (4), pp. 649-56.
Schumpeter, J. A. (1934), *Theory of Economic Development*, (reprinted 1967), Oxford: Oxford University Press.
Schumpeter, J. A. (1935), 'The analysis of economic change', *Review of Economics and Statistics*, 17 (4), pp. 2-10.
Schumpeter, J. A. (1939), *Business Cycles: A theoretical, historical and statistical*

analysis of the capitalist process, 2 vols., New York: McGraw-Hill, reprinted in abridged form 1964.

Shackle, G. L. S. (1938), *Expectations, Investment and Income,* new edn 1968, Oxford: Oxford University Press.

Shackle, G. L. S. (1967), *The Years of High Theory: Invention and tradition in economic thought, 1926-1939,* Cambridge: Cambridge University Press.

Shackle, G. L. S. (1974), *Keynesian Kaleidics,* Edinburgh: Edinburgh University Press.

Shiller, R. (1981), 'Do stock prices move too much to be justified by subsequent changes in dividends?', *American Economic Review,* 71 (3), pp. 421-36.

Sims, C. A. (1972), 'Money, income and causality', *American Economic Review,* 62 (Sept), pp. 540-52.

Sims, C. A. (1977), 'Exogenous and causal ordering in macroeconomic models', in C. A. Sims (ed.), *New Methods in Business Cycle Research,* Minneapolis: Federal Reserve Bank of Minneapolis.

Sims, C. A. (1980), 'Macroeconomics and reality', *Econometrica,* 48 (1), pp. 1-48.

Sinai, A. (1976), 'Credit crunches: analysis of the post war experience', pp. 244-74 in O. Eckstein (ed.), *Parameters and Policies of the US Economy,* Amsterdam: North Holland.

Sinai, A. (1977), 'Financial instability: a discussion', pp. 187-203 in E. I. Altman and A. W. Sametz (eds.), *Financial Crises: Institutions and markets in a fragile environment,* New York: Wiley.

Sinai, A. (1978), 'Credit crunch possibilities and the crunch barometer', *Data Resources Review,* June, pp. 9-18.

Sinai, A. (1980), 'Crunch impacts and the aftermath', *Data Resources Review,* June, pp. 37-60.

Singleton, K. J. (1987), 'Speculation and the volatility of foreign currency exchange rates', pp. 9-56 in K. Brunner and A. H. Meltzer (eds.), *Bubbles and Other Essays,* Carnegie-Rochester Conference Series 26, Amsterdam: North Holland.

Slutsky, E. (1937), 'The summation of random causes as the source of cyclical processes', *Econometrica,* 5 (2), pp. 105-46.

Smith, A. (1776), *An Enquiry into the Nature and Causes of the Wealth of Nations,* London. Reprinted 1979 with revisions as *The Wealth of Nations,* Harmondsworth: Penguin.

Smithies, A. (1957), 'Economic fluctuations and growth', *Econometrica,* 25 (1), pp.1-52.

Solomou, S. (1987), *Phases of Economic Growth 1850-1973: Kondratieff waves and Kuznets swings,* Cambridge: Cambridge University Press.

Solow, R. (1970), *Growth Theory,* New York: Oxford University Press.

Strigl, R. (1934), *Kapital und Produktion,* Vienna.

Tabellini, G. (1987), 'Reputational constraints on monetary policy: a comment', pp. 183-90 in K. Brunner and A. H. Meltzer (eds.), *Bubbles and Other Essays,* Carnegie-Rochester Conference Series on Public Policy 26, Amsterdam: North Holland.

Taylor, J. B. (1979), 'Staggered wage setting in a macro world', *American Economic Review,* Papers and Proceedings 69 (2), pp. 109-13.

Taylor, J. B. (1980a), 'Aggregate dynamics and staggered contracts', *Journal of Political Economy,* 88 (1), pp. 1-23.

Taylor, J. B. (1980b), 'Comment', pp. 191-4 in S. Fischer (ed.), *Rational Expectations and Economic Policy,* A Conference Report: National Bureau of

Economic Research, Chicago and London: University of Chicago Press.
Thom, R. (1975), *Structural Stability and Morphogenesis,* New York: Benjamin.
Tinbergen, J. (1939), *Statistical Testing of Business Cycle Theories,* 2 Vols., Geneva: League of Nations.
Tinbergen, J. (1940a), 'Econometric business cycle research', *Review of Economic Studies,* 7 (Feb), pp. 73–90.
Tinbergen, J. (1940b), 'On a method of statistical business cycle research: a reply', *Economic Journal,* 50 (March), pp. 141–54.
Tinbergen, J. (1942), 'Critical remarks on some business cycle theories', *Econometrica,* April, pp. 129–46.
Tinbergen, J. (1951), *Business Cycles in the United Kingdom: 1870–1914,* Amsterdam: North Holland.
Tinsley, P. A., Spindt, P. A. and Friar, R. E. (1980), 'Indicator and filter attributes of monetary aggregates', *Journal of Econometrics (supplement),* 14, pp. 61–91.
Tobin, J. (1963), 'Commercial banks as creators of money', in D. Carlson (ed.), *Banking and Monetary Studies,* Homewood, Ill.: Irwin.
Tobin, J. (1984), 'On the efficiency of the financial system', *Lloyds Bank Review,* 153 (July), pp. 1–15.
Tufte, E. R. (1978), *Political Control of the Economy,* Princeton, NJ: Princeton University Press.
Tullock, G. (1976), 'The vote motive', *Hobart Paper,* 9, London: Institute of Economic Affairs.
UNCTAD (1987), *International Monetary and Financial Issues for Developing Countries,* New York: United Nations.
Van der Ploeg, F. (1984), 'Implications of workers' savings for economic growth and class struggle', pp. 1–13 in R. M. Goodwin *et al.* (1984), *Nonlinear Models of Fluctuating Growth,* New York: Springer-Verlag.
Van Duijn, J. J. (1983), *The Long Wave in Economic Life,* London: George Allen & Unwin.
Varian, H. (1979), 'Catastrophe theory and the business cycle', *Economic Inquiry,* 17 (Jan), pp. 14–28.
Verdoorn, P. J. and Post, J. J. (1964), 'Capacity and short term multipliers', pp. 179–98 in P. E. Hart, G. Mills and J. K. Whitaker (eds.), *Econometric Analysis for National Economic Planning,* Proceedings of the Sixtieth Symposium of the Colston Research Society, London: Butterworths.
Vining, R. (1949), 'Koopmans on the choice of variables to be studied and methods of measurement', *Review of Economic Statistics,* 31 (May), pp. 77–86 and 'A rejoinder', pp. 91–4.
Volcker, P. A. (1978), *The Rediscovery of the Business Cycle,* New York: Free Press.
Volterra, V. (1926), 'Fluctuations in the abundance of species considered mathematically', *Nature,* CXVIII, pp. 558–60.
Wachtel, P. L. (ed.) (1982), *Crises in the Economic and Financial Structure,* Lexington, Mass.: Lexington Books.
Wallis, K. F. (1977), 'Multiple time series analysis of the final form of economic models', *Econometrica,* 45 (6), pp. 1481–97.
Wardwell, C. (1927), *An Investigation of Economic Data for Major Cycles,* Philadelphia.
Wichern, D. W. (1973), 'The behaviour of the sample autocorrelation function for an integrated moving average process', *Biometrika,* 60, pp. 235–9.

Wicksell, K. (1907), 'The influence of the rate of interest on prices', *Economic Journal*, 17 (June), pp. 213-20.
Wicksell, K. (1934), *Lectures on Political Economy*, London: Routledge.
Wicksell, K. (1936), *Interest and Prices*, London: Macmillan.
Yule, G. V. (1927), 'On a method of investigating periodicity in a disturbed series', *Transactions of the Royal Society*, 226, London.
Zarnowitz, V. (1972), 'The business cycle today: an introduction', in V. Zarnowitz (ed.), (1972).
Zarnowitz, V. (ed.) (1972), *Econometric Research Retrospect and Prospect, Fiftieth Anniversary Colloquium, Vol. 1, The Business Cycle Today*, National Bureau of Economic Research General Series No. 96, New York, London: Columbia University Press.
Zarnowitz, V. (1985), 'Recent work on business cycles in historical perspective', *Journal of Economic Literature*, 23 (2), pp. 523-80.
Zarnowitz, V. and Moore, G. H. (1986), 'Major changes in cyclical behaviour', in R. J. Gordon (ed.), *The American Business Cycle*, National Bureau of Economic Research, Chicago: University of Chicago Press.
Zeeman, C. (1977), *Catastrophe Theory: Selected papers 1972-1977*, New York: Addison-Wesley.
Zellner, A. and Palm, F. (1974), 'Time series analysis and simultaneous equation models', *Journal of Econometrics*, 2, pp. 17-54.

INDEX

acceleration principle 38, 44
accelerator 106, 124
  modified 23, 41
  –multiplier interaction 44–5, 58, 63–4, 71, 86, 105–7, 110, 122–3, 130, 136
Adelman, F. L. 27, 106
Adelman, I. 27, 106, 113–14, 115
adjustment costs 47, 48, 49, 50
adjustment process 111
Aftalion, A. 19
aggregate demand 12, 33, 65, 74, 90, 129
aggregate output 12
aggregate shocks 42
aggregate supply 90
aggregate time series 1, 3–4, 12
Anderson, E. E. 8, 9
'animal spirits' 44, 45, 51, 71, 107
arbitrage 92, 94, 96
assets (liquidity) 68, 84
asymmetry issue 2, 12–19, 125, 126, 138
autocorrelated shocks 6, 21–2, 24–5, 27
autocorrelation function 21, 95, 120–1
automaintained cycle 20
autonomous investment 44, 106, 124–5, 129–31
autoregressive integrated moving average model 23, 25–8, 120, 139
autoregressive process 7
autoregressive shocks 136–7
Azariadis, C. 44–5

Backus, D. 39, 40, 41

balance of payments 96, 98
Balducci, R. 57
bank credit *see* credit
Bank of England 79, 81, 82
Bank for International Settlements 89
banking sector 110–11, 131–2
  central banks 34–5, 57, 65, 87, 89
  core banks 79
  financial instability and 78–84, 89, 101–2
  fringe banks 79–80, 81–2
Barclay, C. 78, 79–80, 83
Barro, R. J. 38, 39, 51
'beauty contest' 41
bifurcation theory 59, 60, 127
'billiard table' nonlinearities 24, 106, 136
Black, F. 47, 48, 49
Blanchard, O. J. 16, 33, 90, 91–3, 95
Blatt, J. M. 4, 12–13, 23, 119, 137–8
Boch, M. E. 137
Boddy, R. 129
boom phase 1, 34, 45, 85–6, 126, 128–9
borrower of the last resort, 73, 75–6, 77, 101
Boschen, J. 46
Box, G. E. P. 4, 7
Box–Pierce test 95
Brady Report 101
Bronfenbrenner, M. 29, 137
Brunner, K. 16, 95, 96–7
buffer role (bank) 101, 102
building cycle 116
bull markets 93, 94, 96
bunching (innovations) 44, 110, 122–3, 125, 130, 131, 132

Burns, A. F. 1-2, 5, 6, 8-11, 13, 16, 114-19
business cycle
  duration 8-11
  modelling (interactive) 140
  pre-Keynesian theory 63-72
  research agenda 135-140
  Shackle on 122-6
business cycle (nature of)
  asymmetry issue 12-19
  definitions 1-6
  Frisch-Slutsky hypothesis 19-29
  Monte Carlo hypothesis 6-12
  post-war changes 29-35
business cycle theory (in 1980s)
  approaches and themes 37-45
  equilibrium business cycle 45-54
  nonlinear cycle theory 54-60

capital
  flight 88, 89
  -labour ratio 12, 56, 129
  mobility 89, 133
  -output ratio 124
  stock 23, 48, 66-7, 68
capital gains 80, 91, 94, 96
capital goods 46, 48, 66, 67, 126
capitalist economies 29-30, 56-7
  Goodwin's macrodynamics 127-33
  Minsky on FIH in 72-8, 86
  Schumpeter on economic evolution 108-13
Carey, M. 64
cartels 78, 79, 81
cash-in-advance constraint 50, 51, 53
catastrophe theory 58-9, 60, 99-100, 127, 131
central banks 34-5, 57, 65, 87, 89
chance function 6, 21
Chang, W. W. 58
chaos theory 59
Chi-squared distribution 7, 8, 9
Chiarella, C. 55, 108
class conflict 56, 57
classical business cycle 133
closed model 24
clustering 110
coherent series 21
commodity prices 116-17
comovements 1-2, 4, 10, 12, 16, 48, 62

competition 78, 79, 80, 81, 83, 98
conservative oscillations 54-5, 56, 138
consumer
  outlay 65
  preference 47, 48, 49
consumer goods 47, 53, 66-7, 68
consumption 13, 115, 130
  ratchet effect 106, 108, 122, 125, 126, 131
'contagion' 101
contingency table test 7, 9
contract model 52
contractionary phase 1, 6-7, 8, 16, 18, 125, 138
core banks 79
covariance-stationarity 16
Cowles Commission 14
credit 49, 83-5, 88, 93, 110, 111, 126
  rationing 42, 81, 89
  role (pre-Keynesian theory) 63-72
crisis, financial *see* financial instability hypothesis
Cross Report 89
Crotty, J. 129
Cusp catastrophe models 59, 99
cycle modelling (overview) 105-8, 129
cycle theory 43, 44

Dale, R. S. 101
Daly, D. J. 11
damped cycles 4, 5, 13, 19, 21-5, 138-9
data
  detrended 10, 12-13, 15, 18-19, 119
  non-detrended 2, 5
  phase-averaging 18-19
  see also information
Day, R. H. 58, 59-60
debt 69-70, 74-5
  Latin America 79, 89
  Mexico 34, 82, 88
decision-making 41, 63, 72-3, 76, 133
  see also risk; uncertainty
definitions 1-6
deflation 69
De Leeuw 28
De Long, J. B. 13-15, 17, 33, 35
demand, aggregate 12, 33, 65, 74, 90, 129

INDEX

demand management 31
depressions 111–12, 117–18, 126, 129
deregulation 34, 101
Desai, M. 56
detrending 2, 5, 10, 12, 13, 15, 18–19, 119
Diamond, D. 84
difference-stationary process 120, 121
Di Matteo, M. 57
'disaster myopia' 88–9, 90
disaster probabilities 90
discount rate 64, 65
discounted present value 75, 76
discredit 86, 87
disequilibrium 2, 38, 45, 64, 74, 107, 122
displacement 85
dollar appreciation 98–9
Driffill, J. 39, 40, 41
Duesenberry, J. 106, 108, 122, 125
Dybvig, P. 84
dynamic economic development
  concluding remarks 131–3
  cycle modelling (overview) 105–8
  Goodwin's macrodynamics 127–31
  growth trend 119–22
  long swing hypothesis 113–19
  Schumpeter on economic evolution 108–13
  Shackle on business cycle 122–6
dynamic specification 19, 24, 25, 28

Eckstein, O. 33
econometric models 5–6, 11–15, 132, 136–9
  Frisch–Slutsky hypothesis 19–29
economic development *see* dynamic economic development
economic evolution 108–13
economic time series *see* time series
efficient market hypothesis 92, 94, 96
Eichenbaum, M. 43, 50–3, 132
Eichengreen, B. 35, 88–90, 101, 133
endogenous
  cycles 4, 5, 20, 29, 135, 136
  shocks 20, 45, 51, 55, 91
  variables 25–7, 32, 41
entrepreneurs 110–11, 125, 126
equal classes/probabilities 9
equilibrium
  new 19, 110–12

Walrasian 40, 122
equilibrium business cycle 2, 32, 37–9, 41, 122
  modelling 45–54
  real 42–3, 47, 49–53, 57, 131–2
Ericsson, N. R. 18
erratic shocks 20, 22
error process 26–7
euphoria, speculative 82–3, 90, 95, 99, 100
Evans, M. K. 11
excess capacity 130
exchange rate 40, 65, 89, 96–7, 98, 99
exogenous
  cycles 4, 5, 135, 136
  shocks 5, 20, 29, 30, 43, 45, 55, 114, 123, 125
  variables 21, 25–9, 32, 137, 139
expansionary phase 1, 6–8, 16, 18, 65, 102, 106, 125, 128, 138
  economic evolution 108–13
expectations 83–4, 123–4
  see also rational expectations
extraneous events 91–2, 94
extrinsic information 96–7

F-tests 118
Fabricant 30, 32
Federal Deposit Insurance Corporation 77, 87, 96
Federal Open Market Committee 39, 49
Federal Reserve Bank 73
Federal Reserve Board 52
Fels, R. 108, 110
filtering 22, 114
financial instability hypothesis 1, 62
  banking sector 78–84
  conclusion 99–102
  Kindleberger's model 85–90
  Minsky on 72–8, 100–1
  money and credit (role) 63–72
  rational speculative bubbles 91–9
'financing veil' 73
first differencing 52, 120, 121, 122
First Republic Bank 96
'fiscal neutrality' 34
Fischer, S. 52
Fisher, I. 2, 6, 19, 69–70, 106
Flemming, J. S. 76–7
Flood, R. P. 90–1

'fluctuations' 2
'fold catastrophe' 59
'forced lending' 89
'forced oscillations' 24–5
forecasts 26, 30
foreign exchange markets 82, 88
four-phase cycle 109
Fourier analysis 21
'free oscillations' 24–5
Frey, B. S. 37
Friedman, M. 16, 18, 33, 42, 49, 52, 97, 121
fringe banks 79–80, 81–2
Frisch, R. 4, 105
Frisch–Slutsky hypothesis 4–5, 19–29, 37, 42–3, 55, 60, 106–7, 119, 125, 132, 136–7
Frisch-type econometric models 12–13
Frisch I hypothesis 20–1, 113, 121, 136
Frisch II hypothesis 20, 21
full employment 67

Galbraith, J. K. 93, 100
game theory 39
Garbade, K. D. 93
Garber, P. M. 51, 90–1
gearing 85
General Agreement on Tariffs and Trades 73
Gilbert, R. A. 87
Glombowski, J. 57
Goldsmith, R. W. 77, 87
Goodhart, C. A. E. 81
goods *see* capital goods; consumer goods; producer goods
Goodwin, R. M. 43–4, 55–7, 60, 106, 108, 110, 132
  macrodynamics analysis 122, 127–31
Gordon, R. J. 29, 32–3, 39, 41, 43
government policy 26, 31, 33
Grandmont, J. M. 57–8, 108
Granger, C. W. J. 3
Granger-causal relationships 50, 51, 52
Great Depression 41
Greenwald, B. 41, 42, 46, 107
Griliches, Z. 137
Grossman, H. I. 46

Grossman, S. J. 46, 53
growth cycles 2, 29–32, 55–6, 133, 135, 137
growth theory 43, 44, 105, 106, 107
growth trend 119–22
Guttentag, J. M. 88–9

Haavalmo, T. 24
Haberler, G. 63, 64, 65, 66, 67–72
Haitovsky, Y. 26
Hansen, A. H. 1, 2, 44, 63, 64, 86–7
Harrod, R. F. 44, 105, 124
Hawtrey, R. G. 64–6, 71
Hayek, F. A. 37, 64, 66, 67–8
Henderson, D. 91
Hendry, D. F. 18
Herring, R. J. 88–9
Hickman, B. G. 27, 135, 136, 137
Hicks, J. R. 20, 44, 71, 84, 106, 129, 131, 138
hoarding 68
Howe, Geoffrey 39
Howrey, E. P. 8, 114–15, 117

impulse problem 19–21, 23–8, 71–2
incoherent series 21
income-expenditure multiplier 122, 123, 124, 126
induced investment 44, 110, 123, 124, 126, 130
inflation 29, 31–2, 34–5, 46, 55–6, 67–8, 76, 80, 82–3, 135
  anti-inflationary policies 39–40
information 41, 53
  asymmetry 42, 46, 84
  imperfect 42, 57, 89, 90, 97, 98
innovations 14, 20, 28, 43, 71–2, 105–6
  bunching 44, 110, 122–3, 125, 130–2
  investment 108–10, 112, 123–6, 128–31
input–output relationships 43, 48, 67, 110, 122, 124, 126, 130, 131, 133
insurance 84, 102
interest rate 34–5, 46, 52, 58, 75, 76, 123
  role of credit 63–72
International Bank for Reconstruction and Development 73

international dimension (of FIH) 85–90
international lender of last resort 87, 89, 90
International Monetary Fund 73, 89
inventions 20, 126
inventories 115, 136
inventory cycle 1, 122
investment 42, 73, 74, 75, 76, 115
  autonomous 44, 106, 124–5, 129–31
  induced 44, 110, 123, 124, 126, 130
  innovatory 108–10, 112, 123–6, 128–31
  over-investment theories 66–8, 70
  pre-Keynesian theories 63, 65–8, 70–2
irrational bubble hypothesis 94–5
'islands' hypothesis 38, 45, 47, 48, 57, 130
ISLM models 72, 86

Jenkins, G. M. 4, 7
Jevons, W. S. 44
Judge, G. C. 137
Juglar cycles 108, 113, 117, 122

Kahn multiplier 122–3
Kaldor, N. 44, 57, 58–9, 106, 108
Kalecki, M. 22, 129
Keynes, J. M. 19, 40, 41, 86–7, 90, 100, 107, 122, 125, 131
  cycle modelling approach 37–8
  General Theory 46, 51, 62, 72, 73, 105, 123
  pre-Keynesian literature 63–72
  see also new Keynesians
Kindleberger, C. P. 62, 72, 76–8, 83, 92, 95
  FIH model 85–90
King, R. 49, 50, 51
Kitchen, J. 117
Kitchen cycles 108, 113, 117, 122
Klein–Goldberger model 113
Knight, F. H. 40, 63, 90, 97, 122
Kondratieff, N. D. 116
Kondratieff cycles 108, 113, 116
Koopmans, T. C. 9–10, 136
Krüger, N. 57
Kuznets, S. S. 114, 116
Kuznets cycle 115, 116

Kydland, F. E. 39, 43, 47–53, 107

labour constraint 128–9
Laffargue, J. P. 76
lag structures 10, 23, 27, 28, 113, 118, 120, 121
land constraint 128
Latin American debt 79, 89
Lavington, F. 70
Lawson, Nigel, 39, 40
lead–lag structure 10, 113, 118
Leijonhufved, A. 59
leisure 47, 48, 58
lender of the last resort 73, 75–8, 86, 87, 101
'lifeboat' operation 82
limit cycles 4, 5, 24, 28–9, 54–5, 106, 121, 127, 139
linear models 4–5, 13, 23, 105–8, 127, 137–9
liquidity 68, 84
Llewellyn, D. T. 81
log linear trends 5, 118, 119, 139
Long, J. B. 43, 47–9, 51, 53, 131
long cycle theory 43, 105, 108
long swing hypothesis 22, 31, 113–19
Lucas, R. E. 2, 5, 9, 11–12, 32, 37, 40, 41–3, 47, 49–51, 62, 107, 121
  critique 54, 132–3
  –Stokey model 52–3
  supply hypothesis 23, 38
Lundberg, E. 29

McCulloch, J. H. 6–8, 9, 46, 77, 120
Machlup, F. 69
macrodynamics (Goodwin's) 127–31
macroeconomic
  dynamics 37, 38
  theory, Keynesian 107
  time series 5, 14, 17, 18
  variables 17
macroeconomics, open economy 133
major cycles 1, 108, 113, 116–18, 122
Mandel, E. 31, 43, 107
mania/manic phase 85–6, 95
Mankiw, N. G. 52
market bubbles 90
market fundamentals 91–2, 94, 98–9
'market islands' 38, 45, 47, 48, 57, 130
Markov processes 13
Marshall, A. 64

Marshall, M. 64
Marx, Karl 56
Matthews, R. C. O. 29
Melitz, J. 78, 88
Meltzer, A. H. 16, 40, 90, 92, 95–7, 99
Metcalfe, J. L. 43, 83
Metzler, L. A. 1
Mexican debt crisis 34, 82, 88
Mill, J. S. 64
Mills, J. 64
minor cycles 1, 108, 113, 117, 122
Minsky, H. P. 45, 63, 80–3, 85–7, 106
 on financial instability 72–8, 88–9, 100–1, 102
Mintz, L. W. 30, 32
Mises, L. von 69
misspecification 6, 23, 25, 27–8, 32, 98, 119–20, 136–7
Mitchell, W. C. 1–2, 5, 6, 8–11, 13, 16, 115–18, 119
modified accelerator 23, 41, 49
'monetary factors' 71
monetary shocks 5, 23, 33, 43, 45–7, 50–4, 107, 132
money
 role (pre-Keynesian) 63–72
 stock 12
 supply 33, 42, 52–3, 57, 83
monotonic dampening 24–5
Monte Carlo hypothesis 2, 6–12, 38, 60, 115, 120
Moore, G. H. 2, 30, 32, 33
moral hazard 77, 84, 88
moving average process 22, 114, 119–20
 see also autoregressive integrated moving average models
Mullineux, A. W. 5, 23, 29, 31, 34, 37, 38–9, 46, 54, 55, 81, 101
multi-sectoral approach 57, 60, 110, 132
 Goodwin's macrodynamics 127–31
multiplier 48, 51
 -accelerator interaction 44–5, 58, 63–4, 71, 86, 105–7, 110, 122, 130
 effect 124, 125
 income–expenditure 122–4, 126
Myrdal, G. 46
Myrdallian theory 110, 123, 124

National Bureau of Economic Research 2, 3, 5–11, 15–18, 29–31, 38, 115–17, 119
Neftci, S. N. 13–14, 15, 16–17, 18
Nelson, C. R. 5, 50, 119–21
neoclassical growth theory 48–50, 107
neoclassical synthesis 72, 73, 86
New Classical models 23, 38, 41, 46, 57
new equilibrium 19, 110–12
New Keynesians 40–2, 45–6, 58, 107, 122, 131, 133
New York Stock Exchange 93, 100
no arbitrage hypothesis 92, 94, 96
non-detrended data 2, 5
nonlinearity 14, 16–18, 131
 cycle theory 4, 21–2, 24, 54–60, 106, 108, 121, 138–9
 equations 127, 138
 type I 21–2, 24, 106, 127, 136
 type II 21, 22, 106, 136
nonstationarity 8, 119–22
Nordhaus, W. D. 37, 107
null hypothesis 7, 8, 15

OBE group 27
'observational equivalence' 54
OECD countries 14–15, 33, 34, 35, 107, 128, 133
oil price shocks 29, 31, 33, 37, 43, 51, 107
Okun, A. M. 46
open economy 12, 133
open model (exogenous case) 24
optimism 71
output 23, 48
 see also input–output relationships
overlapping generations model 44, 58
overtrading 64, 85, 87

panic phase 85
Patinkin, D. 73
pessimism 71
phase-averaging (data) 18–19
Phelps, E. S. 38, 45
piecewise linear analysis 127
Pigou, A. C. 71
Plosser, C. I. 5, 43, 47–51, 53, 119–21, 131
political business cycle 37, 39

Ponzi finance 75-6, 77, 82, 102
population 9
Portes, R. 35, 88-90, 101, 133
portfolio redistribution 92
Post, J. J. 139
post-war changes 29-35
post-war cycles 135, 137
pre-Keynesian theory 63-72
pre-war cycles 135
predator-prey model 56, 108
preference function 47, 48, 49
Prescott, E. C. 39, 43, 47-53, 107
price bubbles 70-1, 91, 94-6, 97-8
prices 107, 116-17
　see also oil price shocks
primary cycle 19
producer goods 67-8
production 13, 115
production possibility hypothesis 47
profit 78-81, 128, 130
propagation model 4, 6, 22, 33, 107-8, 121, 138, 139
　equilibrium business cycle 43, 45, 48-9, 51-2, 54, 132
　problem 13, 19-21, 23-5, 28, 71
　simulations 25-9, 136
property sector 80, 82, 96
'psychological' theories 70-1
Punzo, L. F. 43, 108, 132
purchasing power 110, 111
　parity 97, 98, 99

'quantity theory' 52

random shocks 6, 10-11, 20-6, 48-9, 105, 121, 136, 138
random walk 94-5, 96, 97, 120
ratchet effect 106, 108, 122, 125, 126, 131
rational bubble hypothesis 94-5
rational expectations 37, 38
　equilibria 44-5
　hypothesis 39-42, 46-7, 57, 122, 133
　speculative bubbles 63, 77, 85-7, 101
Reagan administration 34
real business cycle 42-3, 47, 49-53, 57, 131-2
recession 15, 29-32, 34-5, 45, 74, 111-12, 125, 129

reference cycles 10, 11, 15-18, 116, 118
refinancing 74, 75, 97
research agenda 135-40
'reserve army' 129
'resorption' 111
Revell, J. 78, 80, 81-3
revulsion 85, 87
risk 63, 74, 80, 88, 90, 97, 101-2
　aversion 42, 75, 98
　premiums 76-7, 79, 84, 89
Romer, C. D. 30-1
Rotemberg, J. J. 18, 52

Salent, S. 91
Samuelson, P. A. 56, 105, 106
Santoni, G. J. 93-5
Sargent, T. J. 3, 4, 9, 12, 21, 23, 54
satellite models 26, 139
Savin, N. E. 9
savings 66, 67, 68, 100
Scheinkman, J. A. 54
Schumpeter, J. A. 1, 20, 43-4, 56, 79, 102, 106, 117-18, 130-2
　economic evolution 105, 108-13
Schwartz, A. J. 18, 33, 52
secondary cycle 19
sectoral analysis 133, 136
Securities and Exchange Commission 93
securitisation 89
self-sustaining cycles 20
Shackle, G. L. S. 40, 43, 46, 72, 102, 130-2
　business cycle 105, 108, 110, 122-6
Shah, A. 56
shocks
　autocorrelated 6, 21-2, 24-5, 27-8
　autoregressive 136-7
　correlated 23, 32
　endogenous 20, 45, 51, 55, 91
　erratic 20, 22
　exogenous 20, 29, 30, 43, 45, 55, 114, 123, 125
　external 20, 31, 109, 112, 125-6, 131
　-generation 19, 24, 25, 28
　internal 112, 123, 125
　monetary 5, 23, 33, 43, 45-7, 50-4, 107, 132

164 INDEX

random 6, 10–11, 20–6, 48–9, 105, 121, 136, 138
real 5, 23, 33, 43, 51, 54, 107, 120, 132
sources 6, 19, 27–8, 43, 107
stochastic 40–1, 49–50, 120
supply side 33, 137
technology 43, 48–9, 51, 53
signal extraction problem 38, 41, 46, 47, 48, 49, 53, 121, 122
Sims, C. A. 25, 52, 132
Sinai, A. 33
Singleton, K. J. 43, 50–3, 97–9, 132
Slutsky, E. E. 4, 6, 105
  –Yule effect 21–2, 24, 113, 114
  see also Frisch–Slutsky hypothesis
Smith, Adam 64
Smithies, A. 106
smoothing procedures 8, 22, 113–14, 119
Smyth, D. J. 58
Social Science Research Council 29
socialist economies 29–30
South Sea Bubble (1720) 100
specific cycles 6, 10, 11, 116, 118
spectral analysis 8, 9, 113–15
speculative euphoria 82–3, 90, 95, 99, 100
speculative excesses 63, 85–7, 90–101
speculative finance 75–8, 82–3, 89, 102
spurious cycles 22, 114
stabilisation policy 135
stationarity 16, 121
Stiglitz, J. E. 41, 42, 46, 107
stochastic models 4, 13, 18
stochastic shocks 40–1, 49–50, 120
stock market crises (1929) 77, 100
stock market crisis (1987) 34, 87, 88, 93, 94
Stokey, N. L. 50
Strigl, R. 68
structural neutrality hypothesis 46
'stylised facts' 4, 12, 31, 38
Summers, L. H. 13–15, 17, 33, 35
sunspot theories 44, 45, 96, 97–8
supply 23, 38, 90
supply side policies 31
supply side shocks 33, 137
symmetry issue 12–19

synchronisation (of cycles) 133

taxation 34, 40
Taylor, J. B. 46, 49, 53
technical progress 56–7
technology matrix 130, 131
technology shocks 43, 48–9, 51, 53
tertiary cycle 19
Texan crisis 96
Thatcher government 34, 40
Third World debt 33, 89
Thom, R. 58
'time to build' 48, 49, 50
time series 9, 13, 23, 44
  aggregate 1, 3–4, 12
  macroeconomic 5, 14, 17, 18
  models 15, 16–17
Tinbergen, J. 136, 139
trend-stationary process 120–1
trend cycles 17–18, 24, 116, 119, 121
Tullock, G. 37
two-phase cycle 109

uncertainty 40–1, 44–6, 63, 72–4, 76, 90, 97–9, 122, 133
unemployment 29, 31–2, 42, 47–8, 128–9, 135
  benefit 34, 57
  series 13–14, 15, 17, 120
unvariate autoregressions 17

Van der Ploeg, F. 56
Van Duijn, J. J. 31, 107
Varian, H. 58, 59, 99–100
vector autoregressive models 14, 17, 44, 132, 137
venture capital 110
Verdoorn, P. J. 139

Wachtel, P. L. 90
wages 45, 51, 56, 107, 128–9
Wallace, N. 26
Walrasian equilibrium 40, 122
Wardwell, C. 116, 118
Watson, M. W. 16, 33, 90, 91–3, 95
wealth shock 100
Weiss, L. 46, 53
Wicksell, K. 46, 66

Wicksellian theory 66, 123, 125, 126
Wood, G. E. 87
working capital 42, 66

Yancey, T. A. 137

Yule, G. V. 21-2, 24, 113, 114

Zarnowitz, V. 2, 27, 29-31, 33, 37, 40, 46-9, 54, 55, 132
Zeeman, C. 58